British Rail

The Nation's Railway

TANYA JACKSON

FOREWORD BY CHRIS GREEN
FORMER BRITISH RAIL MANAGER

The
History
Press

Cover Illustrations. Front: Illustration of an IC125. (Author's collection/Science & Society Picture Library) Double Arrow Trade Mark 2107832 used by permission of the Secretary of State for Transport. *Back*: *Left*: A Britannia. (Ray Vincent/The Transport Treasury) *Right*: 86215 in InterCity Executive livery and EMU 321-364 in NSE colours. (John Lewis)

First published 2013
This paperback edition published 2014

The History Press
The Mill, Brimscombe Port
Stroud, Gloucestershire, GL5 2QG
www.thehistorypress.co.uk

© Tanya Jackson, 2013, 2014

British Library Cataloguing in Publication Data.
A catalogue record for this book is available from the British Library.

ISBN 978 0 7509 6076 2

Typesetting and origination by The History Press
Printed in Great Britain

Contents

Foreword
By Chris Green; an ex-British Rail Managing Director

I t is easy to forget that Britain's railways have been in private hands for many more years than in public ownership. The sweep of history reminds us that our railways were private for over a hundred years from the age of George Stephenson before being nationalised for just half a century. They now seem set for a second long spell in the private sector, but this time in a much more restrained public-private style, in which the private operators are regulated and part-funded by state institutions.

My own career straddled the public sector and public-private phases, and I found both to be equally effective in their different ways. I joined British Rail in 1965 with a strong belief that a public industry could be made to perform as well as a private company – and I believe that we eventually demonstrated this when we were set free as business sectors. However, we never found a solution to the infuriating stop-go investment funding which seems to be an inevitable feature of public sector life.

My subsequent experience in the private-public era showed that, after an appalling start, the new industry was capable of attracting levels of investment that BR could only have dreamed of. The emerging Network Rail has the stability of five-year funding agreements, whilst it escapes the old stop-go funding by being allowed to raise debt in the private market. Its performance is also closely regulated by an independent Office of Rail Regulation, whilst the Department for Transport holds train companies to their legally binding franchise commitments.

Tanya Jackson's new book takes us through this dramatic seesaw history of railway ownership from the pioneering days of the mid-nineteenth century to the becalming of the industry in the Great Depression. Then on to the high-minded rail nationalisation of 1945 to the golden age of the business sectors.

And finally back to today's more sophisticated compromise of private operation with public regulation.

Her well-researched book captures the atmosphere of Victorian travel perfectly, from the outrageous early extremes between first- and third-class travel to the huge human efforts that went into delivering an ever more complex and labour-intensive service. She reminds us how travel habits changed almost imperceptibly up to the Second World War with the gradual introduction of corridor coaches – and the means of reaching a toilet at last – electric lighting, the end of slip coaches, not to mention railway porters and closed compartments. The Great Depression saw the private companies unable to provide investment and becoming penniless by the end of the Second World War.

She then turns to the half century of the nationalised railways through which many of her readers have lived. She rightly reminds us that nationalisation brought a gigantic modernisation plan worth £25 billion in today's money – which had been unavailable to the Big Four. She then traces how this was squandered, with the result that Whitehall lost confidence in rail travel and abandoned rail to Dr Beeching whilst it diverted investment to the motorways.

British Rail did however belatedly get its act together in its final decade when it entered a golden age in which lively new brands such as InterCity, ScotRail and Network SouthEast appeared, bringing with them household names such as Inter-City 125, Sprinters, Networkers, Railcards, Travelcards and Savers.

Tanya Jackson concludes her scholarly narrative with a look at the current era, starting with the Big Bang which fragmented the industry into a hundred companies. She traces the appalling start that resulted in a spate of accidents before politicians and the rail industry managed to work successfully together just in time. There can now be no doubt today that we are living in a new golden era of rail on a scale that we have not seen since the mid-nineteenth century boom.

Passenger travel in Britain has *doubled* in the fifteen years since privatisation and has now reached unprecedented levels and is predicted to keep on growing. The big change is that Whitehall is now backing rail as a business with a future again and there seems to be all-party agreement that long-term investment is needed to develop rail capacity to meet and encourage the growth trend.

The future of the railway looks better in 2013 than it has done in any period since the nineteenth century – when the industry was untroubled by road or air competition. This book offers a timely review of the roller coaster that the industry has had to ride since the 1830s to get to this stable and encouraging position.

Introduction

This book started out with the working title of *British Rail: A Passenger's Journey*, because it is an account of passenger services on British Rail. In discussions with the publisher it was agreed that that the original title was slightly confusing and didn't really explain what the book was about. So I suggested *British Rail: The Nation's Railway*, as I had always wanted the book to show BR as a national asset, as 'the people's railway', one that served the entire country. The focus of the book, however, remains on passenger services.

It could be argued that this is quite appropriate since one of the most important changes that came about in the BR era was that the British railway system became predominantly a passenger railway, with freight very much in decline. The point to be made is that the enthusiast's habitual focus on the Beeching cuts and the demise of steam traction has hidden a much more significant story of the railways and their part in our wider social history. The time of BR was to see a revolution in the way we used the railways, and the way in which the railways were changed to suit modern needs and conditions. That is what the following is really about.

Research for this book really started when I was appointed British Rail carriage steward of the Historical Model Railway Society. That is an odd story in itself, as initially I applied for another stewardship. Two of these became vacant at once: the 'private owner wagon stewardship' and the 'carriage stewardship'. Having had a lifelong interest in private owner wagons I wrote to the committee offering to fill that post, only to be told that, very unusually, two people – myself and another – had applied. They pointed out that often no volunteers came forward to fill such posts. I took this as a subtle hint that the carriage steward vacancy was uncontested. As I am also interested in the subject of railway carriages and passenger services on British Rail, and also wanted to appear accommodating, I withdrew my application for the wagon stewardship and applied to be British Rail carriage steward. It has all worked out very well, I think. My 'rival' for the

PO wagon stewardship turned out to be none other than John A. Arkell, someone who already knew far more about PO wagons than I did then, or indeed possibly had more knowledge on that subject than I ever will. I hope that I have made myself useful as British Rail carriage steward during my time in the post.

Soon after I found myself part of the Historical Model Railway Society (HMRS) team that helped sort the British Rail Board residuary archive at Porchester Road. This was a colossal task in which the National Archives, the National Railway Museum and then the HMRS took turns respectively to record historically significant material from the mass accumulated by BR. I had my hands on real railway history at last! It is impossible to describe the volume of material we sorted through or to portray the atmosphere at Porchester Road archive, a dim Victorian building with bars on the windows, reminiscent of a prison, or perhaps a workhouse, or even possibly an asylum! It had originally been constructed by the Great Western Railway right beside the main line from Paddington. It is a great shame that the archive was broken up (the building has now been converted to luxury flats) but at least it has made much of the useful material accessible to future generations. The rest – we couldn't save it all – had to be destroyed, and I am sure I am not the only one who still has nightmares about that. Those were the rules – there was no fourth sift. Taking it home was not an option, but it was tempting.

One of the most important resources available to me for this book was a set of copies of *Modern Railways*, dating from the time the magazine changed its name from *Trains Illustrated* towards the end of the BR era. A large part of the collection – whole years – was donated to me by Alan Norris of Woking Railway Correspondence and Travel Society (RCTS), to whom I am very grateful indeed.

I had always had great respect for *Modern Railways* as both a popular magazine and one which carried serious professional insight into the industry, but that view was reconfirmed when I started turning the pages. In his *100 defining Aspects of BR*, Roger Ford listed *Modern Railways* itself as number 100. As someone who helped make the magazine what it is, some might think him biased in his praise, but I can quote his words with objectivity: 'In turn enthusiastic supporter, candid friend or severe critic, this magazine grew up with BR. In return the railway used these pages to fly kites, grind axes or pursue vendettas. For 34 years all BR life was there.'

Thanks are due to James Abbott, the current editor of *Modern Railways*, who gave me *carte blanche* to quote from the magazine. Thanks are also due to the publishers who have given me permission to quote from their works, particularly Ian Allan Publishing Ltd who have been most gracious in their assistance.

Thanks are also most certainly due to the Railways Archive http://www.railwaysarchive.co.uk/ which has made the task of accessing material so very much easier than it would have been. Many thanks also to many people, and I am not sure I have remembered them all in the list below – *mea culpa*.

Colin Divall; Susan Major; Terry Gourvish; Alan Norris of Woking RCTS; Malcolm Peakman; Bob Reid; Robert Carroll; Ashley Butlin; Irene Rabbitts of Woking RCTS; Adrian Vaughan; Chris Green; Peter Rayner; Terry Silcock (who has done sterling work for years as RCTS librarian); Stephen Poole; Helena Wojtczak; Howard Sprenger; Graham Feakins; Mark Brinton; Neil Flower; Douglas Lindsay; Adrian Curtis; Mike Robinson; Kit Spackman; David Halfpenny; John Atkinson; Ernest Bate; Jim Snowdon; Geoffrey Coward; Sophia Brothers of Science and Society Picture Library; Bill Bedford; Colin Boocock; Laurie Mack; Jonathan Wagstaff; Peter Stanton; Richard Gaff; Geoff Noakes; Hesham Gneady; Adrian Curtis; Anthony McDiarmid; Lawrence Mack.

The company stewards of the Historical Model Railway Society, particularly John Lewis, Paul Bartlett, Ivor Lewis, many members of the RCTS, the Southern email group, the LMS email group, and the Trackwork email group.

Indexing with the aid of PDF Index Generator: http://www.pdfindexgenerator.com.

Apologies to anyone I should have thanked but have overlooked.

1

Towards National Integration

By 1851, just twenty years after the opening of the Liverpool and Manchester Railway, over 6,000 route miles of railway had been constructed in the British Isles. A transport system connecting most of the major towns and cities of the United Kingdom had come into being within the lifetime of a single generation. In that year thousands of people from all over Britain travelled to the Great Exhibition by special excursion trains. The success of the Great Exhibition would not have been possible without the railways,[1] nor would the many railways then operating the system have been able to cope with the task had there not been an organisational system in place.

How had this happened? In the 1830s it was not at all certain that the railways then constructed would link up physically, let alone that railway companies would co-operate with each other in providing a national service. There had been at least one visionary seeing the need for a national system. The monomaniac Thomas Gray – a suitable candidate for the title of the world's first railway anorak – had published a series of pamphlets urging 'the establishment of a General Iron Rail-way' with lines running throughout the nation. Yet the early engineers created railways that didn't link up, and sometimes were of different gauges; not only was there Brunel's broad gauge of 7ft ¼in but there was also the 5ft gauge (until 1844) of the Eastern Counties Railway. Brunel arrogantly predicted that there would be no need for his Great Western Railway to exchange vehicles with other companies, as it would be entirely dominant in the west of England.

In Britain there was no planning of the railway system. Instead, railway schemes were each considered individually, supposedly each on its own merits. They were initiated by private individuals or companies sponsoring a private bill in parliament. Parliamentary powers were needed to compulsorily purchase other people's land. Private bills were by tradition considered by committees with little or no debate in the actual House. Only the committee members voted to pass the bill and, contrary to the norm of today, they were picked because they had a specific

interest (stake) in the matters concerned – in other words, they held constituencies local to where the railway was to be built, or were involved with the railway
company itself. This may seem objectionable to modern eyes but contemporaries,
such as the Prime Minister, Peel, were willing to defend this robustly. In 1844 a
rule change prevented MPs whose constituents were affected by proposals from
participating, but that just left those with financial interests in the schemes to fix
matters amongst themselves.[2]

The committees saw themselves primarily as umpires between the interests of
the landowners whose properties were to be affected and the railway companies
themselves. Apart from that the main aim seems to have been to guarantee the
fairness of tolls upon the railway. This was because it was originally envisaged that
the railways would be run like the existing turnpikes and tramways, such as the
failed Surrey Iron Railway. Railways were simply a new type of road upon which
all would be able to drive their vehicles, as long as the appropriate amount was
paid to the company that owned it. In 1840 a parliamentary committee recognised the impossibility of this:

> The intention of parliament cannot be carried into effect; the payment of
> tolls is only a very small part of the arrangement necessary to open railroads
> to public competition; any person with the mere authority to place an engine
> or carriages on a railway would be practically unable to supply his engine with
> water, or to take up and set down passengers … The safety of the public also
> required that upon every railway there should be one system of management
> under one superintending authority. On this account it is necessary that the
> company should possess a complete control over their line of road although
> they should thereby acquire a complete monopoly … [3]

But this didn't change anything in the way that railways were authorised.

Mark Casson finds that parliamentary decision-making tended to the creation
of the worst possible options. Main trunk routes could find themselves compelled
to have several additional branch lines tacked on and this created inefficient hubs
which were poor value in distributing traffic. Lines that should have been built
sometimes weren't because they faced fierce opposition from existing powerful
interests. Such a case was the proposal for a line from Oxford to Cheltenham.
The GWR put up its own rival scheme, never undertaken. On the other hand,
the system favoured aristocrats seeking to build uneconomic 'vanity lines' for
their own purposes – the Lewes–East Grinstead 'Bluebell' line would be a good
example here. Competition between railways led to the creation of surplus hubs,
some in locations remote from places actually served.[4]

Sometimes the process of getting a bill through parliament did forge successful
alliances to allow successful proposals and this resulted in useful lines, such as the
Great Northern and its loop line through South Yorkshire and Lincolnshire, but it

also resulted in multiple lines between those same places. In theory this should at least have brought the virtue of competition, but, as we shall see, the railways did their best to work together to avoid undercutting one another.

All this activity prompted the following criticism, addressed to Robert Peel in 1837:

> the great mistake … consists in viewing these vast projects as local measures, and in referring them to local committees. No one can doubt that they are far too important in a national point of view to be so considered. It is in fact this very thing which leads to the infusion of a local, consequently a restricted and not infrequently a selfish and exclusive, spirit in these undertakings.[5]

There was one attempt to scrutinise the bills presented to parliament and recommend the best according to an overall plan. During the winter of 1844 Lord Dalhousie, then President of the Board of Trade, had chaired a committee sorting through and recommending which railway bills should be authorised and which should not. The final say was parliament's, however, and this was where the plan fell through. Dalhousie opposed the extension of the broad gauge into the Midlands, yet the Oxford, Worcester and Wolverhampton Railway (OWW) wished to be a broad-gauge line. When it came to a vote the Prime Minister, Peel, voted for the OWW, leading Dalhousie to resign in objection to his recommendation being ignored. The idea of planning Britain's railway system outside the chaos of parliament's bill-by-bill approach vanished with him. Ironically, the OWW subsequently changed its mind and was built as a 4ft 8½in gauge line. The failure of Dalhousie's plans happened right before the 'Great Mania' – the second and most serious major influx of railway bills – when parliament seriously needed some guidance on which schemes to approve.

As early as 1844 the chairman of the London and Birmingham railway, George Carr Glyn, was to look back with regret and comment 'if a new start were being made, I would be for a state system'.[6]

Some commentators have put the lack of government guidance and intervention down to the trend of *laissez-faire* economics popular at that time, but Henry Parris, who made a study of the parliamentary proceedings, wrote that 'Nothing is more striking in these debates than the infrequency with which the voice of economic orthodoxy is heard.'[7] The conflicting causes of protecting the rights of landowners and free trade were themselves the subject of a wider national debate that was to result in the split of the old Tory party. Another possibility suggested is that victory in the Napoleonic wars was considered to have demonstrated the superiority of British liberty over state control.[8]

If parliament's approach to the construction of the railway system was disorganised, then its attempts to regulate them was laggardly. The first major piece of legislation was the Railway Regulation Act of 1840. This was not a government bill but was introduced on behalf of a select committee that had been appointed in 1839 as a result of traders' protests at the monopolistic behaviour of the London and Birmingham Railway Company. The act authorised the Board of Trade to appoint inspectors of railways and require companies to give the board one month's notice before a railway was opened. In 1842 a further act allowed the board to suspend the opening of a line if it wasn't satisfactory. Serious accidents were made reportable and drunkenness by staff constituted an offence.

It was in 1843 that the first published call for railway nationalisation emerged. This was a book entitled *Railway Reform*, written by William Galt. Galt was actually a proponent of *laissez-faire*, but excluded the railways from the free market, seeing them instead as a basic service that the state should provide to all.[9] Galt was a witness before Gladstone's Select Committee on the railways in February 1844, and as a result a railway bill was published giving the state the power to purchase any railway fifteen years after its inauguration, for a sum equating to twenty-five years of the net profits accrued by the railway. In the Commons this was changed to a clause enabling the government to purchase railways established after 1845, but not allowing this before 1 January 1866, and for a payment amounting to twenty-five years' profits averaged over the three preceding years. This power was never invoked, but there could have been little point in the government purchasing a fraction of the system anyway. Another proposal was passed, and this gave the act the alternative title of the 'cheap trains Act'. It required the railways to run workmen's trains, one in each direction once a day, at a fare of not more than a penny-a-mile and at a minimum speed of 12mph. It also set minimum standards for passenger carriages, including the requirement that they had roofs.

In 1845, faced with an upsurge of railway bills, parliament passed the Railway Clauses Consolidation Act, which set out standard clauses to be inserted into all new railway acts. This was at least a form of standardisation, but it left a number of routes that were authorised on a different basis.

In the early days of the railways passengers were the prime users of trains, as opposed to freight, but there was already concern for those using railways to transport goods. The Common Law had set out the role of a Common Carrier, with various duties and responsibilities, but this was largely dispensed with by the Carriers Act of 1830, which set such a role on a statutory footing. It was never tested in court whether this act applied to the railways, so, as the railways quickly became a dominant monopoly, parliament made sure of the railways' duties.[10] Section 90 of the Railways Clauses Consolidation Act had required that railways should treat customers equally, but of course it only applied to railways built after 1845. 'Cardwell's Act' – officially the Railway and Canal Traffic Act 1854 – stated that they should not 'make or give any undue or unreasonable preference or advantage to or in favour of any particular person or company, or any particular description of traffic …'[11] The companies now had to 'afford all reasonable facilities for the receiving and forwarding and delivering of traffic …' In other words, railways now had to provide suitable facilities to carry whatever was presented to them unless particular exceptions were made. An act of 1868 required that charges be 'disintegrated' – meaning that the railways had to be open about what they were charging for and itemise their bills. A further act of 1873 compelled the publication of all rates in force and their disintegration upon request by any interested person. A body of 'Railway Commissioners' was also set up, with the purpose of hearing cases of dispute over railway charges and their obligations.

A further Railway and Canal Traffic Act was passed in 1888, after two select committees reported. This set up the Commissioners on a permanent basis and renamed them the 'Railway and Canal Commission'. This was the prototype body of the Transport Tribunal that oversaw the pricing structure through much of the British Railways era. At a time when the railways were in a monopoly position this affected them little, but later, when they faced competition, restrictions on pricing led to protests from the railways that the law was unfair.

Parliament was very slow to regulate in terms of safety. Numerous horrific accidents occurred whilst it turned its face against interference in the railways' affairs. The number of company directors in parliament, or the number of MPs who became company directors, is a plausible explanation for this, but there were also technical disagreements over which safety devices should be applied. (The companies couldn't even agree over what type of couplings should be used.) Sometimes these issues boiled down to self-interest as well; for instance, several senior locomotive engineers in the companies had their own patents on braking systems.

In the mid-1860s two high-profile murders aboard trains, in successive years, led to the adoption of a standard system whereby passengers aboard trains could raise the alarm. In 1868 parliament finally made such a system compulsory on all passenger trains.

But it took the Armagh disaster of 1889 to seriously change parliament's attitude regarding the need for regulation to prevent accidents. A public outcry ensued after this event and parliament was finally stirred to regulate.

By this time technology existed to enable the brakes on each vehicle of a train to be controlled from the locomotive or guard's van, and to automatically apply the brakes if the vehicle became detached from the train, or if some other fault occurred with the braking. This was now made compulsory in the Regulation Act of 1889, as also was block signalling and interlocking of points and signals.

Even so, the act did not specify which type of brake needed to be fitted, only that it needed to be automatic and had to be of a type approved of by the Board of Trade (BoT). Here the BoT could have imposed uniformity by choosing only to approve one type, but it did not. The Westinghouse air brake and the vacuum brake were both approved. Most companies opted for the simpler vacuum brake, but some, like the London, Brighton and South Coast Railway, opted for the air brake. This inevitably led to problems with the interworking of stock. Another issue that arose was that, after all this negotiation, the companies were unable to agree on the size and position of the connecting hoses on stock.

One most important piece of legislation parliament did manage to implement was the Railway Clearing House Act of 1850. This gave statutory recognition to the Railway Clearing House (RCH), the most important unifying organisation of the British railway system until the creation of British Railways.[12]

Originally formed by the companies in 1842, the RCH was inspired by a similar organisation that facilitated stagecoach travel. This was based at the Golden Cross near Charing Cross in London and enabled accounts to be settled between stagecoach companies. Tickets sold by one stagecoach company often authorised passengers to use the coach of another company on a part of their journey. Revenues accrued were divided between the companies on a mileage basis through the Clearing House. Such a system greatly aided travel and the railways realised they needed something similar.

The RCH pioneered a ticketing system to facilitate through travel. This was devised by Thomas Edmondson. It involved a robust form of ticket made of card and measuring 1¼in by 2¼in. Issued complete with serial numbers and date-stamped, the ticket was a token in an accounting circle, being carried by the passenger throughout the length of the journey; it authorised travel until it was surrendered to the ticket collector at the end. Then it was bundled up with others to be sent to the accounting department. If the passenger's journey had been confined solely to the lines of the ticket's issuing company, then its journey ended there; if not it went to the Clearing House for an 'inquest' to determine the correct apportioning of revenues due.[13] The Edmondson system required that stations be 'closed'. This meant that no one was allowed on to or off the platforms of a station without a ticket check, or surrendering a ticket at the end of the journey. This system was essentially for the apportioning of revenues when many companies existed, but survived well into the BR era, 'open' stations only becoming common as the level of staff dwindled. Main-line stations did not become open until the 1980s, and Southern terminals at Waterloo still have a ticket check at barriers.

The Clearing House adopted the Edmondson system and made it compulsory for all members. In doing so they achieved their aim of enabling through booking from one company to another, to yet another, wherever the passenger needed to go.

By 1845 more than half a million people had been booked straight through to their destinations at great convenience to themselves and minimal cost to the companies.[14] The Clearing House also solved the problem of through coaches, proving that Brunel was wrong in his belief that companies would not trust their carriages and wagons in the hands of others. From January 1842 a system of charging by the mile was introduced, by which one company would in effect 'hire' a coach from a foreign railway when it passed onto its rails. Now customers could relax and get comfortable in their carriage, since it would take them for the whole journey, whichever railway's line they were to end up on. As we shall note later, that is a level of comfort that has been dispensed with. Similar arrangements allowed freight wagons to travel onto rival lines. There were, inevitably, some disputes about accuracy of charges centring on such things as the accuracy of maps but, on the whole, thanks to the RCH, sanity had broken out and the system had passed a most essential hurdle in integration. As well as providing the facilities for revenues to be distributed between the companies it also provided a neutral ground where managers of different companies could meet and sort out matters of mutual interest or settle disputes.

From 1851 the RCH played an important part in organising excursion traffic, with the Great Exhibition functioning as the spur and Joseph Paxton himself urging matters be taken in hand. Excursions had been a feature of the railways since at least the early 1840s, but from 1851 the trade grew with the assistance of the Clearing House. Many would have got their first experience of rail travel on a journey to the Great Exhibition.[15]

Although Thomas Cook is usually credited as being the inventor of the railway excursion there are other candidates. Cook's clientele were the middle classes, but cheap trips were also offered by such entrepreneurs as Henry Marcus, who served as agent for the LNWR and was proclaimed as the 'father of cheap trips' in a later testimonial.[16] The cheap excursion was to be a feature of the railway system for well over a hundred years, until they were finally abandoned in the profit-driven 1980s.

To further facilitate through services from 1850 the RCH co-ordinated time-tables between the companies at monthly meetings, an arrangement that stayed in place until nationalisation. Given this you would have thought that the publication of a national timetable would have been possible and that the RCH would have been the organising body, but that was not so. It was left up to private individuals and Bradshaw was just one of several publishers who provided such a guide.

In September 1847 the Clearing House Committee resolved to recommend that its members adopt Greenwich Mean Time (GMT) as a standard. Prior to this every town in the country had its own local time, based on the position of the sun at that location. This standardisation of time was speedily adopted by the members of the RCH. Even the GWR, not yet a member of the Clearing House, adopted GMT by the early 1850s. Clock towers sprang up across Britain as time became a 'modern' preoccupation.[17]

The RCH could and should have also been a forum where important safety measures were agreed but here the individuality and resistance of its member companies meant that little headway was made in an area that did not promise to increase profits. Such issues would have to wait – and wait – on parliament for regulation.

What the Clearing House did achieve though, was to bring about a (sort of) universal Rule Book (note the capitals, it is the Rule Book).

For those unfamiliar with the railway Rule Book, it is the basic regulatory document upon the railway, laying out regulations on conduct, safety, signalling and basic working practices whilst operating lines and trains. The railways of Britain, having grown up individually, were very inconsistent in terms of things like signalling practice, and such variations led to accidents. A classic example is that red discs were used on some railways to indicate proceed, while the same colour discs were displayed by other companies to indicate danger.

The first Rule Book issued by the RCH started out amidst concerns regarding crews' working trains over 'foreign' lines, that is, lines of another company where they would otherwise have to be issued with that company's rule book as well as that of the company they worked for. Thus was born the 'Rules of Working Over Foreign Lines'. It was to serve as an appendix to be bound in with the companies' own Rule Books and was drafted so as to 'avoid any interference with existing rules'.[18]

This situation did not last for much longer (too long, of course, for those who died in the intervening time). By 1874 there had been enough carnage to even ruffle parliament, which was threatening legislation. In March 1874 the General Managers' Conference approved a far more comprehensive set of rules, this time expressed in authoritative terms. Although individual peculiarities remained, the RCH rules now had supremacy over those of individual companies.

One of the most debatable aspects of the RCH was its function in stifling competition amongst the railways – or in ensuring the survival of competing services – you can take your pick.

The RCH became the mechanism by which the railways came together and agreed on rates and fares, this co-operation sometimes having the effect of eliminating competition between them.

The Select Committee of 1872 on Railway and Canal Amalgamations stated that:

There has on different occasion been effectual competition between railway companies in the matter of charges, and it is probable that the charges now made still bear the traces of that competition. But it may be taken as a general rule that there is now no active competition between different railways in the matter of rates and fares.[19]

It seems that early on the general managers recognised a truth that was to be summed up, many years later, by Sir W. Guy Granet, general manager of the Midland Railway, 'The paradoxical position under the rule of unlimited competition is that competition must be restricted or ruin will inevitably follow.'[20]

In order to maintain some sort of competition parliament resisted, to some degree, attempts to amalgamate companies. Some amalgamations made sense, such as the one that created the LNWR – giving single control to the main trunk line from London to Manchester to Birmingham (also known as the West Coast Main Line) and this was authorised in 1846 – the first big merger. Other attempted mergers were thwarted as they made little sense apart from preventing competition. Nevertheless, there was a gradual move towards combining operations from larger companies. An alternative was the creation of joint lines which, as Mark Casson points out, were often attempts by multiple companies to poach a rival's traffic. Where competition did break out – as between the South Eastern Railway and the London Chatham and Dover Railway (LCDR), the results were not necessarily for the good. Parliament had to accept a forced marriage of the two companies when the LCDR came close to bankruptcy. The Midland Railway, forming the major part of one of three routes to Scotland, competed by the strategy of promoting its third-class passengers to the grade below first (the term 'third class' was retained and 'second' abolished) and at the same time reducing its first-class fares to those of the former second class. This stole a march on competitors and was a manoeuvre which helped seal the Midland's reputation for comfort.[21]

By the latter half of the nineteenth century the Clearing House was thoroughly established as the main binding ingredient of the British railway system. Simply to operate the requirements of Cardwell's Act membership of the RCH was required. It was bureaucracy – in 1883 Frederick Williams reported that there were 2,100 clerks working for the RCH.[22] It had risen from six in 1843 and 600 in 1861. By the start of the First World War more than 3,000 persons were employed by the Clearing House as clerks or else as number-takers, monitoring the movement of wagons at many junctions around the country. These were the bureaucrats needed to support a system of many hundreds of privately owned railways. Could it be organised more effectively, people wondered? The argument for railway nationalisation never really went away.

In his book *The Political Economy*, republished in various editions from 1848 to 1871, John Stuart Mill stated that there was no reason why the railways should not be owned by the state but leased out to private companies to run for limited periods – an idea which sounds remarkably like the present system of franchising. In 1864 Galt prepared and distributed an updated version of his *Railway Reform* and the issue of state purchase was smuggled onto the agenda of the Royal Commission on Railways of 1865. This commission decided that Gladstone's 1844 Act had in fact made the issue of railway purchase more difficult, and pointed up a number of other problems.[23] The government declined to act in the face of the committee's report but in 1868 purchased the telegraph system from the private companies that operated it and placed it under the control of the Post Office. This was regarded as a success and spurred on calls for railway nationalisation.[24]

By the late nineteenth century those calling for railway nationalisation were joined by the socialists and the Amalgamated Society of Railway Servants, whose

Congress voted to press for nationalisation of the railways.[25] In 1894 the Railway Reform Association was established, in 1895 the Railway Nationalisation League was formed and in 1908 the Railway Nationalisation Society came into being, this latter enjoying the support of members from all three political parties: Labour, Liberal and Conservative.[26] In the same year the Labour Party committed itself to nationalisation. In 1913 the Liberal government appointed a Royal Commission to investigate railway nationalisation, but the war intervened.[27]

During the war the railways came under control of the government via a committee of railway managers. Strictly speaking this was not nationalisation but rather a case of 'borrowing' in the national interest. After the war the coalition government under Lloyd George returned to the issue of reforming the railways. In 1919 the Ministry of Transport was established with the Conservative politician Eric Geddes as the First Minister. Plans were laid for changes to the ownership of the railways and at a Cabinet meeting of 7 June 1920 three proposals were outlined. The first was complete nationalisation: the state would take over both ownership and operation of the railway system. The second was to allow the railways to go back to their pre-war position. The third was viewed as a middle course: to continue with private ownership but force an amalgamation of the existing companies into larger groups, together with a mixture of direct and indirect state supervision. It was the third option that was adopted.[28]

The justification for this was 'found in the history of the railways of this country. They had grown up in an unsystematic and parochial fashion, with the result that they were now very expensive and wasteful.'

And the minutes continue:

> A number of comparative figures were laid before the Cabinet, showing that the efficiency of our railway system was inferior in many respects to that of other countries whose commercial and industrial development had been more or less parallel with our own. The nation could not afford to perpetuate this inferior system, and it was therefore necessary, while retaining the advantages of private ownership and permitting competition between the areas served by groups, to frame a policy which would enable a gradual levelling up process to take place.[29]

The proposal was accepted by the Cabinet, initially on the basis that there would be five or six groups. In the intervening months, before a bill was presented to parliament, there were discussions with traders and the companies during which the proposals were thrashed out.

The suggestion of a London Group involving 'the passenger carrying railways local to London, such as the District Railway and the Tube railways'[30] was abandoned, Geddes believing that the problems of London's transport were better dealt with in a scheme that involved the bus and tram services as well.[31] He supported the idea of a Scottish Group but in this he was over-ruled, but his view that the East Coast Main Line should be owned by one group rather than split between two companies was carried forward. In the end, four companies emerged; these were designated in schedule one of the act as the Southern Group, the Western Group, the North Western, Midland and West Scottish Group and the North Eastern, Eastern and East Scottish Group. The act designated constituent and subsidiary companies for each of the groups, the constituents being the major players and the subsidiaries the small fry that got scooped into the net.

We know these groups better by the names they adopted for themselves. They are: the Southern Railway, the Great Western Railway, the London Midland and Scottish Railway and the London and North Eastern Railway. In fact the Great Western Railway was the only survivor of the act, compelled by it to amalgamate with many of the other railways that had entered its sphere of operations. Brunel had been wrong about the Great Western achieving a monopoly in the west, but it still outlasted its contemporaries due to its overwhelming dominance.

The North Western, Midland and West Scottish Group became the London Midland and Scottish Railway; it consisted of the London and North Western, and the Caledonian: those companies that formed the West Coast Main Line. Also included were the Lancashire and Yorkshire (which the LNWR took over the year before) and the Midland Railway.

The North Eastern, Eastern, and East Scottish Group became the London and North Eastern Railway. It consisted of the Great Northern, the North Eastern and the North British – the three partners of the East Coast Main Line. The North British was also the partner of the Midland on the Midland Main Line to Scotland, leading to co-operation between the two companies. Also included in the LNER were the Great Eastern and the Great Central.

The grouping south of the Thames became the Southern Railway, consisting of the London and South Western Railway, the London Brighton and South Coast Railway, the South Eastern Railway and the London Chatham and Dover Railway – by that time run by the same organisation and known collectively as the South Eastern and Chatham Railway.

The three new companies lasted only twenty-five years, but nevertheless have achieved considerable status in the public consciousness. Perhaps this is because they are still within living memory for some; others undoubtedly believe they were older than they were. In between the wars the four companies did manage to stamp their identities on the network, and overcoming this to form a national system would be one of the problems that would face British Railways.

Geddes's view that the issue of London public transport needed a separate solution was taken forward by the London Traffic Act of 1924. Amongst other measures it set up an advisory committee that recommended that London public transport operations should come under single management with a common fund.

This would have been a private company so it was vigorously opposed by Labour. In 1929 the bill was defeated in parliament.

The next year Herbert Morrison submitted his proposals to take London's passenger transport operations into public ownership, run by a public board. After much discussion London Transport and the London Passenger Transport Board (LPTB) were born when the London Passenger Transport Act was passed on 13 April 1933.

Although not a national system, the scale of the LPTB's operation was still enormous and undoubtedly comparable to the national railway systems in many other countries at that time, or even today. London was a sprawling metropolis and the tentacles of the Underground system, the buses and the trams were quickly spreading to the outer limits of the great conurbation and into the Home Counties. The LPTB was the first experiment to be conducted in this country where public transport of several kinds was being operated by a single public body. Under its dynamic leaders, Frank Pick and Lord Ashfield, it was to become a notable success in unifying and expanding London's transport system and in giving it a common brand image. Its success could only have encouraged those who believed in public ownership that its expansion would be for the better, and perhaps those who were less than enthusiastic as well.

The Labour government that had made it happen was to last for only a single term. The Conservatives took control of parliament again but did nothing to roll back the advance of public ownership regarding London transportation. In 1939 the country was yet again at war and the companies suddenly became 'essential military equipment' once more, for a second time run by a committee of railway managers on behalf of the government. As in the First World War the Cabinet was formed by coalition, this time a mixture of Conservative and Labour ministers. Thus the Labour Party was in a position to put forward its ideas for nationalisation.

Oddly enough it was not a Labour MP who initiated the planning of what was to become the British Transport Commission. This idea can be traced to the work of Sir John Reith,[32] previously the founding Director General of the BBC, where he had established the principle of public service being quite distinct from a market-driven philosophy. Amongst other things, Reith had resisted Churchill's attempt to take over the BBC and use it as a government mouthpiece during the General Strike of 1926.

Sir John had gone on to be chairman of Imperial Airways before being invited to participate in the wartime coalition Cabinet, becoming the Member of Parliament for Southampton to enable him to do so. He was the Minister of Information under Chamberlain, then Minister of Transport under Churchill.[33] He set in motion the planning of a National Transport Corporation that would serve the wartime needs of the country and also its peacetime needs after the war. Churchill gave his blessing to the exploration of these ideas and the Deputy Secretary of the Ministry, Sir Alfred Robinson, and Dr William Coates (from ICI) thrashed out some proposals.

Meanwhile the idea was discussed in Cabinet but met strong opposition – particularly from Lord Beaverbrook. On 3 October Reith was relieved of his post as Minister of Transport but nevertheless the Coates-Robinson Report appeared a couple of weeks later. The proposal was for a body with a complete monopoly of internal road, rail and air services. It was to consist of nine to twelve members with subsidiary regional boards and management committees.[34]

Reith was succeeded as Transport Minister by Moore-Brabazon and then by Lord Leathers, neither of whom showed overwhelming enthusiasm for the Coates-Robinson plan, but it was drawn to the attention of Lord Leathers by another civil servant in the ministry: Cyril Hurcomb. Leathers authorised a further exploration of the ideas by Coates and a further report was delivered in 1942.

In the same year the annual conference of the Labour Party passed a resolution urging that the government should co-ordinate road, rail and inland waterways under national ownership, with a special emphasis on meeting wartime needs. The next year it published a pamphlet calling for the socialisation of British transport and even quoting Lord Leathers in support of the idea.

Although the concept of a body with a national monopoly of all transport had been dismissed by the wartime Cabinet, the idea of railway unification – indeed nationalisation – clearly met with approval. A memorandum of a meeting attended by, amongst others, Attlee and Leathers was discussed by the whole Cabinet on 15 July 1941. The document was entitled 'The Future Of The Railways' and showed that there was much discussion about the future of the railway after the war and that the general feeling was that unification, or nationalisation, was desirable and would be the most likely outcome. The debate in that meeting, and the question posed to the wider Cabinet, was not whether it would happen, or should happen, but at what point the announcement would be made. The announcement was put off.[35]

With the war ended the coalition broke up and each party set out its stall for the 1945 general election. The 1945 Labour Party manifesto promised to place inland transport in public ownership, contending that co-ordination could not be achieved without unification and the setting aside of sectional interests.[36]

Meanwhile, the Conservative manifesto came out against the creation of a state monopoly, but then hedged its bets with the suggestion that an independent tribunal was the appropriate remedy if such a thing existed. It promised a transport system of the highest efficiency – details still to be worked out.

It was the Labour Party who caught the national mood and triumphed with a landslide victory in the general election of 5 July 1945, gaining 393 seats to the Conservatives' 197. Perhaps surprisingly the nationalisation of transport was not mentioned in the King's Speech of 15 August 1945, which outlined the legislative programme of the new government. A draft announcement of the nationalisation was made in the House of Commons by Herbert Morrison (Lord President of the Council and Chairman of the Cabinet Committee) on 19 November. It was to be almost two years before the Transport Act was passed in 1947.

During that time the railway companies sought to resist the plans for nationalisation with posters and pamphlets. At this point an interesting suggestion emerged from the LNER. It was the 'Landlord and Tenant Scheme'. Under this plan the government would purchase the track and structures and would then lease them back to the companies. The proceeds would be used to modernise the entire system whilst the rent charged would be calculated so that the railways were on an equal footing with road transport – the track would effectively become another form of government-maintained road. It was a scheme that was in some ways similar to that devised by the government in the 1990s.[37]

Meanwhile the new Minister of War Transport (as he was then), Alfred Barnes, considered the options. Cyril Hurcomb drew his attention to the Coates-Robinson proposals and these formed the basis for the new plans. The idea of regional boards running all transport facilities in a particular area was viewed as too difficult in terms of organisation, and also it was thought that the railways – then still the most popular mode of transport – would become the dominant force in each of them. With that view taken, thoughts turned to a board for each mode of transport working under an umbrella organisation. At various turns, these became 'executives' and the umbrella organisation became a 'commission': the British Transport Commission (BTC). The executives were to be the agents of a commission in whom ownership of the transport concerns – railways, road transport, docks and canals – were to be vested. This was the scheme presented to parliament via the Transport Bill of 1946. One point of contention was the powers of appointment in terms of the executive members. Hurcomb believed strongly that for the commission to be an effective organisation it needed the power to hire and fire the members of the executives, but political pressure was brought to bear to secure these powers to the minister himself.[38] Hurcomb was to be stuck with the minister's appointments for the executives, and in the case of the head of the Railway Executive, he didn't like it.

Although the idea of regional boards had been dismissed there was of course one that came readymade: the London Passenger Transport Board. Under the act this now became the London Transport Executive (LTE), all of its assets now vested in the BTC. The LTE was in a way a microcosm of the BTC, covering all forms of transport but for London alone.

Apart from the LTE there was a Railways Executive, a Road Transport Executive, a Hotels Executive and a Docks and Waterways Executive (it was said of this last that all that the docks and canals really had in common was water). Of these by far the largest undertaking was the Railway Executive, despite the fact that the railways were now to be shorn of many of their assets. The many docks they had built up, such as the Southern Railway's docks in Southampton, were to be transferred to the Docks and Waterways Executive. Some of their road transport undertakings went to the Road Transport Executive. The many hotels went to the Hotels Executive. This was far from satisfactory from the point of view of those who had worked to build up the railways as industrial empires.

Also set up by the act was the Central Transport Consultative Committee (CTCC) and the Transport Users Consultative Committees (TUCCs). The TUCCs were regional and set up with representatives from 'agriculture, commerce, industry, shipping, labour and local authorities', all to be appointed by the minister.

Most of the parliamentary debate on the bill was taken up with the question of compensation to the shareholders, who were to be dispossessed of their assets. Little attention was given to the structure of the organisation or whether it was necessary at all. Conservative MP Tufton Beamish protested at this lack of discussion, and the use of the parliamentary guillotine, commenting: 'I submit that the Government have not adduced a scrap of evidence that the transport industry is, in fact, inefficient. Nor for that matter has any hon. or right hon. Member on this side of the House sought to prove that there was not room for improvement.'[39]

2

Some Sort of an Organisation

When we reorganise, we bleed.

Gerry Fiennes

Just a few months before the nationalisation of Britain's railways, on 15 August 1947, India had gained its independence. This was surely one of the defining symbols of the decline of Britain's place in the world, and its prosperity. BR was born into a post-war world where its priorities were to be defined not by serving an industrial heart with guaranteed markets throughout the world, but by functioning in an entirely new economic reality, where Britain's industries were going to have to compete on equal footing with those of other nations. There was now to be competition from the roads and from the internal airlines.

Despite the changing situation the nationalisation of the railways did not originally bring accompanying changes to the economic legislation by which the railways were bound. The Railway Rates Tribunal was renamed the Transport Tribunal, and for more than a decade after nationalisation retained its powers to tell the railway how much it could charge for its services. There was also to be political interference in railway charges. The requirements and restrictions of the Railway and Canal Traffic Act of 1854 also remained in force – the railways still had to 'afford all reasonable facilities for the receiving and forwarding and delivering of traffic …' despite no longer having the monopoly that the act was designed to counter.

Yet, in theory at least, the railways were still to be viewed as a business and the British Transport Commission was intended to break even, with the rider (which no one seems to have really understood) 'taking one year with another'. They were to find themselves caught in the middle and increasingly squeezed, as legislative demands for them to provide services conflicted with their ability to raise enough money independently to pay for it all. Did the successive governments really believe that the railways could break even? Churchill,

Conservative Prime Minister from 1951 to 1955, stated that 'it doesn't matter whether the nationalised railway shows a deficit, though of course every possible economy should be used in their administration'.[1] Essentially the railways were, if necessary, to be run at a loss as a public service; it was only when the deficit grew to alarming proportions that panic set in and remedial measures were seen to be necessary.

The 1948 Act was not to be parliament's last word on how the railways were run – far from it. The Railway Executive's reign was to be brief, though it did accomplish rather a lot. It had largely rebuilt the main-line track work to pre-war standards by 1953.[2] It designed and built some new steam locomotives, carriages and wagons. It undertook experiments with lightweight diesel multiple-units and paved the way for the 25,000V electrification system to be adopted as standard.

The Railway Executive (RE) also set up the administrative areas known as 'regions'. There were initially six: Eastern, London Midland, North Eastern, Scottish, Southern, and Western (In 1967 the Eastern and North Eastern regions were combined). The regions were essentially echoes of the inter-war companies but now with Scotland administered separately. It may have been that this was only ever intended to be a temporary measure in order to retain the operating structure of the old companies whilst something new was sorted out, yet the regions were to prove that they had staying power. Under the Executive those in charge of the regions were merely chief officers and the real power lay with the Executive. Each member of the Executive was head of a system-wide department; for instance, Robin Riddles was the executive member responsible for mechanical and electrical engineering.

The 1947 act required the commission to 'provide, or secure or promote the provision of, an efficient, adequate, economical and properly integrated system of public inland transport and port facilities within Great Britain for passengers and goods …'[3] It also empowered the commission to take necessary steps for extending and improving the transport and port facilities. In the pamphlet *The Organization of British Transport*, published by the BTC in 1948, Hurcomb wrote that the different modes of transport had different characteristics, making them suitable for different purposes. Simply, Hurcomb considered that railways were best used for long journeys and/or large numbers of people or volume of goods, with roads more suited to making short journeys and/or carrying smaller numbers of passengers and volumes of goods.[4] He doesn't sound at all unlike Beeching. Had Hurcomb's scheme proceeded it would undoubtedly have resulted in many lines being closed and given up to buses in the name of integration and efficiency, rather than for reasons of economy and market forces. One difference is that Hurcomb's BTC may have arranged better substitute bus services than the BTC of Robertson and Beeching, or the British Railways Board.

The RE did make some attempts to identify surplus resources, as we shall see in Chapter 6, but it was overtaken by political events.

The Conservatives won back power in 1951 and in 1953 they passed another Transport Act. As a consequence the Railway Executive was abolished and the BTC was put in direct charge of the railways. At this point the railway regions were raised in status and local boards were set up to give more input. The politicians now insisted that the railways undertake *Modernisation* – replacing much of the locomotives, infrastructure and rolling stock. At the same time as this was implemented the railway's finances started to descend into the red. Remedial action involved yet another Transport Act in 1962. This abolished the British Transport Commission and created the British Railways Board. The infamous Dr Beeching became the last chairman of the Commission and the first chairman of the board.

In 1968 the Labour government changed the whole way in which the railway was financed. It created a system of grants for socially necessary services as well as empowering the minister to create 'Passenger Transport Authorities' and 'Executives' to operate and subsidise public transport in major urban centres outside London. From 1974 there were seven of these. The 1968 Act represents a consensus that has not truly been changed by any party in Britain – that some railway services must be funded by government for social purposes.

The modernisation plan had involved high levels of spending, but after that BR was put on a drip feed with practically every investment scrutinised by the Treasury and having to be justified on commercial grounds. There was continual pressure for BR to operate some parts at a profit and to be more businesslike. To this end a major change in how BR operated came in the early 1980s when the business sectors began to emerge – InterCity, Provincial (later Regional Railways), London and the South East (later Network SouthEast) as well as the freight sector. These sectors grew in power and importance throughout the 1980s and led, at long last, to the abolition of the mighty regions.

During its existence BR was to undergo a very large number of reorganisations at local, regional and commission/board level. It is hard to select a time when BR wasn't reorganising, usually to satisfy its political masters in respect of gaining greater efficiency savings. There were also a very large number of investigations, courts of inquiry, parliamentary select committee reports and all manner of people poking their noses into railway business. In the 1950s, as mentioned previously, fares and charges were decided by the tribunal but not only that, railway wages were decided by several courts of inquiry, basing their findings on abstract notions such as fairness. Of course the railway was left to pay for it all. Then, as you might expect, there were problems in trying to close uneconomic operations – more on this in Chapter 5.

When things were going seriously wrong parliament set up the Stedeford inquiry, led by a leading businessman, to investigate the railways. This was in addition to the usual investigations being carried out by parliamentary committees. As well as being the era of the 'Beeching reports', the 1960s was almost one long investigation of BR by the government, and also a time when the Treasury had begun to squeeze railway investment and force BR to justify every penny – a situation that continued for the rest of its days. In the 1980s there was the Serpell Report which threatened to complete what Beeching had started and reduce the railway to a truly basic, skeletal trunk route system. This was vetoed by the politicians but BR came under increasing pressure from the Conservative government to cut costs and to make a profit on those areas where this was seen to be practical.

On top of all this there seemed to be an endless supply of economists launching into print seeking to establish their reputations by criticising the nationalised industries, and particularly BR. Everyone wanted to 'play trains', even if it was only with a pen and paper. Now the railways were nationalised and belonged to the people, it seemed as if all and sundry could offer suggestions for improvement. After all, the commentators reasoned, 'Everyone knows how they should be run, surely it's obvious?'

The people in charge of the railways over the years came from a variety of backgrounds. Right at the top was the Transport Minister, or the Secretary of State for Transport, or for the Environment, depending on the government departments' remits. The post is usually given to the type of politician who is coming into, or falling out of, favour. For this reason the minister responsible was always in the position of Hoffnung's hapless bricklayer: either on the way up or on the way down, and always in imminent danger of receiving a severe blow. This unhappy scenario is something that did not change after privatisation, as the fiasco of the West Coast Main Line franchise has shown. Even the department responsible for transport has been phased in and out of existence. In the early 1970s this organisation became part of the Department of the Environment, only to become a ministry again in the early days of the Thatcher regime and to be relegated to a mere department shortly afterwards.

Responsible to the minister was the chairman of the BTC, or later the BRB and, of course, from 1948 to 1953 there was also the post of Chairman of the Executive.

The first head of the British Transport Commission, Cyril Hurcomb, had of course been the civil servant who had helped create the organisation. He was to clash forcefully with the first Chairman of the Railway Executive, Sir Eustace Missenden. Missenden was a career railwayman with a distrust of civil servants and, it would seem, those who had a better educational background than his own. Sir Eustace had joined the railways straight from school, whereas Hurcomb was an Oxford graduate and a high-flying civil servant who was unaccountably jealous of the railway managers. This clash of personalities bedevilled the first years of the BTC, but came to an end when Missenden retired and was replaced by John Elliot, another Southern man but one who had a more relaxed outlook.

Hurcomb himself retired in 1953, making way for Sir Brian Robertson. With a distinguished military and diplomatic career behind him, Sir Brian had retired from the army because he was passed over for the post of Chief of the General Staff, due to the fact that he had never commanded an army in the field. In many ways the chairmanship of the BTC was a consolation prize. Robertson, however, did not realise what he was getting into. He was later to confide in John Elliot that when he had accepted Churchill's offer to run the railways he had no idea that the management had been 'destroyed' before he arrived.[5] In place of the void left by the Executive Robertson created an extensive bureaucracy which often thwarted the purposes of the organisation it was meant to serve. Robertson's chairmanship was overshadowed by a growing deficit when increased labour costs and a decline in freight traffic forced an already difficult financial situation into the red. Despite the financial problems, Robertson fought valiantly for the electrification of the West Coast Main Line, and this achievement, if nothing else, stands today as his great legacy.

When the Conservative Lennox-Boyd was offered the role of Transport Minister by Churchill he commented that it sounded like a job for a 'rather unprincipled person'.[6] Subsequently they actually managed to land one, because in 1959 Ernest Marples was appointed to the role. Marples was a founder of the firm Marples Ridgway, which, amongst other things, specialised in road building. Under Marples's tenure of the post, the motorway network was authorised, with Marples Ridgway benefiting from massive motorway construction contracts. When the issue was raised in parliament Marples made a written statement in which he did not deny his vested interest.[7] He also keenly believed that the railways should compete with the roads. It was Marples who was to be given the task of sorting out the deficit that British Railways was accruing and Marples who appointed Richard Beeching to make a report, and he also piloted the 1962 Transport Act through parliament. As stated above, this is examined in more detail in Chapter 5. Marples and Beeching had a good and productive working relationship, but the policy of rail cuts was unpopular in the country and probably contributed to the Conservative Party's loss of power in the 1964 election. No further significant *statutory* change of the railway's controlling body and structure was made until the privatisation of the 1990s.

Richard, subsequently 'Lord', Beeching had previously worked for ICI, as technical director with a seat on the board. He had originally been appointed to the Stedeford Committee that had investigated BR's problems and after this he became the last chairman of the BTC. As an added inducement to lure him from his position with ICI, he was paid £24,000 per annum, as against Robertson's £10,000.[8]

Beeching was in turn succeeded by Sir Stanley Raymond. Raymond had been raised in an orphanage and had made his way up through the ranks, an achievement of which he was very proud.[9] He was to cross swords with the Labour

Transport Minister Barbara Castle, who eventually terminated his employment by telephone. When this happened he was in the middle of negotiating with the unions and, according to one of those present, took the news of his dismissal with considerable equanimity.[10]

Barbara Castle initially wished to appoint Peter Parker, a businessman with left-wing credentials, but when invited initially he turned down the role.[11] Sir Stanley Raymond was succeeded by Henry Johnson, the former General Manager of the London Midland Region, who had overseen the successful electrification of that region's flagship West Coast Main Line. Johnson was another career railwayman who had started on the LNER.

When Johnson retired in 1971, the Conservative Transport Minister chose Richard Marsh as his replacement. This was something of a surprise, since Marsh had been the Labour Minister for Transport who had succeeded Barbara Castle. Marsh was a notoriously temperamental personality, who was characterised as a 'whinger' by *Modern Railways*.[12] However, he did fight his corner to try to get investment for the railways; some considered that the time for complaints – or even a row – was overdue.

In 1977 Marsh was succeeded by the man who had originally turned down the role when Barbara Castle had offered it to him in 1967. Peter Parker was to over-see something of a renaissance in the railways with the IC125 coming on stream and British Rail embracing a new commercialism. There were now railcards, a catchy advertising slogan 'This is the Age of the Train' and television adverts fea-turing the now disgraced Jimmy Savile, who was at that time a highly popular, family-friendly, television personality.

Parker was also to argue the case for increased rail investment through such avenues as his Commuters Charter – this was in fact a discussion document about where the money was to come from to fund socially necessary rail services. He originated the phrase 'crumbling edge of quality', when he told the Commons Select Committee on the Nationalised Industries that 'Investment is a crumbling edge. If you do not do it, no one really notices, but things get tattier and less safe.'[13] Parker's attempts to ignite a new discussion on rail funding in Whitehall were to result in the infamous Serpell Report of 1983. This study contemplated such options as a drastically reduced railway network, for which reason it was hardly likely to capture the backing of any politician who knew about the British public's affection for their railways – something which Margaret Thatcher was well aware of. However, this report did force the board into a defensive position, when it had hoped to have clear recommendations for more investment.

Parker stepped down as chairman in September 1983 and was succeeded by the first of two chairmen who were, by a strange coincidence, both called Robert Reid. To avoid confusion in subsequent pages I will follow the convention estab-lished by Terry Gourvish, who designated them as Robert Reid I and Robert Reid II.

Robert Reid I was another career railwayman. Born in 1921, he had come up through the LNER graduate training programme after taking a degree at Oxford. Whereas Parker had been a great motivator of people, Reid was rather different, being characterised by *Modern Railways* as 'Neutron Bob' Reid – 'the one that takes out the people while leaving the buildings standing'.[14] Parker was also inclined to left-of-centre ideas, whereas Reid's sympathies were with the right. Reid had good relationships with both Nicholas Ridley, the Transport Secretary, and also with Denis Thatcher (Prime Minister Margaret Thatcher's husband).[15] Reid listed golf as one his hobbies in the 1982 *Who's Who in the Rail Industry*, a hobby also enjoyed by Denis Thatcher. He even found a supporter in Mrs Thatcher herself, who was usually disdainful of those who came from within the nationalised industries. He managed to persuade Nicholas Ridley – who was very much an opponent of nationalised industries – to support higher investment in the railways in exchange for greater efficiency which would in turn result in a reduction of rail subsidy. The money was forthcoming, but ironically it came from the sale of railway assets, including property and a number of businesses (see Chapter 14).

The first Robert Reid's period as chairman was characterised by a rather more robust attitude to the unions than previously, as well as a business-led approach, with 'Sectorisation' becoming established as the new organisational structure. From January 1982 the railway was divided up according to specific traffics served: InterCity for the trunk route passenger business, London and South East for the London commuter business, and Provincial for the other metropolitan areas and rural services. The freight sector was divided into sub-sectors according to traffic served.

Reid's period of management, particularly up to 1987, is often characterised as being a 'golden age' in which BR was firing on all cylinders, meeting its government-set financial targets, investing in its infrastructure and rolling stock and still managing to be one of the world's most cost-effective railway networks. After 1987 things went somewhat downhill with a series of railway accidents (notably the high-profile disaster at Clapham) and a bitter strike in 1989. Reid retired feeling tired and drained by his hard exertions, echoing Peter Parker's feelings on relinquishing the post.

In 1990 Robert Reid was succeeded by none other than Robert Reid! This new Robert Reid was an outsider who had just spent five years as chairman and chief executive of Shell UK. In the view of Terry Gourvish it was unlikely that an insider would be picked after the various complications of the last years of Robert Reid I's premiership. Reid II was specifically recruited by government minister Cecil Parkinson and he enjoyed a remuneration package that was twice that of his predecessor.[16]

Coming from the oil industry as he did, Reid II already had a commitment to safety and now made it a priority for the board's specific attention. He also saw through the final changes in BR's management structure that had begun with Sectorisation. 'Organising for Quality', as it was called, had begun in 1988 and involved the abolition of the Regions and the assigning of responsibilities for costs and profits to specifically designated 'profit centres' within the sectors. The profit centres of the passenger businesses were to form the nuclei of the franchises when the system was privatised.

Given the hassles and interference from outside sources it is a wonder that British Railways achieved anything, but nevertheless it did. Sometimes progress was delayed. As an example, it would have seemed reasonable to create a nation-wide timetable soon after nationalisation, but this was not actually done until 1974.[17] However, when BR did get its act together it could be spectacularly successful. These successes, together with the occasional failure, are the subject of the rest of this book.

3

Old-Time Passenger Services and Comforts

Let us cast our mind back, without any nostalgia (all right, maybe just a little bit) to how things were approximately sixty-plus years ago, at the birth of the nationalised railway network that came to be known as British Railways, or British Rail. Railways were then the pre-eminent mode of land transport. Mass private car ownership had been very much delayed by the war. Britain's road network was then a cat's-cradle of archaic, twisting thoroughfares, ancient highways that funnelled traffic in and out of narrow streets in town and city centres that had been planned, if at all, to accommodate horses and carriages. There were few stretches of dual-carriageway, or bypasses, to sweep you past all those places you didn't actually want to stop in. There were no motorways, and would not be for another decade. Despite this, road transport had already begun to gnaw away at the freight side of railway operations and to a certain extent to reduce the number of railway passengers. The more opulent long-distance traveller could probably now afford a car, and buses and trams competed for passengers for short-distance journeys. For most, though, the railway was still the only practical means for the medium to long-distance journey.

At the start of the British Railways era steam was still the primary traction method on the railways. The internal combustion engine had yet to make a serious entry and only one company – the Southern – had electrified any main lines. Steam engines were dirty, comparatively slow and not as popular in their own time as they are today. Even the express trains of the time were slow by modern standards and steam haulage had something to do with this, although poor track-work right after the war didn't help. The track was better in the thirties but even the high-speed expresses of that era were slow by modern standards. *Mallard* may well have reached 126mph on its record-breaking run on a selected piece of track, but that was very far from the pre-Second World War average speed. The first non-stop run of the *Flying Scotsman* service in May 1928 averaged just 49mph. At that time the West Coast–East Coast speed limit agreement was still in force, but even when it was set aside it did not yield anything comparable to today's fast trains. The *Silver Jubilee* service, Britain's first streamlined train, inaugurated in 1935, was booked to average 70.4mph and on its inaugural run twice obtained a maximum speed of 112.5mph.[1] This was an exception though and, as we note below, this speed was achieved at a cost.

Steam engines might seem attractive and innocuous on today's heritage railways but these trains are usually very much 'underworked'. In comparison, a hard-working steam locomotive on a 'real' railway would produce a lot more smoke and sparks. Getting a spark in your eye or having clouds of smoke enter a carriage through an open window in a tunnel were amongst the hazards for passengers of the past. A present-day warning notice on the preserved Bluebell line spells out the horrors to a generation unfamiliar with them:

SAFETY NOTICE
Steam locomotives can blow coal dust, cinders, ash, steam,
water & oil over the train and platforms.

The filth and grime generated by steam locomotives would undoubtedly be a prime target for vigorous environmental concern if such conditions still existed to the degree they once did. Another danger to passengers was outlined in the British Railways General Appendix of 1960:

WATER ENTERING CARRIAGES FROM WATER TROUGHS

Owing to the risk of water entering carriages when locomotives are taking
water whilst passing over water troughs, passengers in the leading vehicles
should be warned of the advisability of keeping the windows closed when
troughs are being approached.

Although locomotives slowed down to take on water, the forces involved still meant that a torrent would cascade down the train sides and into any open window. Those who have experienced it at first hand, presumably as a result of not being warned in accordance with the General Appendix – or else have not heeded the warnings – say that the depth of the water on a carriage floor afterwards could be measured in inches. An often-told story about this involves a railwayman travelling 'on the cushions' (that is to say, in the passenger's accommodation). Knowing that troughs were looming, he stood up and closed an open window beside him, whereupon an indignant gentleman seated opposite promptly got up and opened it again – only to be immediately saturated through his suit to his underpants. The indignant gent went off to the lavatory and was not seen again.

So much for the 'glory days' of steam. But let us turn to the most important things: the services the trains worked and the vehicles of which they consisted.

Although the British railway system had developed from many different companies, the basic realities of railway operation and passenger requirements applied to all of them. The main differences arose from the areas they operated in or their preferred traffic. The southern companies, with their relatively short trunk routes, were driven to exploit the suburban commuter market in south London whilst the railways north and west of the Thames were able to focus on long-distance markets. As I said in Chapter 1, initially the railways eschewed provision for the 'lower orders' until they were required to provide workmen's trains. Some railways, like the Great Western, continued to prefer the up-market commuter to the inner-city working poor.

For purposes of organisation in such documents as working timetables (meaning the real timetables that tell railwaymen what is actually meant to be happening) passenger trains were divided into two groups, 'express' and 'ordinary', the latter also known as 'general purpose'. From the passengers' point of view, then and now, trains can be divided into two groups: those for exceptional journeys, mostly long distance, such as holidays or special business trips, and those for everyday journeys, such as commuting or shopping. But neither of these viewpoints, of operator or user, is particularly useful in discriminating between *modes* of service.

A more insightful view was offered in the book *Modern Railway Operation*, published in 1926 and written by David Lamb, who was then editor of *Modern Transport Magazine*.[2] Lamb's breakdown of passenger services describes a set of operations that had become established by the late Victorian period and which can still be recognised on a modern railway. Basically, he divides them into four types: urban, suburban, intermediate and long distance.

What Lamb means by 'urban' is now covered by the modern term 'rapid transit' – that is, an intensive, frequent passenger service on a line dedicated solely to it. This kind of operation is ideal for distributing passengers around an inner-city area, since it is operated by trains all running at the same speeds and all making the same stops, essentially functioning like a conveyor belt. The London Underground is a prime example, and this is the example Lamb himself uses to illustrate this type of working. British Railways ran few lines that could genuinely be classified under this heading.

Under 'suburban', Lamb notes two different modes of operation: the slow train that stops at all stations and also what Lamb terms, rather misleadingly, as 'non-stop', more commonly known as semi-fast. These are trains that collect passengers from outer-lying stations and then travel at express speed, without stopping at the intervening ones. This has undoubted advantages in terms of delivering passengers from a greater distance more quickly to their destination, as well as averting overcrowding, by deliberately dividing the passengers into separate groups of trains.[3]

Most of the Great Western Railway's commuter traffic came to be long distance suburban in nature, the company preferring the higher class long-distance commuter over the folk who lived in the inner suburbs. The other group era companies all operated trains of the semi-fast type within their suburban portfolio.

The services that Lamb terms 'intermediate' are those that travel comparatively short distances and connect up stations between the more important towns. They include branch-line trains, a branch line being a line that links a place or places of modest importance to a trunk or secondary route. At the time when Lamb was writing, these services had minimal variations in traffic with the heaviest being carried on Saturdays and market days, in response to the availability of cheap tickets. Lamb also states that they act as feeders for the long-distance services – Dr Beeching should have taken note of this.

It was these services that were to be targeted as unprofitable by the nationalised railway system. In many cases their axing was to go along with the closure of the lines upon which they ran; in other cases they were withdrawn from lines that were kept open with only the stations that the stopping trains served being closed.

When it comes to long-distance trains most people think of named expresses, the popular image being of those such as the *Flying Scotsman*. In fact, long-distance trains were not all glamorous titled trains running non-stop. There were many important main-line services that went undistinguished by a title, and many express trains that took a rather long time to reach their destination, even by the contemporary standard. The express train headcode was also used for fast parcels traffic and even for some fast freight trains. But at one time or another all of the railways sought to provide prestigious express trains that caught the public's imagination. This had been a feature from the early days and continued with the Big Four, although the practice of officially 'naming' trains (by official I mean with the name appearing in timetables, on headboards or carriages) did not really come into vogue until the group era – much later than most people would suppose. The Midland did not run any named trains, and the LMS did not name any of its services until 1927. Even the *Flying Scotsman*'s title did not gain official recognition until after 1923, despite having run since 1862.

Top-flight expresses that ran non-stop or at record breaking speeds were generally publicity gimmicks for media consumption and were nonsense in terms of efficient operation. They sent slower moving traffic ahead of them scurrying for refuge in sidings and sidelines, whilst leaving a void of underused rail behind them.

Having said this, long-distance services did tend to be of the 'fast' type, bypassing many stations. This made sense for the convenience of passengers, as they reached their destination quicker and few people were likely to make the whole-length journey if the train took too long. The notion was that passengers changed to other services that served intermediate stations (see below) and that these services operated as feeder services to the long-distance services – a theory that was to be challenged. How many stations an express train should stop at, and how many stops turns an express train into a stopping train, are questions which must vex modern writers of timetables as they must have concerned those doing the same job many years ago.

As Lamb points out, long-distance services were subject to the greatest seasonal variations. Indeed summer loadings often required that relief trains be run – effectively one service was split into several portions for reasons of economy and passenger comfort. A very long train would have to 'draw up' at stations, in other words the platform would not be long enough to accommodate the whole train at once, therefore it would have to allow one portion to be loaded and unloaded and then pull ahead to bring the other section up to the platform. Generally this was not an uncommon problem on the British railway network. Many stations were originally built for shorter trains and shorter carriages, meaning that by the twentieth century many platforms were not long enough.

The *Flying Scotsman* was one of the trains that were provided with a relief in the summer season to cope with demand. In post-war days it was the *Scotsman's* relief trains – then increased to two and both named the *Capitals Limited* – that provided the non-stop service. In 1953 the *Capitals Limited* was renamed *The Elizabethan* in honour of the coronation of Queen Elizabeth II.

The heaviest summer loadings were inevitably destined for the coastal holiday resorts. As railway travel became more comfortable towards the end of the nineteenth century more people were persuaded to travel long distances and the railway companies exploited this growing trend. From 1904 the *Sunny South Express* from Manchester and Liverpool to Brighton and Eastbourne was run jointly by the London and North Western and the London, Brighton and South Coast Railway. The idea proved lucrative and similar services followed, including the famous *Pines Express*, whose origins lay in a service that started in 1910. Going on holiday by train became commonplace and seaside towns expanded with large stations built to receive the many thousands of passengers that came during the season. In the 1950s and 1960s British Railways continued to nurture this traffic, and to encourage people to 'See Britain By Train', as the advertising slogan phrased it.

Holiday guides (in the late 1950s also entitled 'Holiday Haunts') were produced for each region and were thick books, sometimes approaching 300 pages, with details of resorts, places of interest, a picture section and a lot of adverts, mostly for hotels and guest houses. Despite the adverts these were not free, originally costing a shilling. There was also the British Transport Films unit, which included travelogues amongst its varied output.

Because of the holiday traffic, summer months on the railways were once hectic, particularly in areas like the West Country, where trains from many places in Britain brought holidaymakers. On a summer Saturday the railway station of any British coastal resort was likely to be truly bustling. In his book *The Day of the Holiday Express* Richard Woodley says:

> To move the holiday crowds on a summer Saturday in July 1960, British Railways Western Region needed to run over twice the usual number of daily express trains. Normally about 190 long distance expresses were scheduled for each day. On an early July Saturday this total increased to around 450 trains … [4]

Saturation point on the Western Region had been reached by 1957 and a serious breakdown in the quality of service took place regularly on summer Saturdays as processions of trains queued for platforms at busy termini or for paths through such bottlenecks as the Severn Tunnel. According to David St John Thomas and Simon Rocksborough Smith the most chaotic day ever in the West of England was 27 July 1957. Between 8.24 a.m. and 9.37 p.m. eighty down passenger trains arrived at Newton Abbot and were an average of 122 minutes late. Every train arriving between 1.15 p.m. and 5.15 p.m. was more than two hours late. The 8.50 a.m. from Paddington reached Exeter St David's after the 10.35 a.m. Waterloo–Padstow train. The 10.00 a.m. train from Paddington reached Exeter two hours after the 11.00 a.m. Waterloo–Ilfracombe *Atlantic Coast Express.*[5]

Such malfunction was a serious embarrassment to staff, a frustration to passengers and a classic lesson in the basic, immutable facts of running a railway – or any transport system: the more services you pack in, the more customers you move, the slower you actually move them. Choices have to be made between serving a few passengers well, or providing a large number of travellers with a less efficient service, or alternatively spending a lot of money to improve infrastructure – investment that may not be recouped for a very long time, if at all. This is an important theme that I will return to again.

A chief virtue of Lamb's breakdown of service types is that it corresponds with the revenue take. Suburban trains and branch-line trains may travel similar distances but suburban trains are much more lucrative, due to the higher density of passengers. Long-distance trains are the most profitable. It is the intermediate trains – both the branch-line trains and the stopping trains on the trunk or secondary route – that are the least profitable, and can even make losses. It was these that were to bear the brunt of the cuts in the Beeching era.

Suburban services, and the more well-subscribed branch lines, were likely to earn the distinction of having a time-interval, also known as a 'clockface' service. This is where trains run from a specific place to a specific destination at specific intervals, say every half-past-the-hour. There was little new to this style of service when Herbert Walker introduced it together with the new London and South Western Railway's suburban electric services in 1915, but Walker came up with a classic one line argument for it, 'People don't like timetables, make it easy for them.'[6]

The clockface service was to become associated first and foremost with Walker and the Southern Electric, but longer-distance services, such as on the GWR, also benefited from such timetabling.

Another type of train service that is outlined in Lamb's book is the so-called 'cross-country services'. The category that these fall into really depends on the distance travelled by the particular train. Cross-country services run between the main trunk routes, often linking major destinations but via secondary lines. In a country where many of the railway lines have a bias towards north-south alignment, many of these services provide east-west connections. A cross-country route once existed between Oxford and Cambridge. The one linking Reading with Tonbridge still exists. There were named expresses that fell into the cross-country grouping, as well as the express and through train categories, including many holiday expresses such as the *Sunny South Express* and the *Pines Express*.

As well as the scheduled services there was another type of passenger service: the 'special' or 'excursion'. The railways had long sought to maximise the use of their assets by encouraging people to travel outside peak hours, hopefully for long distances. One promotional idea had been to offer people the chance to charter their own special trains. People were also encouraged to travel by regular services purely for leisure. Both forms of trip were advertised by British Railways in brochures entitled *Party Outings*. Again British Transport Films joined in the publicity campaign, showing how the railways could facilitate specialist interests, such as in *Cyclists Special* (1955), which shows how a special train with suitably equipped cycle vans conveyed a group of cyclists from Watford and Willesden to Rugby for a day out. Also of interest is the film *A Day Of One's Own* (1956) in which a number of women from various parts of the country are shown taking a day off from their usual routine in order to travel by rail.

The *Party Outings* brochures advertised:

Day outings – parties of 8 or more.
Guaranteed day excursions – parties of 400 or more.
Guaranteed half day excursions – parties of 300 or more.

The day outings were accommodated in regular services, 'where practicable, accommodation will be reserved on trains free of charge'. The guaranteed excursions involved special trains: 'For large parties travelling by special trains, corridor and/or open vestibule coaches – the latter fitted with tables and allowing freedom of movement on the journey – together with restaurant and buffet or Cafeteria car facilities can generally be provided.'

The use of the term 'guaranteed' distinguished such excursions from so-called 'advertised' excursions which were organised by the railway itself. Often falling into this latter category were services for sports events such as football matches or race meetings. The organisation of guaranteed specials to some events was specifically barred by the railway, as they organised their own. The 'football excursion', later known as 'Footex', was to be amongst the last type of such excursions run, long after the horse-racing community had become motorised.

Excursionists benefited from cheap fares but often were given the rolling stock to match. On the railway of old the price you paid for your ticket determined the quality of carriage you rode in. The best stock was kept for premium, long-distance work, whereas excursionists on cheap tickets were likely to experience carriages that had seen better days.

Although excursions could run to anywhere on the railway network, in BR days they were organised by the regions. The *Party Outings* brochures bore the brand of the issuing region and gave contact addresses at its main stations. An exception was *Party Outings from London and the Suburbs*, which gave a central (London) contact address for each region (except the Scottish) as well as the 'Chief Passenger Travel Representative, British Railways' at an address in the Charing Cross Road. The brochures generally ran to the same script, obviously centrally co-ordinated, and emphasised Britain's places of historic interest and beauty spots, seaside resorts and other attractions such as zoos. They targeted specific markets – 'Clubs, firms, societies, schools. Etc.' but commercial promoters were also free to charter trains and offer tickets at their own risk. For those who needed some priming before their big adventure, films and lantern slides were available, and 'it may be possible in certain circumstances for a Railway lecturer [sic] to give a display ... which will pave the way for a really good outing.'[7]

If catering vehicles were not available on trains there was a packed lunch service. Packed lunches consisted of sandwiches or filled rolls, cakes and bars of chocolate. Also available was 'tea in insulated urns (to take with you) and paper cups can be supplied to parties numbering more than 60 persons having packed meals for an additional charge of 5s per gallon (equivalent to 20 cups).'

By the mid-1950s individual TRAY MEALS were provided, for ORGANISED PARTIES (BR used capital letters to describe both of these). These consisted of a 'Main Course, Sweet, Roll, Butter, Cheese, together with Cutlery and Condiments with space for Fruit Squash Carton and Straw' (presumably the latter not actually being included). Then there was 'An innovation for small private parties'. This was the COMPAKT [sic] MEAL BOX, containing a 'complete cold meal' and a 'hot beverage in vacuum flask' which was 'Neatly packed and easily carried'.[8] Another booklet describes the COMPAKT meal as 'a "de-luxe" packed meal for small parties or the individual traveller', and continues 'The container is made of anodised aluminium, and when fastened, can easily be carried like an attaché case.'[9]

Amongst the railway-organised, 'advertised' services were such archaic oddities as 'hop-pickers' and 'hop-pickers' friends' specials. Hop-pickers were usually working-class women, often with children, taking a working holiday during the hop-picking season in September. They often took their furniture with them, requiring several vans to be added to the rear of the trains. The hop-pickers' friends were usually the husbands, visiting at weekends.

Trains from London Bridge ferried hop-pickers from the East End to Kent where a railway 'Hop Control' was operated at Paddock Wood station throughout the season. Services also ran from Portsmouth and Southampton to the hop-grow-ing area around Alton in Hampshire. On the Great Western Railway hop-pickers from the Black Country travelled to Herefordshire and Worcestershire.

The special services had originally been organised to keep the notoriously violent and drunken hop-pickers from troubling other passengers – in 1863 the Mayoress of Maidstone had been assaulted by hop-pickers on a platform at London Bridge.[10] Hop-pickers' tickets were overprinted with the letters 'HP' as well as the year, and were valid only for the special trains. These ran at night, pre-sumably also to keep the *hoi polloi* at a safe distance from 'decent folk'.

On the Southern Railway this had clearly amounted to a considerable traf-fic, although figures are somewhat sketchy. For 1925 they show seventy-one 'Hop-pickers' specials' (five in the daytime, sixty-six at night), carrying 34,448 passengers. In 1938 there were only thirty-four 'specials' (whether day or night service is not recorded) carrying only 13,514 hop-pickers. In the same year sev-enty-four 'special' trains carried 27,906 'hop-pickers' friends'. In the war years the numbers increased substantially – no doubt the wish to escape the bombings was a contributing factor. In 1944, 164 'specials' carried 79,000 hop-pickers. By 1958 the number had dwindled to just two 'specials' carrying 1,986 hop-pickers and the service had died out before Beeching needed to do anything about it. The last recorded 'hop-pickers' specials' from London Bridge ran in 1960.[11]

In Chapter 1 I mentioned that from early on the railway companies had recog-nised the virtue of running through services – ones that started on one company's rails and ended on another's, sometimes travelling over a third company's rails in-between. Due to the spaghetti patchwork nature of the early railway system this was a practical necessity for many passengers on long journeys and the pre-group railways entered into agreements where certain sets of carriages were jointly owned, such as the East Coast Joint Stock. They also operated individual or small groups of carriages which were detached from one service and attached to another at company meeting points. By the twentieth century the 'through coach' had emerged as a major form of railway operation.

There was a time when every major station had its own station pilot, a small locomotive dedicated largely to removing vehicles from one train and attach-ing them onto another (as well as the necessary empty stock movements that loco-hauled operations required). Before nationalisation it would have been possible to see trains consisting of several companies' stock as well as coaches many miles from their parent system. For the sake of passenger convenience the through coach was also adopted within company systems and provided a solution to serving the rural byways, where they often ran up and down branch lines as a stopping service, being attached and removed from an express train at a major junction. A classic example of this was the *Atlantic Coast Express*, a train consisting of several through coaches detached at various points. In the winter of 1955/56 it boasted no fewer than sixty-five destinations without change as its carriages were detached at various points and made their own ways along the system.[12] There was something civilised about being able to remain in your carriage whilst you were shunted from one train to another, without having to carry your luggage up a footbridge and down again to board another vehicle.

However, the through coach was doomed. They required complex operations that obstructed traffic paths in stations, and, worse than that, they led to delays. Whereas a connecting service could be let to go on its way if a train connecting to it was late, a through coach had to be waited for or else the system was thrown into chaos – that coach would be in the wrong place, at the wrong time, for future movements. There were other issues too which complicated the diagramming of stock for such uses; I have already explained in Chapter 1 how a number of mismatches of couplings, brake systems and corridor connectors could obstruct the passage of a coach from one system to another. These technical hassles lasted well into BR days as pre-nationalisation stock continued to be used.

For a single coach to function as a through coach a special type of vehicle was required – a brake composite; that is to say, one with a guard's compartment and accommodation for all classes of passenger. Constructing and maintaining these involved an additional expense above simply operating the service. Given all the hassles, the axe would soon be out to end the days of the through coach. The move to fixed sets of carriages and multiple-unit operation would hasten its decline still further. Although the through coach's total demise was often exaggerated, the term 'through coach' was proclaimed obsolete in the 1992 edition of Alan A. Jackson's (no relation to me) *The Railway Dictionary*.

The most extreme form of through coach, still made use of by the Western Region until 1960, was the 'slip coach'. The slip coach was uncoupled on the move and drifted into the intended destination shortly after the train it was detached from had sped through. Like the normal through coach, the slip coach was then often taken on to other points by another train. Slip coaches dated back to the nineteenth century and it was a peculiarly British form of railway practice, although it was tried for a while in Holland and France. Historians have traced its origins to the LB&SCR but at one time the Midland and GWR were enthusiastic users. Other companies, such as the NER, refused to have anything to do with slip coaches.

In his article 'Service by slip',[13] Marcus Newman gives three principal reasons why slip coaches were used by the companies, some of which also went for ordinary through coaches.

Firstly they were to serve sizeable towns not touched by a trunk route.

Secondly slip coaches were used to serve an intermediate town on trunk routes and bring attractive 'foreign' targets within its range – such as the GC's famed Sheffield non-stop train, which slipped a carriage at Leicester that meandered to Nottingham and on to Grimsby and Cleethorpes.

Thirdly slip coaches were operated to pay court to influential suburbs, such as the GWR's slip at Slough for the Windsor line.

In grouped days all four railways used them at first, the LMS abandoning them in 1927, the Southern in 1932, and the LNER doing so in 1936. The GWR greatly reduced its usage throughout the 1930s and ceased using slip coaches altogether during the war. The surprise is, perhaps, that slipping started again after the war with the Western Region perpetuating the use well into British Railways' days. They started again in the winter of 1950 with the *Cornish Riviera Express* scheduled to slip for Westbury. Other slip services in the 1950s were for Didcot, Bicester and Reading.

The carriages used for these slips were all pre-war, but the Western Region had some of its post-war 'Hawksworth' carriages modified for slip working as late as 1958. It seems that those who commissioned this work were out of the loop regarding further plans, because slip coaching was already well in decline in the region.

As with through-coach working, slip-coach working had drawbacks which made it uneconomical and eventually told against the practice. Beyond the need to accommodate the guard-driver and all classes of passenger, the coaches had to have special equipment to disconnect the draw gear and the pipes for brakes and train heating (in the case of the automatic brakes, doing things without triggering them). This made the coaches more expensive. The mode of service was inflexible in that slip coaches only worked one way, and were usually worked back to their point of origin in normal trains. They usually lacked gangways connecting the coach to others, meaning that passengers on the slip portion had no access to dining car facilities. Telling against the slip coach was the greater strength of modern locomotives (steam, then diesel and electric) to stop and start a train, enabling more intermediate stops without having to jettison a vehicle *en passant*. What is more, if the whole train stopped, passengers could be picked up as well as dropped off. Also, greater speed meant more paths and more capacity to run ordinary services to the places served by slip coach. On the other hand, some of those places once served by slip were abandoned by the railway altogether.

Although the slip coach contravened the basic principles of railway safety by allowing two movements to occupy the same section there were only two serious accidents recorded, and no fatalities, in the whole history of slip-coach operation in the British Isles.

On 9 September 1960 the last slip coach was detached from the 17.10 Paddington–Birmingham train and drifted quietly into Bicester station. The occasion was not marked by any ceremony.

The demise of the through coach was one part of a double blow affecting the comfort of passengers. As from 1958 there was no one to help people with their luggage on the station platform. For over a century the railway porter had been available to carry bags and push trolleys but that service came to an end when the British Transport Commission decided that a porter was no longer obliged to do such things. Despite objections raised by the ever toothless Central Transport Consultative Committee (set up by the 1947 Act[14] as the passengers' watchdog) the helpful railway porter was despatched to history. Thus the railway lost a vital point of contact with its customers, a personal touch that could add immensely to the value of the service. Doubtless the increasing wage bill had much to do with this decision.[15]

As I said in Chapter 1, the division of classes of travel was very complicated in the Victorian era. Generally – but not universally – there was first, second, third, a workmen's class and, in pioneer times, a number of distinctions within those classes (for example 'inside' or 'outside'). By 1923 the classes had been boiled down, with a few exceptions, to first and, nonsensically, third. This was because second class, where it had existed, had slowly been phased out in the late Victorian period, and as well as this its provision had been patchy for some time. The Great North of Scotland Railway had never provided it; the London and Greenwich Railway had temporarily experimented with dropping it. Eventually the Midland took a stand by abolishing second, reducing its first-class rates to those that had previously been second, and upgrading third class to the standard of second. Some companies, such as the LNWR, were slow to follow and in the London area of the LNER second-class travel was not abolished until 1938.

So British Railways inherited the basic structure of first and third, although an exception existed in the London area, where many services only offered the lower class (this followed a wartime abolition of first-class travel in the London area).[16] The other exception was boat trains; because the European railways retained first, second and third classes, some of these services on the Southern Region had all three classes and British Railways built coaches to provide for this requirement.[17] This ended in June 1956[18] when classes on the European railways were streamlined to two, and in Britain the British Transport Commission renamed third class as second. In 1987 the BTC, at last showing some sensitivity to the self-esteem of its customers, renamed second as 'standard'.

I have already touched on the issue of catering. At the start of the British Railways era train catering was quite often restaurant-style silver service, being based around one entire car containing the cooking facilities and restaurant saloons either side – one for first class, the other for third. This was an arrangement that was not to survive for very long; it increased train weight considerably and also meant that a lot of resources were committed to a single train. In the prewar era catering cars had led relaxed lives and only the LMS, with its long West Coast route, was really able to justify such extensive facilities on a single train.

The Second World War had brought great changes in the way people lived, and the way they ate. Many people had been introduced to the idea of fast food and self-service after experiencing wartime canteens. In 1951, 114 services previously offering full restaurants were converted to serve light refreshments.[19] From 1952 BR started to convert a large number of pre-nationalisation coaches to cafeteria cars – some sixty-five in total,[20] but these were not a success. The amount of provisions on display meant that people spent a long time choosing and queues built up – this was acceptable in a platform café but it proved inconvenient in the restricted space of a train. As any schoolchild knows, nothing encourages you to make up your mind like a finger-tapping dinner lady standing over you, so the self-service idea was abandoned in favour of the staffed buffet counter.

In the days when railway carriages had windows that opened it was common for refreshments to be served to passengers from trolleys on the platforms while they waited for departure. So it seemed an obvious move to put the trolleys on the trains themselves and a picture from 1948 shows that this was being done.[21] Lord Inman, newly appointed as the chairman of British Transport Hotels, took the idea up and in April 1949 announced in the magazine *Caterer and Hotelkeeper* that it was to be introduced to all lines. As it turned out, the trolleys were unsuc-cessful and also controversial. As the trolley made its way along the corridors it was awkward for people to squeeze around it, and when the 'food on wheels' encountered groups of standing passengers it was brought to a halt. Passengers and staff complained and the idea was dropped, only to be resurrected by the Midland Region in November 1960. Fifty-three services were provided with trolley facilities but the old problems resurfaced. Although the advent of open saloon stock had eased the problems regarding space, the NUR raised the issue of safety because the trolley was still seen as a potential obstacle to staff and pas-sengers in the event of an emergency. Given that the trolleys were rather top heavy, transporting urns full of boiling water, the union did have a point. NUR members refused to be involved with trolleys. For main-line use the trolley idea was abandoned – for the moment – but cross-country services often featured a trolley that had its home in the brake van, rather than a buffet car, and would be stocked from a platform refreshment room in advance.[22]

The man who had led the post-war renovation of the platform refreshment rooms was E.K. Portman-Dixon – or 'PD' as he was more usually known. He had come from a background of contract catering to transform the fortunes and image of the refreshment rooms of the LNER, which was at that time burdened with the poorest reputation on the network. In 1948 he was made chief of the refreshment rooms in the new Hotels Executive which was responsible for railway catering, on and off the trains. PD soon began to improve profits and service standards. In 1953 he was put in charge of the cars as well and until his retirement in 1969 he was to prove a dynamic force behind the catering side of British Railways, laying the foundations for an important component of the Inter-City brand.

For a long time the market leader in railway catering in Britain had been the Pullman Company (although in America Pullman was primarily known for its sleeping cars). The Pullman car was the notion of George Mortimer Pullman who started his Pullman Palace Car Company in America in 1867. In 1873 he entered into an agreement with the Midland Railway to bring his ideas to Britain. This particular venture was not wholly successful but Pullmans subsequently found favour with the Great Northern Railway and the London Brighton and South Coast Railway. In 1894 the British Pullman Palace Car Company was formed, later succeeded by the Pullman Car Company Limited from 1915.

The Midland's Pullman trains had only featured catering in the form of pre-packed hampers. The honours for the first British railway dining car on which actual cooking took place ultimately went to the Great Northern when it had an existing Pullman sleeper rebuilt as the *Prince of Wales*, which went into service in November 1879. Two years later the Brighton Company introduced the car *Victoria* which featured a pantry and buffet. Later it had the car *Maud* converted to a full diner.

Pullman cars were wholly owned by the Pullman Company, who also supplied attendants. The railway companies were responsible only for external washing and maintenance. Passengers were charged a supplement to ride in the cars but what they got, in later years, was an 'at seat' service of meals, snacks and drinks. Pullman service was available in first- and third-class varieties.

With the formation of British Railways the Pullman Car Company remained privately owned but in 1954 the BTC bought the ordinary shares of the company for £700,000 and thus gained a controlling stake. Before it took control the BTC had exploited its monopoly of the British railway network by delaying the signing of new contracts. Now Pullman was to become a flagship for British Railways passenger services and both the BTC and the British Railways Board (BRB) invested substantially in the brand. In 1958 British Railways was running twelve all Pullman services and operating 204 Pullman carriages, thirty-eight formed into electric multiple-unit stock on the Southern Region and the other 166 being loco-hauled. Pullman car staff served 1.5 million passengers with nearly 4 million meals and light refreshments.[23] In 1962 the BTC bought the preference shares of the Pullman Company and when the board took over it became the Pullman division of BR.

You would have thought that logic dictated that the Hotels Executive ran the sleeping cars as well as the catering cars. Not a bit of it — the sleepers were under the control of the railway managers, starting with the Railway Executive (RE). As it turned out the fortunes of the third-class traveller were very much improved under the RE, so perhaps the arrangement was no bad thing. In fact, genuine third-class sleeping accommodation had not been offered by any British Railway company until 1928, when the LMS, LNER and the GWR (the Southern did not operate any sleeping cars) simultaneously introduced third-class vehicles.

These cars featured four-berth compartments, with only a rug provided for bedding, but from the early days of British Railways work began to convert the existing third-class sleeping accommodation to two-berth and to provide full bedding. You still had no choice but to share with a stranger if you could only afford the lower class accommodation, but at least you only had to share with one person. From 1948 to 1952, fifty sleeper cars were built to a design of the former LMS, but the third-class vehicles had two-bed compartments as new, as well as pressurised ventilation for both classes. These features were repeated in the BR standard vehicles of 1957.

If anything exemplifies the traditional thinking of Britain's railways, then it must be the layout and design of the British passenger coach, particularly in the form of the 'closed compartment carriage'. Closed compartments are those consisting of facing rows of seats spanning the width of the carriage and accessible only by side doors from the platform. This design should have been beyond its sell-by date at the turn of the century, but BR was to perpetuate its use into the post-nationalisation era and to build its own examples, although in the switch-over from the conservative Executive to the BTC there was to be an about-face in this policy. Despite this, some of the carriages built by the Executive had to last many years in service.

The closed compartment was a hangover from the dawn of the railway age when stagecoach bodies had been mounted on flat rail trucks and had thus set the style of the internal structure of the accommodation. In America this had very quickly given way to the open style 'day coach', with its many advantages for passengers and traincrew. It had also allowed the Americans to devise the end vestibule – a transverse passage at the ends of the car – to be used for loading and unloading. Thus they were able to place the outside doors at the ends rather than in rows down the sides. As a consequence the construction of the American railroad car became very much more rigid and able to withstand impacts. By contrast, the British railway carriage remained flimsy and prone to crushing in accidents. This is a matter I shall return to, at relevant points, throughout this book.

At the end of the nineteenth century the railway passenger carriage became a much more complex vehicle. In this era a range of innovations came together and significantly upped the comfort level, and also the weight of the carriages, forcing locomotive engineers to build larger and more powerful engines. The bogie carriage started to become common, slowly displacing the four- and six-wheeled carriage, which had been used even on long journeys. The side corridor was introduced for long-haul use, giving passengers access to a lavatory. Gangway connectors, enabling passengers to walk safely from one carriage to another, started to appear and in 1892 the Great Western Railway introduced a train with a continuous corridor running its entire length on its Paddington–Birkenhead route. Oddly enough the GWR did not take advantage of this by including a restaurant in the formation. The first corridor train with full dining facilities was

introduced on the West Coast Main Line in 1893. Previously it had been necessary for passengers to stay in the dining car for the whole journey, or else to
change coaches when the train stopped if they wished to dine on board. From
that time onwards it was possible to leave your compartment on the move and
take your seat for breakfast, lunch or dinner. Train heating became common at
this time, powered by steam from the locomotive. As we have seen, the law in
England already required that passenger trains should be fitted with continuous
brakes and a communication cord.

By the turn of the twentieth century the passenger train had gone from being
a collection of carriages strung behind a locomotive to an integrated system in
which one carriage was part of a whole. Yet still carriage designers in Britain stuck
to the closed compartment as the basic unit of design for short- and medium-
haul work and even into the twentieth century some principal trains still featured
closed compartments. Doubtless the economies of loading had much to do
with the preference for this type of vehicle, where many more passengers can be
packed in for the tare weight of the carriage. Also, those plentiful but structure-
weakening side doors really were an advantage when having to load and unload
a lot of people quickly.

In terms of the ordinary experience of the railway traveller the greatest
inconvenience – or perhaps better put, lack of any convenience – of the closed
compartment was the denial of access to a lavatory. C. Hamilton Ellis was of the
opinion that the lavatory was the greatest of blessings introduced into railway
carriages and deplored the way that its provision in Britain had been so slow
and grudging.[24]

The Great Western in particular must be singled out for criticism for the use
of closed compartments on long-haul runs, but all railways were inclined to press
closed compartment stock into use on schedules that tested the human blad-
der to its fullest. In Victorian times third-class passengers were wont to express
their displeasure at the lack of a commode (at a time when chamber pots were
commonly kept in many rooms of the house) by relieving themselves in the
compartments. This reached such a stage that, in approximately 1873, the South
Eastern Railway actually sank iron funnels into the floors of third-class carriages
to aid with the flushing out.[25] Hamilton Ellis states that he encountered the same
behaviour whilst travelling with hop-pickers in Kent,[26] which must have been at
a much later date, since he was born in 1909. Generally the behaviour of railway
passengers in this respect improved with the generations – and perhaps also as a
result of the better provision of WCs.

Closed compartments gained the reputation of being unsafe as regards attacks
by strangers – although I do not know of any statistics that prove either way
whether personal safety was more of an issue in closed compartments than in
any other form of carriage. Certainly there was always the fear that you could
find yourself alone with a psychopath sitting opposite you and have to face many

miles before reaching the next station. I was always careful not to get into compartments that were occupied by single men, or by men who looked like they were travelling together. The fact that few cases of murder are actually cited in the historical literature, and that the same tragedies are referred to more than once, suggests that murder on board a train was actually a rare occurrence. The most repeated story is the murder of Thomas Briggs by a German named Franz Muller which occurred in 1864 on the North London Line. Muller was executed, but his name survived in railway parlance because of the so-called 'Muller's lights': circular holes cut in the partitions enabling occupants of neighbouring compartments to view each other and communicate. These did not last long, and certainly not into British Railways' days, since the communication cord superseded them as the primary safety device.

There have been many fictional accounts of murders on the railways, more than occurred in reality, I hope. A good study of this is provided by Ian Carter in his book *Railways and Culture in Britain*. Carter points out that a moving train is an intriguing variation on the 'sealed room device', a literary technique which entails throwing a variety of individuals together in an isolated situation prior to a murder.[27] When you add to that the crime writer's obsessive compulsion regarding detail and the scope of material made available for this by railways in the form of timetables and so forth, you begin to grasp why the railway is an attractive venue for fictional crime. Whilst concluding that the closed compartment may well have an exaggerated reputation for murderous danger, it is also worth noting that many of the best known murder mysteries set on railways take place on corridor trains, such as Agatha Christie's *Murder On The Orient Express*. The long-distance corridor train, in fact, gives a writer many more opportunities for the drama to unfold in different on-board locations, for people to be alone, and thus to be murdered, and to conspire to murder. This may be a considerable distortion of reality, though. Surely people are likely to be more vulnerable in the closed compartment with fellow passengers who have paid for short journeys in untraceable cash, and who are without aristocratic titles, associations with heiresses and the like.

A good account of genuine incidents on the Victorian railway is given by Ivor Smullen in his book *Taken For A Ride: A Distressing Account of the Misfortunes and Misbehaviour of the Early British Railway Traveller*.[28] On page seventy-two Smullen reproduces a Punch cartoon showing a very useful technique for discouraging other passengers from joining you in your compartment. This involves use of that most invaluable of travellers' aids, the false baby. A speaking doll held up to a misty window when at the station 'may generally keep your compartment select'. Whatever the century, the prospect of sharing a compartment with a noisy infant is enough to put anyone off.

The suspicion of strangers in closed compartments was often a matter of simple prejudice. In their book *Windrush: The Irresistible Rise of Multi-Racial Britain*, which refers to immigration from the West Indies, Mike and Trevor Phillips cite the case of John Richards, one of the first wave of West Indian immigrants who was later to work for BR. Richards relates how when he first came to Britain in the late 1940s and rode on trains from Orpington to London Bridge no one would come into the compartment he was occupying – he could actually fall asleep and no one would bother him. After a couple of years, he says, things did change.[29]

Closed compartments were the scene of other sorts of abuse, including what one correspondent of mine terms 'gentlemen's clandestine activities', which he witnessed in the late 1960s and early 1970s in compartment stock on late-night trains out of Victoria:

> … light bulbs were removed in the compartments. On the Central Section 4-SUBS [multiple-unit trains], with lighting in series, removal of both light bulbs in one compartment would result in the whole coach going dark, so that, upon arrival at Clapham Junction for example, most of the intending passengers made for the three remaining illuminated coaches. On the South Eastern side, however, removal of the two bulbs in a single compartment only meant that that particular compartment went dark. This meant others involved in such activities would have to remove the bulbs in their 'own' compartments in the coach …
>
> There was a period when I was asked to house-sit in Bromley. That last Orpington train out of Victoria demonstrated all this very well. I could never quite understand at first why, at that time of night, chaps used to wander up and down platform 2 at Victoria alongside the coach with most compartments darkened right up until the whistle blew. The scenario seemed even more bizarre when, at Brixton, many alighted, and raced about and boarded the train again into another compartment.

Of course, such behaviour wasn't confined to the gay community. According to one ex-BR manager, 'Lamp bulbs out and a quick go with a girl was common on many lines.'[30] In the 1860s the privacy of the closed compartment on trains between Cannon Street and Charing Cross had even been turned to commercial advantage:

> Some ladies of the streets had found that the SER's first class compartments, combined with the uninterrupted seven minute run provided ideal conditions for their activities at a rental that represented only a minute proportion of their income. The number of drawn blinds on these services noticeably decreased after the opening of an intermediate station at Waterloo [East], at which most trains stopped, on January 31st 1869.[31]

Vandalism was also a problem. In 1859 the LSWR highlighted the slashing of seats in carriages by exhibiting such damage and threatening that if it continued cushions would be withdrawn altogether.[32] In 1867, before a House of Lords committee, managers of various railways north and south queued up to testify regarding the nuisance and damage caused by third-class passengers.[33] One hundred years later and a Pathé newsreel from 1960 shows the same sort of damage in the closed compartment of a 4-SUB at Wimbledon Park depot.[34] By the 1970s BR had had enough of this and, with the trend towards open carriages prevailing, many closed compartment carriages were removed from those multiple-units that had them and the surviving loco-hauled carriages of the type finally bit the dust.

One positive aspect of the closed compartment should have been to separate smoking and non-smoking passengers more efficiently and to enable the smokers to keep the smoke to themselves (that was, of course, when smoking was permitted on trains). In reality, though, with no through-corridors or gangways on crowded trains, people often had to occupy any compartment, so many non-smokers had to endure the smoke of the smoking compartment, and many smokers had to wait a goodly length of time in the non-smoking before finally lighting up on the platform at their destination.

In passing I may as well note that originally many railways had banned smoking altogether, as is now the case for all. In 1868 the provision of smoking accommodation was made compulsory by parliament in the Regulation of the Railways Act of that year. It stated that: 'All Railway Companies, except the Metropolitan Railway Company, shall, from and after the First Day of October next, in every Passenger Train where there are more Carriages than One of each Class, provide Smoking Compartments for each Class of Passengers, unless exempted by the Board of Trade.'[35]

For those smokers amongst you who were hoping to seize on this as a legal way to reclaim your right to smoke on the train, I am afraid the clause was repealed in 1959.[36] The same act in 1868 also prohibited railways from organising trains for prize fights.

Compartments were also used to officially segregate the sexes as well as to bring them together – unofficially – in the ways we have already outlined above. Ladies-only compartments were provided on many pre-nationalisation railways. British Railways was to build further examples of multiple-unit stock and loco-hauled stock designed to have such compartments. More than that, rule 161 of the *British Railways Rule Book* provided that: 'When ladies are travelling alone the staff must, if requested, endeavour to select a compartment for them (according to the class of their ticket) in which other ladies are travelling. If ladies wish to change compartments during the journey the staff must enable them to do so.' This rule, with a variation on the wording, dates back at least as early as the *Book of Rules* issued by the Railway Clearing House in 1876. (Rule 242 of that book forbade staff to place members of the female sex in smoking compartments.)

Rule 161 remained in force until October 1972 when documents record that it was transferred from the Rule Book to the General Appendix.[37] However, it does not actually appear in the General Appendix issued at the same time – it seems to have been neatly 'disappeared'. My mother was a regular traveller on the railway as a single woman, when this rule was in force, but insists that she was never made aware of it.

Ladies-only compartments mostly vanished in the 1960s and 1970s; doubtless the fact that so much compartment stock was withdrawn during this time had much to do with it. It is sometimes said that the Sex Discrimination Act of 1975 was the key factor in ending the practice, but the board had legal advice that the bye-law allowing the enforcement of ladies-only accommodation was 'unlikely' to be affected by this legislation.[38]

The railways had come up with some peculiar alternatives to the closed compartment. One of these was the inter-compartment lavatory coach, which usually served in the semi-fast services mentioned earlier. These had lavatories, usually one on each side of the coach, which were accessible from the compartments that were adjacent to them. In some designs a folding seat obstructed the entrance to the lavatory and this was the source of some jokes that highlighted the social difficulties of asking people if they could make way for 'those in need'. Some carriages of this type provided lavatories for some compartments but not for others, on a seemingly random principle of discrimination and with no clue on the entrance doors. Some of these were built by the LMS as late as the thirties and some survived well into the BR period, finally disappearing in the mid-1960s. A more satisfactory oddity was the semi-corridor option, where two separate corridors ran from each end to separate lavatories in the centre.

The open carriage was not completely neglected by the British companies. Apart from dining carriages and Pullman parlours there were examples to be found even on the pre-group companies. (This of course is to ignore the London transport system, where the open carriage was embraced as a standard during the last century.)

The early years of the twentieth century saw attempts to bring down the costs of urban and rural local services by using steam railmotors. These were basically small steam engines packaged inside a carriage. They formed the bogie at one end and must have given a rough ride to passengers. These enabled the train to be driven from either end so that the costly business of running-round by a locomotive could be avoided. Such vehicles were usually built as open carriages – presumably to economise on weight and also so that a conductor-guard could have free movement checking and selling tickets. Later the trend moved on to a format where separate, small locomotives were equipped to be driven from a cab at the end of a carriage. These vehicles too were often open in plan, as were the pre-war internal combustion powered railcars.

In terms of main-line carriages, the Lancashire and Yorkshire Railway (L&Y) was one of the first to experiment with open coaches. One design produced by this company in 1908-09 actually put the aisle down one side of the carriage, as if it were a side corridor.[39] Eventually the railways managed to get it right, though, and the centre aisle became the norm. From 1913 the L&Y pioneered the use of complete trains of open stock on its commuter services to Southport and Blackpool. The Midland and the Great Central also built examples of open carriages.

After the grouping the LMS became the principal builder and user of the open carriage, regarding them as interchangeable with corridor stock.[40] The other companies populated trains with the occasional open carriage as they saw fit but a train completely formed of open stock was regarded as suitable only for excursions. The L&Y's experience seems to have inspired the LMS, for in 1925 it launched a new service between Bradford, Sheffield and London intended for the Yorkshire businessman. *The Yorkshireman*, as it came to be titled, was a long-distance express that consisted entirely of open stock, the seats organised in bays with tables. *The Railway Gazette* was quick to note that the provision of tables throughout the train not only enabled meals to be taken at every seat but also enabled businessmen to work whilst travelling. The LNER began to venture into such trains in the late 1930s and it was the beginning of the format that was adopted by British Rail for its Inter-City services.

Given that there was a choice to be made regarding coach interiors and that railways were in competition with each other, you would have thought that there would have been some market research into customers' preferences, but there seems to have been very little. One exception was O.V.S. Bulleid, Chief Mechanical Engineer on the Southern from 1937. According to his son: 'Bulleid had always taken a powerful interest in "the carriage side", seeing it as the main testing link between the Company and the fare-paying customer. The company's duty, through its CME, was to supply the best space, comfort and elegance that cash would allow.'[41]

In 1945 Bulleid had a composite gangwayed coach, intended for main-line use, exhibited at Charing Cross. This had three third-class compartments, four first-class ones and two lavatories.[42] As many as 25,000 people viewed the coach and their views were taken on the matter of 'open' versus 'compartment' coaches. They voted three to one for compartments but, of course, it must be noted that in this experiment they weren't given the opportunity to sample an open saloon. Later, when it came to designing electric suburban stock, Bulleid and Missenden (then General Manager) favoured open stock for this purpose in order to aid loading; but the traffic department wanted compartments. Missenden ordered some of each type built and then took a 'statistically significant sample'[43] of passengers' views. A large majority were in favour of open carriages. Given this experiment it is hard to see why British Railways should have gone back to preferring the closed compartment from 1948, particularly as Sir Eustace was head of the Executive. The answer must be in the prevailing LMS influence on the engineering side. It is known that as functional member for engineering, Riddles was given a free hand.[44]

Bulleid had been a pioneer of new designs and new construction techniques. He has been credited with introducing welding as a carriage construction method whilst working as Gresley's assistant on the LNER. He also introduced this practice onto the Southern. His later coach designs set out the basic dimensions that were to be taken on by the designers of the British Railways standard gangwayed carriage. He increased the length to 63ft 5in over headstocks and gave them a distinctive bow-shaped side profile with a maximum 9ft width at waist level.

Despite being revolutionary in form, the bodies of Bulleid's coaches were still built of wood, although post-war shortages probably had more to do with this than the designer's own choice. Wood had always been the traditional material for carriage bodies and many wooden-bodied coaches were in use well into the BR era. Wooden underframes had largely passed beyond the veil at the turn of the century but some wood/metal composites lasted into the 1930s, although none are known to have come into BR stock as passenger vehicles. The LSWR and the GWR had been the first companies to introduce metal cladding onto wooden frames, both before 1923.[45] In 1926 the LMS produced an all-steel carriage but this idea was not generally taken up. Like the other companies, the LMS continued to use wood for the body frames of most of its vehicles.[46] Even then there were exceptions, not least the progressive multiple-units built for the Wirral electrification in the 1930s. These were not only all-steel but also integral and had air sliding doors.

After the war a new emphasis was placed on all-metal construction and this was later to be taken up by the Executive. This initiative came from Derby, which in 1948 published a pamphlet with the scintillating title of *New all steel carriage*. The pamphlet had the British Railways flying sausage on it, but it was an LMS commissioned and designed project. It heralded the true beginning of disposing of wood as a carriage-building material altogether. Despite being described by some commentators as integral it plainly wasn't – as the pictures in the pamphlet show, the underframe was a structurally separate entity. However, all-steel was an advance, and one that the newly formed British Railways would take on in spite of post-war shortages of steel.

The first BR standard carriage, or 'Mark 1' (Mk1), is a much maligned beast that actually represented a serious advance on safety in its own time, even though it was later to be condemned as unsafe. The design was a compromise. It was born out of post-war economies and rationing, and out of a need to produce something that fitted in with the needs of a variegated railway network with different requirements and different technical specifications. It was based firmly on the traditional British carriage design and despite significant improvements in safety it still possessed fundamental flaws.

The development of the British Railway carriage from a stagecoach body on a flat truck meant that the underframe was always constructed as a discrete vehicle, with the carriage body erected separately on top of it, independent of the structure that gave the carriage its basic strength. Together with the flimsiness that resulted from the provision of carriage doors along the sides this had fundamental implications for safety that were to be evident many times over the years, but that were to finally achieve official recognition in the wake of the Clapham disaster. The American design of coach, being integral – that is to say with the strength built into the body and with no separate underframe – was a much sturdier beast from the point of view of collision worthiness. The British Pullman cars we have already mentioned were built to American specifications and the contrast between them and the British design of coach was starkly shown in a number of accidents, such as the Thirsk collision on the North Eastern Railway on 2 November 1892. At Thirsk the Pullman car *India* was written off but its body survived intact in an accident which demolished several of the British-type coaches involved. On the LB&SCR *Maud* was written off in the Wivelsfield accident of 23 December 1899, but wasn't completely smashed like the flimsy Brighton-designed stock which was also party to the collision.[47]

British Railways initially had a debate over whether the standard carriage design should be integral, but in the end the decision went against this.[48] The traditional style of construction had an advantage in that coach bodies tended to wear more quickly than the underframe, and also for the style to go out of fashion. It was common for underframes to be used under more than one generation of coach bodies. In the 1950s BR re-bodied the underframes from old Southern Railway multiple-units, themselves converted from steam stock in the 1930s.[49] Even the prematurely condemned compartment coaches of the Executive, mentioned earlier, had their underframes reused as Motorail car flats. The railway companies were past-masters of 'waste not want not' and 'make do and mend'. A life of forty years was envisaged for the standard carriage underframes, and the bodies were expected to last for half this period.[50] Another reason for the traditional construction method was the flexible and economic use of workshop resources. Underframes were built at Ashford to be fitted with bodies at Eastleigh and Swindon, while York built underframes to be bodied at Doncaster.[51]

As stated earlier, in its time the standard carriage was well thought of as a fundamentally safe vehicle and one that was vastly safer than its predecessors. It had an end buffing strength of 200 tons, which was well above that of comparable pre-nationalisation vehicles. The body framing was steel with the ends strengthened. This made it much more resistant to the phenomenon known as telescoping, when the underframe of one carriage overrides another, demolishing the end of the other carriage and passing through its body. Even in the 1970s the MkI continued to be praised by accident investigators. Lt Col. I.K.A. McNaughton, in his capacity as Chief Inspecting Officer of Railways for the Department of Transport, held that the use of this type of carriage had been a major contribution to the fall in accident casualties since 1955 due to its strong ends and use of buckeye couplings, which were standard on BR passenger stock from the time of the Executive.[52]

Although all structural members were of steel the interiors were constructed using plywood and blockboard, with hardboard or thin ply for the ceilings. The floors were covered with linoleum and only first-class areas had carpets. Other surfaces had decorative laminate bonded to them: a wood pattern for the vertical surfaces and off-white for the ceilings. This meant considerable savings when it came to painting. Later the wood panelling made way for melamine in second class. The seats had loose cushions originally stuffed with rubberised horsehair, as per ancient tradition. They were covered with moquette, a hard-wearing fabric consisting mostly of wool with a dense pile. Several different patterns of this were used, the designs changing over the years to reflect changes in fashion.

The Railway Executive had decided on steam as the method of locomotion so the loco-hauled MkIs were fitted with steam heating. Later on this was to bring its own problems as locomotive policy changed to favour diesel and electric loco-motives. Steam heating had its own problems with which the regular traveller of yesteryear would have been familiar. Because the steam inevitably lost its heat as it distributed it down the length of the train there was a tendency for it to go cold before it reached the last carriages. Locomotive drivers tended to pump up the supply of steam to the train to compensate for this, so there was a 'Goldilocks' effect: the front portion of the train could be too hot, the middle just right and the end too cold.

The original bogies for the standard carriage were based on long-established British practice, largely drawn from Great Western designs. They had leaf spring primary suspension and axle boxes with static bearing surfaces. Modern roller bearings were considered too expensive for carriages although they were used on the standard locomotives. On the bogies for the main-line carriages the trusted Moulton-Gresley double bolster arrangement, dating from the turn of the cen-tury, was used for the secondary suspension. Unfortunately a poor choice of bearings for swing links turned out to be a serious liability that prevented the carriages being authorised for 100mph running without expensive regular main-tenance. In its early days this was by far the most serious setback for the standard carriage, yet it set BR on an investigation that was to lead to one of the organisa-tion's greatest triumphs; as it did often, BR was to pull success out of failure, but that story is for Chapter 7.

Another matter in which the standard carriage was traditional was the manner in which it disposed of toilet waste – straight onto the track. This was in its time the source of a variety of music-hall style songs and jokes based on the notices in the lavatories that read along the lines of 'please do not flush the toilet whilst the train is standing in a station'.

It has been demonstrated in various trials throughout the years that this is not a hygienic way of disposing of such material, whether the train is stationary or on the move. If the train is travelling fast enough the material will in fact be liquidised into a fine spray which will coat the outside of the carriages, including the door handles. It could also result in mishaps – there is the case of the signal-man who was walking along a platform on a West Country station when he was slapped in the face by a used condom flushed from a passing sleeper.[53]

Waste storage tanks had in fact been fitted on carriages of the London, Tilbury and Southend Railway as early as 1911[54] for those trains passing along the District Line on Ealing–Shoeburyness services, but several generations of BR stock were constructed before these were fitted as standard. In fact, at the time of writing, there are still vehicles in service that deposit toilet waste onto the track – and on lots of other places.

The standard carriage was built in the greatest variety of all the BR standard coach types, being conceived to quickly replace a wide variety of outworn pre-war stock, in large numbers, in many different roles. It was built in two different lengths: 63ft 6in and 57ft 0in. It was built as compartment, semi-corridor, corridor and open versions. Standard carriages were also built as three types of sleeper, with the same body shell used for each. It was built as 'gangwayed brakes'.

The non-gangwayed suburban vehicles were produced with considerable variations. They were built on both lengths of underframe, in both open and compartment formats and with different densities of seating, depending on the traditions and requirements of the region they were destined for. The Western Region even had theirs built with chains to hold the couplings out of the way should they be used for slip coach operation. Also in the standard range were the very last brake composites. Ironically the last of these emerged in 1964, just when the tide was turning substantially against the through coach.

Amongst the oddities of the standard design was the window of the centre second-class compartment of the CK (corridor composite) which opened inwards to enable a stretcher to be passed through the window. This feature was demonstrated in a publicity photograph probably dating from 1951.[55] It was the only concession made to the disabled or incapacitated in Mk1 stock, but at this time little consideration was generally given to the disabled traveller on the railways (there had been purpose-built invalid carriages in pre-nationalisation but these were for the wealthy).

The standard carriage was to make one of its greatest and longest lasting contributions in the form of catering vehicles. It was built as several different types, some subsequently converted to others. To this day Mk1 catering vehicles continue to provide yeoman service on Britain's preserved lines. Because many of the Mk1 catering cars, and all the sleeping cars, were built late in the production run there were no Mk2 versions of these types. The next generation of loco-hauled catering vehicles were Mk3s built in 1979. Mk3 sleepers were built from 1981, and the Mk1 vehicles served long and hard – and often well.

From 1951 the gangwayed standards began to appear on premier services such as the *Flying Scotsman* and five named trains were launched to showcase the new stock; but for most passengers the standard carriage was slow to come on stream.

Post-war government restrictions, particularly on steel, continued to apply and construction was curtailed in 1952 due to this material's short supply.[56]

In the meantime BR had to make use of 40,000 or so carriages it had acquired as at 1 January 1948. Of these, some 12,000 had been from the pre-grouping companies and were thus twenty-five years of age or older. Many, inevitably, had been built to antique designs and had seen a variety of uses in their lifetimes. They had, as the terminology has it, been 'cascaded' down the ranks.

Cascading is the process by which the railway companies recycle stock during its life, moving it 'downwards' from line to line, and service type to service type according to a list of declining priorities. In the steam era carriages were moved down the ranks into secondary services and from there moved ever further down until passengers on rural branch lines could enjoy the antique comfort of some truly salubrious vehicles. Cascading still happens today as companies fight to get as much use as possible out of their stock.

One use to which superannuated stock was put was the large variety of 'specials' and 'excursions' which I mentioned earlier. BR and its predecessors always had stock on hand to service such requirements, stowed away in numerous carriage sidings. Often these vehicles were of low quality and unsuitable for regular use – an instruction by the GWR in 1936 ordered that only third-class carriages of the 'oldest type' should be used for hop-pickers, and under no circumstances should contain first-class compartments or lavatories.[57] Retaining this ageing fleet was a costly option, as however often or seldom they were used – whether it was once a month or once every six months – they still needed to be maintained to a standard where they could run without incident. Axle boxes would still have to be greased, brake gear tested, and all machinery overhauled.

The coaches that had formed the super-trains of the thirties – those from *The Coronation*, *The Coronation Scot* and others, were not returned to those duties. The age of the de-luxe 'hotel on wheels' was over and the carriages from those sets were distributed amongst other services and sometimes converted to other purposes. The other main-line vehicles of the Big Four were gradually ousted by the new standards but were not to see such extensive reuse. The new fleet of diesel multiple-units took on the duties that had previously been given to old stock and so a generation of coaches hit the scrapheap after what their designers would have considered an unprofitably short life. Of course, this was not entirely a bad thing as most of these coaches were wooden bodied. The diesel multiple-units (DMUs) were steel framed and integral. For a change the customers down the pecking order were getting something new rather than main-line hand-me-downs.

As the new DMUs came on stream purges in the 1950s and 1960s saw off the pre-group, and then the Big Four stock in turn. In 1957 there were 14,000 wooden-bodied carriages still in service, and BR was planning to replace them all by 1962.[58] British Railways proudly boasted of its success in reducing the *total* number of coaching vehicles year on year, for instance saying: 'The reduction made in 1962 in the number of passenger carriages was the largest in a year so far, 4,927 being withdrawn from service. At the same time 685 new carriages were delivered.'[59] The last passenger-carrying vehicles from the Big Four to see BR service were specialists – sleeping cars and catering vehicles. In 1976 a handful of LNER buffet restaurants and LMS second sleepers were still in service. All had wooden members in their structure. By 1980 they were all gone.[60]

When the ageing carriage had rattled its way to the bottom of the cascade chain there were still options to extend its life. One was to use it as a 'departmental' vehicle, meaning that the track or signal engineers would use it as a tool van or sleeping accommodation. There was a chance, though, that it could stay in passenger use as a camping coach 'for delightful and inexpensive holidays', as the brochures said. This was an idea first devised by the LNER in the early 1930s, when it fitted out some redundant coaches at holiday resorts to serve as stationary accommodation for holidaymakers. The requirement was, of course, that you travelled to the destination by train:

> Camping coaches are booked on the condition that tenants purchase in advance not less than four adult ordinary return rail tickets for a six berth coach and six ordinary return rail tickets for an eight berth coach (two children counting as one adult) from their home station to the station serving the camping coach.[61]

But once you got there your 'home away from home' awaited you on a nearby siding set aside for the purpose.

According to the brochures camping coaches provided:

> Holidays in specially selected places in England, Scotland and Wales.
> Out-of-doors camping holiday with the comfort of well-appointed living accommodation at reasonable cost.
> A cheap and ideal holiday for the family.[62]

The railway did not pass up the chance to entice the occupants to further travel on the railway as 'holiday runabout tickets' and 'cheap day tickets' were offered at most camping coach stations. The leaflets advised you to 'make a friend of the station master who will be glad to help you in any way he can to make your holiday a success. He knows the locality and can advise on outings, fishing and golf and in many other ways.'

A leaflet from 1955[63] shows camping coaches available in 107 locations throughout Britain, both on the coast and inland. In 1960 British Railways introduced a new kind of camping coach: the Pullman. These coaches were genuine ex-Pullman cars, that is to say, cars built, owned and once leased to the railways by the Pullman Car Company, now of course part-owned by the BTC. Pullman camping coaches were something of a gimmick though, trading on a name, while the basic ingredient that made a car Pullman – the 'at seat' service – would not have been available. This was probably the one and only time that a Pullman 'car' was called a coach.

Railway-owned camping coaches were offered to the public for the final time in 1971. There is no evidence that they declined in popularity, and the growth of caravan holidays in the 1960s and 1970s would seem to indicate that there was a market for such self-catering accommodation. Doubtless the decline in station staff needed to look after them had something to do with their withdrawal. The coaches also needed to be fully maintained as roadworthy, as they were hauled back to depots in the winter for service – which must have been expensive. The LMS did briefly try grounded bodies but the idea was not continued.

Such was the nature of services and comforts that the railway provided on the eve of the 'reformation'. Soon the railways would be changed almost beyond recognition and much of what we have outlined above would vanish as a consequence. The reformation was to come in two stages: a radical, wholesale, expensive (and, some would contend, unnecessary) change in equipment, and then a change in ethos – in the very notions of how the railway was meant to be operated and what its purpose was.

4

Reformation I: 'Modernisation'

n December 1956 a report emerged from the Eastern Region's headquarters at Liverpool Street that warned of the potential threat of competition to the railways from internal airlines. The report recognised that 'For most passengers speed must always be one of the principal factors influencing the choice between rail and air travel.'[1] Like the rest of British Railways the Eastern Region was faced with a problem: the existing stock of steam locomotives simply weren't up to the job of pulling trains at a competitive speed.

By the time this report was written British Railways had already embarked on a full scale modernisation programme, the most expensive investment programme ever undertaken across the entire railway network. It was the result of the sea-change in policy that had begun with the Conservative election victory of October 1951 and had seen the abolition of the Executives and the placing of the Transport Commission in direct charge of the railway.

There had been much disquiet in political circles over the failure of the Executive to embrace modern technology. Yet the delay was quite understandable, at least in terms of diesels. The man in charge of designing and commissioning new locomotives, Robin Riddles, already had experience with diesels through prototypes that had been built by the LMS and the Southern Railway. These had not proved successful – they were too heavy, too long and very underpowered. Also, they had to heat the contemporary steam-heated coaches with special boilers, because diesel locomotives do not produce surplus steam as a by-product. These heating boilers had been unreliable to say the least, meaning that the diesels had not been used for passenger trains during the winter.[2]

The supporters of diesels in Britain had been misled by the example of overseas railways. It was relatively easy for engineers in other countries to place a large diesel engine and a generator set in a locomotive body. They did not have the restrictions of height, width and weight that George Stephenson and his contemporaries bequeathed to the pioneer British railway system. The diesel power plant that was both small enough and powerful enough to suit British requirements just didn't exist in the early 1950s, and there was no money made available to develop it. Riddles also believed firmly that the future of railway traction lay in electrification – at that time ruled out on grounds of expense – and that if diesels were allowed to intervene as a stopgap they would then be used as a reason to delay electrification yet further.

In 1948 no one could have doubted that the railways were in great need of repair and renovation. So little work had been done since the onset of war, nearly ten years before, that modernisation would be a natural part of the rebuilding of the railways. R.C. Bond, Chief Mechanical Engineer of British Railways from 1953 to 1958, expressed the view that modernisation should be a continuous process based on annual programmes incorporating contemporary equipment.[3]

Much of the war-destroyed European system was being rebuilt with the most up-to-date equipment facilitated by American money given as a result of the Marshall Plan. Many in Britain doubtless felt left out. Others, such as those in the Railway Executive, were aware of the drawbacks regarding innovation for the British system, or else realised that in Britain the money simply wasn't going to be available for such expensive projects as electrification. When the Executive took over in 1948 its main priority was to renew the locomotives, rolling stock and trackwork of the railway with the emphasis on affordability and reliability, with the tried and tested technology at the fore.

So, Riddles had opted for trusted steam locomotives, a quick and reliable way to make sure that the railways were restocked with much needed new power before the politicians withdrew the offer of the money.

The lack of progress in modernising traction was also a source of friction between Hurcomb and the Executive. In 1948 Hurcomb had ordered that a report should be prepared on alternative traction. He took care to specify that no engineers should be on the panel that was writing it. Missenden ensured that it was 'kicked into the long grass' and the panel didn't return a report until 1951. Not surprisingly Hurcomb was irritated over the delay, but when he asked Riddles when he was to have it Riddles told him: 'In any case, you know that the only alternative form of traction is electrification, and you say that we cannot afford it; so what are we worrying about?'[4]

There was a real need for new spending and new equipment for the railways; the problem was the assumption that new equipment was the sole solution. There was idealism that went unchecked about the ability of technology to solve problems.

To fully understand the reasons behind this it is necessary to understand the attitude to technology and modernity prevalent at the time. In the 1950s and 1960s modernisation was not just a buzzword but an implacable faith that what is new is *automatically* better. Visions of 'The Future' predominated in magazines, books and films. Architects set out to create 'Cities of the Future', technologists did their best to invent devices that would transform human life. Such notions became dominant in transport policy as much as anything else. Some of them were very fanciful, to say the least. Lord Cherwell, Secretary of State for Air in the early 1950s (who had previously doubted the existence of the German V2 programme and the very possibility of rockets), believed that transport problems would be solved by everyone having their own personal helicopter and that railways were obsolete.[5] According to the government's *Traffic in Towns* report of 1963, it was commonly believed that personal jetpacks would be the answer to urban congestion.[6]

With the abolition of the Executive in 1953 the BTC was given a full political mandate to modernise regardless of any objections. At this point Riddles rather wisely chose to retire.

Although the impetus for the modernisation was political it was to be the railways' own money that was to be spent on the equipment. The government allowed the railways to borrow money but it had to be paid back, the expectation being that the equipment would earn back its cost through efficiencies.[7] The next few years were to be a steep learning curve for BR as it encountered the very real problems associated with getting diesels to work on the British system.

In 1955 the BTC published a document entitled *Modernisation and Re-equipment of British Railways*. It boldly stated:

> The aim must be to exploit the great natural advantages of railways as bulk transporters of passengers and goods and to revolutionise the character of the services provided for both – not only by the full utilisation of a modern equipment but also by a purposeful concentration on those functions which the railways can be made to perform more efficiently than other forms of transport, whether by road, air or water.[8]

It envisioned improved track to make higher speeds possible on the trunk routes and new signalling (pretty coloured lights) with track circuits, automatic train control, modern power boxes and traffic control with modern telephone systems – cost £210 million.

Then of course there was the motive power issue – a rapid deployment of several thousand electric or diesel locomotives – cost £345 million.

The next idea was to withdraw much of the existing steam-hauled passenger stock and replace it with multiple-units, diesel or electric, and modernise the rest of the rolling stock. Passenger stations and parcels depots would also require 'considerable' expenditure – cost £285 million.

The freight services were considered next. Continuous brakes were now to be standard. Larger wagons were to be introduced. Larger marshalling yards would replace many smaller ones. Loading and unloading methods would be modernised – cost £365 million.

The BTC also envisaged various sundry ideas: improvements at the packet ports, staff welfare, office mechanisms – oh, and at least £10 million for development and research work – cost £35 million.

The total cost was estimated at £1,240 million.[9]

In fact the report casually adds, 'SAY £1,200 million'. But then what's £40 million or so when you are splashing out?

All that was, of course, £1,240 million in 1953 money. In today's money you needn't expect much change out of £25 billion.

Oh, and by the way, do make sure you get a receipt.

The plan promised a transformation in all forms of service offered by the railways. Passenger services were to become fast, clean and regular in all the great urban areas. 'Inter-city' and main-line trains were to be accelerated and made more punctual.[10]

Services on other routes were to be made 'reasonably' economic or transferred to road. The plan claimed that the economic benefit would be of a 'decisive order'.[11]

One of the problems with the British railway system is the number of curves and gradients that obstruct high-speed running. To make the best of the short runs of straight, level track on any route locomotives have to be capable of great acceleration. This is what steam locomotives lacked and was the advantage it was hoped that diesel traction would bring.

There is, of course, also the issue that other slow-moving traffic such as freight trains and local passenger services obstructed fast trains; this problem was to be solved in the next decade simply by the abolition of many of these services. Emphasis was for now placed on the acceleration of these services by new traction. There was a plan to equip all freight vehicles with the vacuum brake, which would enable greater speed to be achieved as the trains could be braked more effectively. This ultimately fell through due to cost. In the next decade the air brake would be embraced as the BR standard for new stock and as a consequence unfitted, vacuum braked, air braked and dual braked stock soldiered on together for many years as yet another example of where the various parts of the system did not join up due to policy changes.

The Executive had not been idle with respect to the track but due to the arrears of maintenance that occurred during the war it had mostly been playing catch-up.

The Railway Magazine reported in September 1953 that the main-line tracks of British Railways had been restored to their pre-war standards and that speeds as high as 90mph were being permitted in some cases. Although the return to pre-war conditions was not yet entirely complete, the magazine was proud to point to several 'high speed' services averaging 60mph on the London Midland Region.[12]

One important change that the Executive did make was to the type of rail. The British railway system had long used the bullhead profile, whereas the rest of the world had largely moved on to the flat bottom (FB) rail. Indeed, most of the American system had been built using FB rail. The FB profile had definite advantages, particularly in terms of its greater resilience and load-spreading capabilities. The changeover in Britain, made as soon as 1948, was a far-sighted decision that was to have important consequences and laid the foundation for high-speed travel and heavier freight trains.

The work so far had been achieved despite the problems faced in recruiting track workers and getting the necessary materials in the face of post-war short-ages. The problems of manpower had been partly solved by the increasing use of machinery. Another tactic was simply to instigate better training by offering even-ing classes for permanent way staff and also by making films[13] that were shown in special 'cinema coaches' that toured the country.[14]

Signalling was an important issue as the traditional manual signal boxes were extremely limited in their ability to control traffic. Mechanical controls based on rods did not work well over long distances. Add to that the limitations on the practical number of levers in a box and the limitations on the men operating them and it was easy to see why modernisation with automatic colour lights would speed up operations. Indeed it did, and in busy areas it was most welcome. Yet, in the opinion of some, such as Alan Williams – who was a trained signal engineer – expensive new systems were often installed with little real justification when the old system would have done the job just as well.[15] Colour lights were expanded to areas that did not need such signalling and where the old manual installations had stood the test of time, and would have carried on doing so. Crude cost-benefit analysis favoured signalling schemes over other improvements because on paper they reduced manpower and thus costs, but they didn't necessarily add any real value to the service being provided.[16] Nevertheless, it became the case that no 'modernisation' of a line, or an electrification, was complete without a new set of 'railway traffic lights' – rather like a boy scout's 'Job Done' sticker.

The 'dieselisation' started off in a well-organised fashion with a set of pilot scheme locomotives that were supposed to be evaluated. Unfortunately as the deficit caught up with the BTC the possibility of saving money through the new technology proved too great a temptation and the pilot scheme was all too hastily abandoned. Large orders were placed for designs that had not been properly tried and tested.

For high-speed passenger work what BR needed was some diesel locomo-tives with some welly; what it got were inadequate to the task. There had been little or no development in British diesel technology since the prototypes of the late 1940s and the first 'high-power', so called, 'Type 4' diesels – those in the 2,000–2,999hp power range – were simply using the same late 1940s technol-ogy recycled with a different look. Two versions were designed and built, one by English Electric and the other by British Railways at Derby, using a Sulzer engine. Both were hampered from the outset by the track engineers' limitations on axle weight, meaning that both designs were placed on a 4-axle bogie that was originally designed by O.V.S. Bulleid for the Southern diesel prototypes. The

Type 4s were cumbersome, lumbering machines produced in a hurry after years of wasted time. They still have their fans, and I count myself as one – they are a milestone in British locomotive development, but they were still bad designs.

Something that they were able to improve – a bit – was the steam heat boilers. These were now at least reliable enough to risk on a cold winter's day, even though on occasions some passengers ended up frozen like fish fingers. The improvements did, however, lead to the laughable spectacle of 'modern' locos drawing water from tanks and pumps intended for the steamers. It also meant that a second man was required to tend the untrustworthy boilers. A principal idea behind diesels was to eliminate the need for a fireman, whereas now they had an extra person just to maintain the train's heating.

Most of the diesels commissioned by the BTC were of the diesel–electric variety – they had low-speed diesel engines powering an electric generator. In Germany an alternative to this arrangement had been developed: the diesel-hydraulic. The BTC decided to try out this option and the Western Region was chosen as the test bed.[17] These locomotives used high-speed diesel engines to power the axles using hydraulic fluid. It brought a weight-saving advantage as the electric generator was eliminated. The downside of this was that they didn't generate electricity for train heating or air conditioning and this was to be a significant reason for their downfall. That and the fact they were non-standard meant that they were withdrawn very early, some having had less than ten years' service.[18]

The Executive had looked into the issue of diesel multiple-units (DMUs) for branch lines and had even commissioned some. The first units were deployed in the West Riding and west Cumberland from 1954 and were a considerable success. In the West Riding passenger receipts increased fivefold in four years. These schemes were the pioneers of the hundreds of diesel multiple-units that were to be unleashed by the BTC as part of the modernisation plan. They were also to provide false hope to many, inside and outside the BTC, that uneconomic lines could be made to pay by using 'more modern' equipment. In the West Riding even the substantial growth in receipts was not enough to make the service viable or even to cover the cost of the units. It was discontinued ten years later.[19]

The modernisation plan called for a wholesale changeover from steam traction to DMUs in a very short timescale, with the expectation that the savings would cover the initial outlay. A massive 4,600 vehicles were originally envisaged, of which 4,171 were eventually built from the mid-1950s to the early 1960s. Withdrawals started wastefully early; by the end of 1970 only 3,621 remained in service.[20]

During the time of construction the withdrawal of services and closures of lines caught up with the programme and some units found themselves being moved as the line they were operating, or were intended to operate, was closed.

The original idea of the diesel railcars was that they would be used for rural areas and thus be a step in the direction of saving branch line services; however, the BTC now came to see the DMU as an outright replacement for steam on suburban and other heavily trafficked routes. Three types of unit were originally planned. Firstly suburban and local services, secondly cross-country services, and thirdly inter-city services.[21] As with the locomotives, this programme required that BR contract the design and construction to outside builders as well as its own workshops. Outside builders designed and built 2,000 vehicles.

The original Derby design produced under the Executive was an integral vehicle, based on the standard carriage underframe but without its underfloor trussing and with the sides bearing the load. This idea became compromised by outside manufacturers, particularly when it came to the suburban stock for which the specifications required a door for every seating bay (see Chapter 3). This significantly weakened the body and when heavily loaded the carriage would bow slightly in the centre.

Ironically, the June 1955 issue of *Trains Illustrated* which detailed the modernisation plan also announced the introduction of the new loco-hauled suburban stock, which the modernisation plan had condemned.

For the Southern Region an entirely different type of diesel unit was developed in conjunction with English Electric. This was a diesel-electric multiple-unit, originally for the Hastings line, and similar power cars eventually found themselves being used also for three-car units in Hampshire, Berkshire and other places. Some closed compartments were sneaked into these as well and they must have been the very last in service in British Rail – some of these lasted into the twenty-first century.

On top of the construction of the DMUs there was much political pressure to try out railbuses as a solution to the most unremunerative branch lines. They were already being used in Germany.[22] Five manufacturers were commissioned to produce examples for the British system, including the German manufacturers Waggon und Maschinenbau.

There were differing attitudes from the regions to the idea; the Scottish Region lobbied hard for a large allocation but the Southern would have nothing to with them on the grounds that a single-vehicle train was impractical. The idea that some of the units could be single manned, meaning that the driver issued tickets, was scotched by the London Midland, who argued that nowhere on the system was there anywhere suitable for such operation.[23] In Germany they were able to stop at any point along the track to pick up passengers who hailed them. In Britain this was of course impossible as, unlike on the Continent, British law requires that railway lines have to be fenced in.

The main issue was that in Britain the railways still had to operate Cardwell's Act, requiring them to run a sundries good service which the passenger trains operated by taking packages and parcels in their guard's vans or even by hauling additional vans – or, in the case of milk traffic, tankers. The railbuses did not have sufficient space inside for freight and the only ones for the British system fitted for towing a vehicle were the German-built ones – these vehicles only being ordered at the insistence of the Eastern Region.[24] This was very odd, almost as if someone were intending to limit the railbuses' usefulness and thwart their purpose from the start. The Eastern Region was supposed to get trailers for the German railbuses but these never materialised (the infamous Sentinel railcars of the LNER had once hauled trailers – Eastern memories of these would still have been fresh).

The attitude of BR's engineers to railbuses is best summed up in the words of E.S. Cox when speaking to a conference at Witwatersrand University in 1961: 'if your service only warrants one of those little fellows you might as well let that bit go to the road, because the little 4-wheeler will not bring you much grist to the mill.'[25] Dr Beeching was of exactly the same opinion in the Reshaping Report, damning the experiment by comparing costs with road buses.[26] By this time the experiment had already failed to save branches on the Scottish and Eastern regions and the railbuses were likely doomed anyway.[27] As will be explained, BR had not finished with the railbus concept; different financial arrangements – meaning operating with a subsidy – were to change the prevailing view once more.

Electrification was another key plank of the modernisation plan and it was here that the BTC was to achieve its greatest success, although it was not to survive to see it to fruition.

The electrification projects that had been undertaken by the Executive had just been continuations of LNER plans that had been aborted due to the Second World War. These were the Liverpool Street to Shenfield and the Manchester–Sheffield–Wath line, often called the Woodhead route. These were electrified at 1,500 volts DC (Direct Current), with an overhead line, a standard that had been endorsed in the 1920s and 1930s.[28]

By the time of the modernisation plan the arguments of Warder and Riddles for AC (Alternating Current) overhead electrification at 25,000 volts, 50 hertz had won the day. In November 1955[29] the BTC bravely endorsed this as the new standard for all future electrification, apart from on the Southern Region, where the third-rail system was deemed too extensive to be supplanted.

The West Coast Main Line and several other projects were authorised: the Eastern Region lines out of Liverpool Street, and, in the Scottish Region, Glasgow suburban lines. In the case of lines out of Liverpool Street this meant conversion of the 1,500 volt DC electrification of just a few years before – 1956 – from 1,500 volts DC to the new standard. The East Coast Main Line electrification was set aside; it was felt that the West Coast Line offered better prospects in that it went through densely populated areas, whereas the East Coast Line had few major population centres on its route.

Due to concern over the more limited clearances available for the wires in suburban areas a dual voltage system was decided upon; 6.25kv would be available in these areas and 25kv outside them, with units capable of switching between them automatically, and having 'dead' sections in-between. This was quite a leap ahead in technology and it is said that the French engineers with experience of 50 hertz raised some eyebrows at the pace of BR's development.

The first AC line to come into service was the 24-mile section from Colchester to Clacton, including the branch to Walton-on-the-Naze. In 1959 this was used as a test bed for the new equipment. In 1960 other sections began to come into use. In September the Crewe–Manchester–Styal line commenced operation. By November the new 25kv service out of Liverpool Street was started and also phase one of the Glasgow suburban electrification. At this point there were teething troubles and it was the dual voltage system which was the cause. Several of the Glasgow trains exploded spectacularly, in one case injuring seven people. It was later to be found that the dual voltage system was unnecessary – it turned out to be possible to run 25kv within the limited clearances quite safely.

For the West Coast Main Line itself it was planned that locomotives would operate the long-distance services, with multiple-units used only for the shorter-distance services. In keeping with the general policy of the modernisation plan prototypes were commissioned from five different companies with at least ten examples built of each.[30] The engineering design was down to each company but on this occasion a front end look was specified that all had to adhere to. This was the work of Misha Black and J. Beresford Evans.[31] So the bodies of the five designs were all built according to very different design principles, from having separate underframes to monocoque construction, but they all looked the same. The engineering that drove them was also very different. They were designated AL1 to AL5. Originally it was intended that some would be low geared for heavy freight, but in the end all were fitted with mixed traffic gearing.

With the tests of the locos successfully concluded a production version designated AL6 was commissioned. The appearance of the front end was slightly altered, but apart from that the look was much the same as the prototypes. One problem that did emerge with these machines was the axle-hung, nose-suspended traction motors – these were not used in the prototypes. They caused significant track damage. This was a serious mistake but also a lesson that would lead to design developments in future high-speed designs.

Having accepted '50 hertz overhead' as a new standard, BR was of course left with many lines electrified at other voltages, using other conducting methods. Conversion was not possible for all of them, but only with one system – the Southern third rail – was major expansion still planned. This decision even today is debatable – doubtless many commuters on a snowy morning curse it – but given the time and the need to get things done it was practical.

Two sets of lines had been left undone by the Southern: the lines out of Charing Cross that reached to Dover and Folkestone, and the Bournemouth line beyond Brookwood. Both of these lines were to be electrified by third rail by 1970, bringing faster and cleaner services. All the new stock for these lines was based on the Mk1 coach. In fact, construction for the Southern Region meant that construction of the Mk1 was prolonged to as late as 1974 – long after other main lines had gone over to air-conditioned carriages (see Chapter 10).

One aspect that was recognised as being important for the modernisation plan was design. The minutes of the Commission meeting for 15 September 1955 refer to 'the importance of incorporating good modern design in all construction and decoration'.[32] Staff were directed to prepare a memorandum on design to discuss with area board chairmen. This memorandum, presented to the Commission on 11 June 1956, made it clear that 'the design of locomotives and rolling stock is a function reserved to the Commission in both its technical and aesthetic aspects'. It stressed that:

It is particularly important that this part of our equipment should not only be modern, but should look, and continue to look, modern – not in the sense of conforming to any passing fashion, but by giving them the kind of basically pleasing form and proportions that will stand the test of time.

It went on:

A criticism frequently levelled at British Railways is that their rolling stock looks out of date and gives no indication of the mark of progress.[33]

The first meeting of the Design Panel took place on 8 August 1956. Amongst those on the panel were the chairman and director of the Council of Industrial Design, W.J. Worboys, as well as Sir Gordon Russell, Christian Barman and E.C. Ottaway, who had direct experience of design work for London Transport.[34]

In 1957, eleven months after the Design Panel was first appointed, George Williams joined the Commission as Design Officer.[35] He was already an industrial designer of some note and was to be a powerful force in shaping BR's design policy.

There was, in the words of Brian Haresnape 'quite a reaction'[36] to the idea of using 'long haired artist types' in the railway industry, and Williams was asked to justify the costs. The challenge was made that they wished change for change's sake and that it was expensive if it meant throwing away existing standards.

The principle of the Design Panel was not to undertake design itself but to oversee the work of outside consultants, who would be contracted for particular jobs. Two consultancies were to dominate in these early days: the partnership of Wilkes and Ashmore, and Design Research Unit. Design Research Unit was ultimately to take on a much larger role in BR's corporate identity programme. Despite its official-sounding name it was a private consultancy started in 1943 with the aim of influencing industrial design practice after the Second World War.

Misha (later Sir Misha) Black and Milner Gray were early members who rose to prominence in post-war British design and were to play an important part in the British Railways design programme.[37]

In the initial pilot scheme there was no design oversight and manufacturers were left free to do as they pleased, often drawing from their own vocabularies and previous experience. It was not originally intended that the pilot scheme designs would go into full production without serious modification, so it seems that no one was really bothered about looks at that stage – this was just a 'try out' exercise. The manufacturers had, understandably, rated ease and cheapness of construction above aesthetic considerations. When the Design Panel got to work it found that the best it could manage was a cleaning up operation on the assemblage of different 'design' ideas that were a *fait accompli*.

One of the requirements for the pilot scheme locomotives was that the locomotives with a cab at each end should have corridor connectors in the fronts of them to enable crew to move between connected units. These were concealed by double doors from which the corridor connector popped out like a cuckoo from a clock. This disfigured the appearance of several of the locomotives. The 'Brush type 2' was based on Brush's previous locomotives for the Ceylon railways, which had a not displeasing appearance. With the corridor doors butting up into the windshield area the aesthetics were destroyed. The Type 4 Sulzer English Electric machines got off rather better in that the doors were neatly placed in the nose ends and didn't protrude.

The modernisation plan also envisioned the 'modernisation' of the locomotive-drawn passenger stock, but apart from the abolition of closed compartments the meaning of this was far from clear. From 1955 the BTC commissioned a number of prototypes for new locomotive-hauled stock, all to be based on the existing standard carriage but to include new ideas on body style and interiors. The design specifications were rather vague – the vehicles were to be economic for distances in excess of 120 miles and the body shell had to be compatible with current BR construction methods. Four outside manufacturers were given a crack at this opportunity and brought in established designers, including Hugh Casson. British Railways also produced its own designs constructed at the Doncaster works. These trials produced some interesting ideas but there was emphasis on greater passenger comfort and amenities whilst reducing seating capacity. At a time when steam locomotives were struggling to keep pace this was not what was required.[38]

The Design Panel's influence grew slowly, but they scored a critical triumph with the first project over which they had any real influence: the Blue Pullmans. These were luxury diesel multiple-units trading on the Pullman brand that operated on the Western and Midland regions. They were withdrawn prematurely in the early 1970s due to the fact they did not fit into the new Inter-City ethos – there were not enough of them to work a full time-interval service, even if enough passengers could have been found all through the day to pay the Pullman supplement. They also 'rode' rather badly once they had worn in.

The postponement of the East Coast electrification was a blow to the Eastern Group, but there was to be a saviour. Aside from the modernisation scheme BR was trialling another locomotive which turned out to have a lot more promise for fast passenger services. English Electric had taken over a company called Napier that had developed the so-called 'Deltic' engine for use in torpedo boats. This consisted of banks of three cylinders arranged in a triangle or 'delta' arrangement. Each cylinder had two pistons which were pushed out in opposite directions by a single combustion. Drive shafts at each corner were each driven by the pistons from the adjoining cylinders and the three drive shafts were connected by gear trains to a central shaft. It all looked like a Chinese puzzle, but it worked.

English Electric put this into a prototype diesel-electric locomotive which, appropriately, they named *Deltic*. Ownership of Deltic was retained by English Electric but it was trialled for a few years on British Railways, first on the Midland Region and then on the Eastern Region. Unlike the conventional Type 4 diesels it had an impressive power-to-weight ratio. As previously stated, quick acceleration is essential on the British railway system in order to make the most of the few high-speed stretches.

By the time that *Deltic* had been trialled to the satisfaction of the BTC the prospect of immediate electrification of the East Coast Main Line had retreated. The Eastern regions were thus left looking for a diesel substitute until electrification could be afforded.

Not all were in favour of the Deltics. J.F. Harrison, who succeeded Bond as CME in 1958, thought it unsuitable for rail traction because it had too many moving parts and he drew attention to the expense of maintaining it. For a few years, according to contract, these costs were borne by English Electric, but later were taken on by BR. By that time T.C.B. Miller had succeeded to the post of CME. Miller acknowledged the excellent performance of the Deltics but described them as a 'maintenance menace', stating that they cost twice as much to maintain as a normal medium-speed four-stroke engine.[39]

Despite Harrison's reservations twenty-two Deltics were built and scheduled to cover 220,000 miles per year. Thus the twenty-two Deltics replaced fifty-five steam locomotives.[40]

In the view of G. Freeman Allen, the inauguration of the first Deltic timetable on the ECML in 1962 was a turning point in British Railways post-war services.[41] The *Flying Scotsman*'s London–Edinburgh timing was slashed by a full hour to just six hours for the 392.7 miles (still only an average of 65mph). The Deltics were still impeded in their best efforts by having to fit into schedules with the earlier Type 4s, and also by the antiquated signalling and infrastructure of the East Coast Main Line. It would not be until the 1970s, a decade later, that the work to remove such impediments to speed as the curves at Peterborough and Durham would be completed. Even then the Deltics needed all their powers of acceleration to make the most of the 100mph stretches.

The Deltics were fitted with water scoops to enable them to pick up water for the steam heat generators.[42] The scoops proved troublesome, as indeed did the steam heat generators, which continued to be the Achilles' heel of the BR diesel classes until steam heating was phased out.[43]

With the failure of the original Type 4s to perform according to requirements, the field was still open for someone to come up with a machine in that power range that could do the job. In the early 1960s Brush, English Electric and the Birmingham Railway Carriage and Wagon Works (BRCW) competed to produce prototypes to fill this role. Brush was the first to produce a working prototype, but this was before a powerful enough single engine came into production, so it used the same 1,400hp high rpm Bristol Siddeley Maybach engines as the Western hydraulic class, again as a pair, with twin alternator/generator sets.

The English Electric machine was called DP2 and was based on a spare Deltic body with a conventional English Electric 2,700hp, 16 cylinder v-type engine. The BRCW entry was called *Lion* and used the Sulzer 2,700hp engine.

Although the Birmingham design was the only one to fit in with the BR specifications, it was not the one chosen. BR chose to go with the Brush 'Falcon' but with an up rated Sulzer 2,750hp engine in place of the twin Bristol Siddeley Maybach engines. Despite this, English Electric were to make a comeback later when DP2 was used as the basis of the fifty Class 50 locos, but for BRCW the failure of their prototype led to the closure of the works. A great name in British railway history was thus extinguished.

The Class 47 was known as the 'standard type 4' but was in reality no such thing. The specifications changed whilst it was in production, leading to a bewildering array of variations between units. There was the bold, belated change to air braking that required a compressor to be installed into an already packed body shell as an afterthought. Then there was the change to electric train heating, and later the requirement that they should power air conditioning as well, which produced further complications. At least they all looked the same, with smart styling by E.G.M. Wilkes. And they had the power – that was the main thing.

The modernisation plan had also called for the updating of passenger facilities, saying that: 'An improved quality of train service may fail to make its proper impact on the public if the standard of accommodation and amenities provided at passenger stations lag behind …'[44] The airlines had new, modern terminal buildings that reflected the jet age. Needless to say, Victorian airports are rather thin on the ground.

The rebuilding and reconstruction of railway buildings to 'modern' standards had been going since pre-war days, the Southern leading the way with its 'deco' style. After the war the Executive had rebuilt some stations, such as Carpenders Park.

In the spirit of the time, modernisation often meant a wholesale clearance of what went before and complete rebuilding. In certain cases this was not unreasonable. Some stations had been expanded from their Victorian originals in such an *ad hoc* way as to render them extremely difficult to use, alter or expand. Old Euston was a classic example; a once impressive frontage consisting of pavilions flanking a propylaeum (known as the Doric Arch) had become obscured and dirty. Behind it the train shed was cramped with expansion obstructed by the Great Hall which had been constructed alongside it. The LMS had already been on the way to demolishing the lot and starting again just before the Second World War broke out; BR finally got on with the job. Not everyone was pleased though, and attempts were made to save the famed arch. The poet John Betjeman became a vociferous critic of what was perceived as cultural vandalism. In the end the Prime Minister himself turned down a plea for financing to move the arch, and it was demolished.

In place of the old rose the new Euston, a building of a fundamentally different ilk. As British Rail's own *Passenger's Guide to Euston* explained:

> Simplicity is the keynote in the design of the new Euston … The main entrance to the station for passengers arriving on foot is through doors in the colonnade which spans the station frontage and includes a number of shops. Inside is the spacious main concourse, the central feature of the new station, covering an area of some 30,000 sq ft. It was planned to accommodate, without crowding or congestion, the maximum number of passengers likely to use the station at peak periods. This concourse is entirely clear of parcels traffic permitting easy and rapid movement of passengers to and from trains …

The new Euston did contain some sensible ideas. There was no more dodging the processions of trolleys being hurried around on the platforms by maniacs on tractors, or red postal vans rushing in like the devil incarnate via the cab road. All of those things, and the customers own cars too (if they could afford the parking charge), were placed down in the basement, leaving the passengers unmolested.

It was a very modern building, with some modern features. As the *Passenger's Guide to Euston* continues: 'The concourse walls are almost entirely glazed with the exception of the north wall which contains the electro-mechanically operated train indicator and illuminated advertising panels.'

BR was particularly proud of the new Travel Centre, situated to the west of the concourse:

> Passengers are able to complete all their travel arrangements without having to visit several different offices. On one side is a ticket counter some 80 feet long flanked by another counter which is used to deal with train and travel queries seat and sleeper reservations and travel to Ireland. Part of this counter is also

used by Hotel Bookings and Information Ltd., who provide a comprehensive hotel reservation service.

Perhaps someone ought to have mentioned that it isn't the length of your counter that matters, but the number of staff serving at it.

What the new station lacked was the money-making development that BR had hoped would arise from it. Protracted wrangles with the London County Council (LCC) had led to BR calling off this part of the modernisation plan and the foundations that were laid were only for the existing buildings. In contrast, the King's Cross modernisation of the twenty-first century has involved the construction of a massive reinforced box underground which can take the weight of just about any building placed upon it within the next 1,000 years. But the new Euston was a fitting departure point for the new electric railway that BR had built. When John Betjeman compared the new Euston to an airport he had, whether he knew it or not, got the point.

Birmingham New Street was also completely rebuilt and Manchester Piccadilly reconstructed. Other stations on the West Coast Route were also demolished, rebuilt or substantially altered. In many of the modernisation era buildings the pre-fab 'concrete' look that had characterised railway architecture from the 1930s to the mid-1950s was replaced by the use of glass, with Barking station being a classic example of this.

Other stations were modernised too. In 1956 York was converted from gas to electric lighting,[45] which was better late than never. There was an acknowledgement that the old would have to do in many places, as in 1961 the Architects Study group of the Design Panel issued a booklet on how to titivate older stations with a view to making them user friendly.[46]

The modernisation of British Railways undoubtedly did improve services. Both speed and efficiency were increased, but the cost was more than it ought to have been. The abandonment of the three-year trial period for diesels led to a chaotic situation where a range of non-standard classes, some of which could not work together, had to be maintained at much greater cost than a standardised fleet. Germany had just one standard locomotive for each power class. BR had several. If BR had taken things more slowly, and not panicked due to the deficit, it would have been much less expensive. Widespread electrification would have been even better.

In 1977 the publisher D. Bradford Barton published a book entitled *BR Diesels Departed*, a thirty-two-page booklet illustrating the many designs of diesel locomotive that had come and gone since the inception of BR. There were the early post-war prototypes, of course, but far more pages were devoted to entire classes, hundreds of locomotives which had been built and then discarded in untimely haste. Serious work had started to whittle down the diesel classes in 1967 and this was to continue into the 1970s. Obsolescence came quickly to the diesels; many barely outlasted the steam locos they replaced.

The electrifications have proved much more durable. Brian Robertson had fought long and hard to get the small amount of projects through, and when he was replaced by Dr Beeching in June 1961 this work still had to be completed. But in the fifth edition of his book, *Titled Trains of Great Britain*, Cecil J. Allen was able to write:

> In the third and fourth editions (1953 and 1955) I remarked that the overall times of some titled trains had receded from the fastest since the 1939,45 war, and at that time very few expresses had retained the speed levels that prevailed in the halcyon days of steam in the later 1930s. But such a criticism could certainly not be levelled today, when the London Midland electric service alone is responsible for 12 daily runs timed at over 80mph from start to stop, 107 at over 75mph and no fewer than 165, with an aggregate mileage of 13,775, at over 72mph, not to mention the numerous high speed runs with diesel power on other regions.
>
> I added in 1953 my hope that the Coronation year, at a time when British punctuality as well as speed was at a low ebb, might see some revival of British prestige in these matters, and that before long we might be able once again to take justifiable pride, on every count, in the express passenger train services of these islands. That hope, I think, has now been fulfilled; as to aggregate high-speed mileage, at long last we have both France and Germany beaten, and so far at least as second class accommodation is concerned, no country on the mainland of Europe can show a standard equal to that of Great Britain.[47]

It might have been expensive, but it *had* worked.

5

Reformation II: A New Creed

I f I had a pound for every time I have been told that Dr Beeching wrecked this country's railway system I would be able to fund the reconstruction of all the lines he closed, and with solid gold rails throughout. An exaggeration, perhaps, but Beeching does have a certain reputation.

The Beeching cuts gained their infamy as a result of Beeching's laudable but unnecessary honesty: his decision, against good advice, to list all stations he had scheduled for closure, and all the passenger services to be discontinued, at the end of his first report. This action was rather like leaving a signed confession at the scene of a murder. He was advised – urged – by civil servants not to do this but obviously felt that, in a spirit of honesty, he owed it to the public. It was a public relations disaster and turned the doctor into the great bogeyman of the railways he has been ever since – the monster that stalks Thomas the Tank Engine in his darkest nightmare, or the villain of *Murder of the Branchlines*! Or perhaps he could even be a suitable adversary for Harry Potter, with the final showdown on platform 9¾ at King's Cross station as Beeching tries to close the line to Hogwarts.

The term 'Beeching Axe' has become a generic term for railway closures regardless of the period being referred to, yet railways were being closed long before nationalisation. More passenger stations were closed prior to Beeching than during his time in charge of the railways. From 1947 to 1960, 1,808 stations were closed, and more than 700 ceased operation between 1955 and the end of 1960; only 1,691 were closed during Beeching's time in office, from 1960–65, although perhaps a part of the 740 closed between 1965 and 1970 should really be added to his tally. So in terms of station closures much of the work had been done before he set foot in a railway office. It is really in sheer reduction of route mileage that the 'Beeching era' excels. From 1948–60 only 1,230 miles were cut; from 1960–65 3,448 miles were closed. There was no breakdown of the route mileage showing that open to passenger trains until 1955, but these figures also tell a story. From 1955 to 1960 more than 900 route miles of passenger railway were closed.

Between 1960 and 1965 almost 3,000 miles were closed to passengers, almost 1,800 in the period 1966–70. Beeching did indeed, it seems, hit the branch lines: those routes where stations were few and far between.[1]

We should not forget, of course, that during this era the purge of the goods depots began in earnest. With the abolition of the requirements of the 1854 Act British Railways was at last free to wash its hands of the inefficient and expensive sundries and wagon load freight business. To those businesses that relied on it – who were effectively subsidised by it – it often meant extinction. The British Railway Board's 1963 Report and Accounts announced that 456 such stations had been closed from 1 June to the end of the year.[2]

My grandfather always used to say that Beeching had been told by the government to 'make the railways pay'. This was in fact not quite true. As mentioned, breaking even was a requirement of the 1947 Transport Act, with the meaningless rider: 'taking one year with another'. It would be more accurate to say that Beeching had been charged by the panicking politicians with stemming the rising tide of losses being incurred by the system. As referred to in Chapter 2, these losses had grown alarmingly in the late 1950s so that savings now became imperative *if* the railways were to continue to be run solely as a business. Beeching's analysis and programme of action was not anything new – he just made a point of letting the public know about it.

Beeching's solution to the deficit problem was extremely similar to Hurcomb's analysis of how to create an efficient, integrated transport system. This was to find out what distinguished railways from other forms of transport, work out what they did best, work out which parts of the network fulfilled these roles, then reshape the system accordingly – in other words, cut out the bits that didn't work efficiently. Beeching, like Hurcomb before him, concluded that the railways were best suited to long-distance traffic and that short-distance traffic and rural areas were best abandoned to road. Beeching also recognised that the existence of unprofitable inner-suburban services restricted the growth of the profitable outer-suburban services.[3]

One seemingly unarguable figure cited by Beeching was that one third of the route mileage carried only 1 per cent of the total passenger miles. Similarly, one-third of the mileage carried only 1 per cent of the freight ton miles of British Railways. The lightly used part of the system included most of the single-track branch lines. An apparently startling fact, but as more sophisticated analysis was to show, the transport cookie doesn't crumble in such clear-cut forms. A comparison might be, what would happen to the motorway network if you cut all the roads that led to it, then all the roads that led to those? It can be seen that maybe things are not that simple.

The Beeching plan was also no different to the unfulfilled promises on page thirty-two of the modernisation plan, which had set out the intention of having marked reductions in stopping and branch-line services.[4]

There are those who maintain that the policy of cuts was unnecessary, and that the figures used to justify them were fiddled, together with a range of other conspiracy theories. This is doubtful, as the railways themselves were responsible for presenting them, and why would they wish to close down profitable operations? Much more likely is that political pressure squeezed the railways at both ends – to run the railway the public want yet with no subsidy. There is ample evidence that the politicians were responsible for the changes. Another interesting accusation that often arises when enthusiasts get together is the one we mention in Chapter 2 – the Transport Minister Ernest Marples, with whom Beeching was friendly, was probably against railways due to his own personal interests. His company helped to construct the M1 whilst the railway system was dismantled. However, on becoming Transport Minister he had transferred all the shares to his wife, so there can't be any accusations of wrongdoing there, can there?

Many of the suspicions of foul play arose through the closure procedure set up by the politicians. BR had to consult the local Transport Users Consultative Committee (TUCC) and then the Central Transport Consultative Committee (CTCC) before closure could officially commence. If the closure was likely to cause hardship then the TUCC could recommend against. Thus the TUCC was the first battleground for those fighting the closure of a line. The TUCCs' role was often perceived as unfair as members of the BTC sat on them and it was thus perceived as being 'judge and jury'. The committees also often refused the public the right to challenge BR's figures. The TUCCs were never intended to be courts of law, though, where evidence is heard and evaluated; they were merely a forum where public views could be aired and passed on to those who made the decisions. Many who protested at railway closures did not understand this. It was, of course, a political decision that it should be that way.

As I have said, the railways were caught in the clinch of having to provide statutory services and break even, with no contribution from the government apart from exhortations to become 'more efficient'. That the law could be applied to force the railways to maintain a service that they wished to withdraw was demonstrated by the case of the Bluebell line, when a lady called Miss Bessemer found a clause in the line's original act which stated that specific services had to be provided upon it. Parliament itself had to change the law and repeal the act before the line could be closed, but not before the local MP, Conservative Tufton Beamish, had caused a rumpus and the case been referred to a public inquiry carried out by the CTCC. A search of Hansard, and other accounts, does not yield any evidence that Beamish called for a subsidy to keep lines open.

It was referred to in Chapter 1 that the British railway system had not been built as an efficient organisation in the first place. There were duplicate lines, vanity lines and other appendages that made little money but sucked revenues from the profitable parts. Those who point to Germany or other countries where railways were planned, often protest that they have not seen anything like the level of closures of railway lines that we have seen in this country. This is true, but they never had the level of redundancy in the first place, and it is doubtful if they would have tolerated it if they did. The Continentals close railway lines too.[5]

No one seriously disputed that some of the system needed to be cut out – but how much, and should it be a purely economic or a political decision? A classic story told by Richard Marsh in his autobiography is how, as Chairman of BR in the early 1970s, he arranged for a computer model that proved that any amount of railway cuts did not result in a profitable system unless a huge amount of money was also spent. Having shown this to the Conservative Transport Minister, John Peyton, Marsh went on to show him a map demonstrating that most of the likely closures would take place in Tory constituencies. For Peyton this was the deciding argument.[6]

As related previously, after the Stedeford Report criticised the government regarding the way the railways were run, and the restrictions placed upon them, the 1962 Act changed the playing field. In respect of closures the TUCCs were now to be forbidden to consider any matters except for hardship and were not to be drawn into financial matters when considering closures. The final say now rested with the minister. This in fact proved to be a lengthy process with the Ministry of Transport drawing out the decision-making process and refusing to grant closure orders in a substantial number of cases. The July 1965 issue of *Modern Railways* reported that the minister had refused to consent to closure of fifteen lines with an annual financial burden to the railway of £925,000 (in contemporary money). The board had spent a further £80,000 on substitute bus services introduced as a condition of withdrawal. In total *Modern Railways* reckoned that the total burden of these ministerial refusals, including all costs, was over £4 million in 1964.

The row over the Bluebell line closure and that of many other lines continues to this day and there will never be any common ground between the warring parties. There are a number of books, particularly Henshaw's *The Great Railway Conspiracy*, which attribute underhand methods and a destructive will to the railways in seeking closures. But why should this be? This point was well made, by the likes of Gerry Fiennes, that railwaymen like running railways, they get money for running railways, and more money the more railways they run. Why should they seek the destruction of their own personal empires?

If you listen to many railwaymen who are or were at managerial level you will find a very different attitude to that of the protesters. They take the view that the changes that Beeching brought about were very long overdue and had been delayed by successive governments, who had placed political considerations in the way of what should have been purely commercial decisions. They point out that that delay was in itself a principal cause of the unprofitability of the railways. Amongst Beeching's supporters are R.H.N. Hardy in his book *Beeching:*

Champion of the Railway and E.A. Gibbins in such books as *The Railway Closure Controversy*. The latter is particularly good at taking on the arguments of those who opposed railway closures, offering references to all his sources; something that is missing from such books as Henshaw's *The Great Railway Conspiracy*.

Aside from the conspiracy theorists and protesters, it should be pointed out that David St John Thomas, in every way a champion of rural transport, accepted the case for the closures of many lines and asks why they didn't happen sooner for the sake of real economy. He also points to a lack of willingness on the part of the railways to consider ways to run lines more economically. There were BR insiders of this ilk, not least Gerry Fiennes, who sought to save some of the services of East Anglia by adopting what became known as 'the basic railway'.[7]

The Reshaping Report itself admitted that 'In parts of Scotland, in particular, and to a lesser degree in Wales and the West Country, road improvement or road construction may be necessary before adequate road services can be provided as full alternatives to the rail services which exist at present.'[8]

Two influential studies about the effects of the withdrawal of train services were carried out at the behest of the Department of the Environment in 1971, one looking at Devon and the other examining West Suffolk. These were subsequently criticised quite heavily by the Independent Commission for Transport (ICT), set up by Hugh Montefiore in 1973. This found that the Devon report's panel was made up of nine people, only one of them a woman, and included interested parties, mostly from officialdom. These included the Transport Co-ordinating Officer of Devon County Council, three officials from the Department of the Environment (one serving as the group's chairman, the other as its secretary) an ex-deputy chairman of the executive board of the National Bus Company and a chartered surveyor. The only woman was the County Alderman. The ICT report concluded that it was unlikely that such people could have an insight into the problems faced by the likes of poor agricultural workers, teenagers or housewives, and that it failed to explore the transport problems faced by the disadvantaged.[9] The ICT said of both reports that their failure lay in the assumption that the problem was with the residue of people who still didn't own cars. The reports saw the solution as lying in voluntary measures, presumably meaning that those who didn't own cars would have to cadge lifts off those who did.[10]

In the late 1970s British Rail commissioned a report on the social consequences of rail closures from the Policy Studies Institute. The study was based on interviews with former rail users, local officials and documentary evidence in a number of areas across the country where rail services were withdrawn. This found little ground for the concerns of protesters that rail closures led to depopulation, a loss of jobs or a decline in business activity in the area. It stated that: 'The impact of the closures on tourism, industrial development and employment prospects seems … to have been minimal.'[11] The study did however point to a loss of mobility amongst certain groups, specifically the elderly, the poor, and women, who were less likely to travel because of the withdrawal of the rail service. It pointed to considerable dissatisfaction with replacement bus services. The main lesson BR took from it, according to *Modern Railways*, was that replacement bus services needed to be more integrated in future, BR saying that 'they need to be run, and seen to be run, as part of the railway system'.[12]

One example where the closure of a railway did affect a local industry was the case of the Tamar Valley branch. This was originally built as a mineral line but during the inter-war years the mineral traffic went into serious decline. However, a new traffic started to grow as the famous Tamar Valley market garden industry thrived. Flowers and fruit were sent from each station on the line. In 1968 all that changed when the traffic collection was centralised at Plymouth. At that point the costs of transport for the market gardeners became unbearable. Road transport was tried but the market gardens industry died out.

The Isle of Wight had its line from Shanklin to Ventnor closed on 17 April 1966. *The Isle of Wight Mercury* (29 April 1966) reported that eleven days after the closure hoteliers in the town were reporting cancelled bookings due to the railway closure.[13] A Ventnor urban district councillor spoke at a meeting of the Ventnor Hotels Association on 25 November 1966 and reported an average drop of trade of around 25 per cent with losses ranging from £400 to £700 in 1966 money.

Again, the hardnosed response would be that these businesses were being supported by the railway, and thus the taxpayer, and that their business plan needed to be remodelled. Why should the taxpayer subsidise holiday resorts? It was not the South East, nor the Miss Bessemers of this world who were to be most deprived by cuts in railway services. The South East was to get off rather lightly in comparison with places like the West Country, Wales and Scotland. It had capacity to spare and so often the lines that were closed were genuinely surplus, whereas in other parts of the country the line closed was the only one for many, many miles. A look in C.J. Wignall's *Railway Atlas*[14] – which shows closed lines in black and those still open in red – reveals the decimation that took place in such areas, both in terms of lines and stations. Scotland was hard hit as it had very few lines to start with, and it had to battle to keep those that are left.

The Waverley route was the Scottish end of one of the three cross-border main lines that had been born out of the competition of the nineteenth century. It had long been relegated to a secondary rate, partly because the main route had been split between the LMS and LNER at the grouping. By 1969, the year of its closure, the Waverley mostly served the local communities that it ran through. On the days before its demise there were many protests as well as bomb threats and even the arrest of a church minister. It was all to no avail. On Monday 6 January 1969, just a few hours after the last service, BR lifted the rails before anyone changed their minds.[15] This was not to be the end for the Waverley route, however, as it is in the process of being partially reinstated as I write this.[16]

As well as targeting unremunerative lines BR targeted unremunerative services: the so called 'stopping trains' of the type I identified in Chapter 3 as the intermediate services collecting passengers from small towns and villages and taking them to central hubs. This of course accounts for the loss of those stations that were closed. Another target was the summer peak services. Beeching's analysis revealed that of 18,500 coaches only 5,500 were in year-round service, with some used as little as ten times a year. An astonishing 6,000 extra coaches were being provided in summer at a cost of £3.4 million, whereas they only earned £0.5 million after deducting movement costs.[17] As Beeching commented, the extra summer traffic was profitable as long as it used regular scheduled services, but quickly became a burden when extra services were to be required.[18]

The solution to the summer service problem was of course to be solved by cutting out branch lines to the resorts. The West Country was to suffer notably from this and plans had already been laid in a report back in 1956.[19] As this report noted, the services provided for long-distance passengers, a lucrative traffic, were being impaired by the need to provide trains to service the many branch lines. Where they entered the main-line system they took up paths and thus obstructed the provision and speed of inter-city trains.[20] The quality of services in the West Country – where they survived – increased significantly after the cuts.[21]

It was only after Beeching departed that a radical scheme to run branches more cheaply was tried. This was the 'open station/Pay-Train' format introduced in East Anglia in 1966.[22] It was expanded to many areas in the following decades. There was nothing new about 'Pay-Trains' apart from the name, which seems to have been in use from 1967.[23] The Great Western had employed 'conductors' on its railmotors and, later on, its auto-trains. These issued bus-style tickets which they also clipped, just as the conductor guards did on BR Pay-Trains. What was new was the use of this to enable the de-staffing of stations on whole lines to save money. This new system was promoted with television advertising,[24] following the successful campaigns of the West Coast Main Line (WCML) electrification and Inter-City – see below. By October 1967 it had also been adopted by the London Midland Region on two lines.[25]

Beeching was much more enthusiastic about the long-distance 'inter-city' services, about which he said:

> As a group, these services make a substantial contribution to system cost, and their profitability can certainly be improved by detailed attention to individual services and trains. There is, therefore, no doubt about the continuation of the railways' inter-city passenger services on substantially the present broad pattern, so long as the main line network remains in being, adequately supported by other traffics.[26]

The Doctor's last major contribution before he left office was the Trunk Route Report in which he identified key routes that he thought ought to be developed, with the rest of the system to be abandoned or left to go fallow. A mere 3,000 route miles were to be selected for development in the years up to 1984.[27] Clearly, Beeching had little faith that either passenger or freight services would justify the retention of much of the network. British Rail was to prove him wrong.

As noted in Chapter 2, in 1964 the political climate changed and the Trunk Route Report was shelved as the Network for Development Plan took its place. One positive consequence of the Trunk Route Report was the recognition of the importance of the east–west routes, in particular the cross-country route linking the West Country with the north-east and eastern Scotland. This was soon to be developed to fit in with the new West Coast Main Line electrification as Birmingham New Street was chosen as the interchange where cross-country and north-south services met.[28] Cross-country services remained something of a Cinderella, however, being given cast-off first generation type-4 locos and second-hand coaching stock. They were last in the queue for the High Speed Trains that at last gave some real recognition of the value of the service. There were also difficulties in getting the regions to co-operate on inter-regional services, despite the fact that by 1972 an inter-regional management group had been formed to improve them.[29]

If Dr Beeching took a bleak view of the branch lines and stopping services then he took an equally bleak view of electrification, and this may well count as the biggest negative mark against him. Whilst on the Stedeford Committee he had questioned whether the electrification of the WCML was worth the money, and even whether high-power diesels like the Deltics were justified. He felt that the system could be run by lower-powered diesels of less than 2,500hp.[30] Because of the doubts cast over the value of the WCML electrification by Beeching and other critics, Marples did not sign off on it until as late as 1961.[31] The only electrification scheme approved during the Doctor's tenure was the extremely cheap third-rail electrification to Bournemouth, given the go-ahead in the autumn of 1964.[32] There was even the notorious de-electrification on Tyneside – about which I shall say more in Chapter 8. Yet, as foreseen in the modernisation plan, it was the West Coast Main Line electrification and high-powered diesels that were to set BR on the path to a much brighter future.

Dr Beeching had left British Railways by the time that the West Coast electrification was completed in 1966 – a full eight years from its inception. Henry Johnson, at that time general manager of the London Midland Region, asked the venerable student and critic of train timings, O.S. Nock, to write a book about the achievement, entitled *Britain's New Railway*. Johnson had every reason to believe that Nock would be genuinely impressed, and he clearly was, writing 'the new services are not merely fast in a relative sense, they are really fast'. He pointed out that:

At one time a journey between London and Liverpool, or London and Manchester, would have been considered as 'long-distance' travel; but in this era, when cities such as Zurich and Rome are within two hours' flying time to London airport the new railway services have been geared to the tempo of this modern age ... [33]

One of the important features of the new services is the way in which intermediate centres will be catered for by direct stops of the Liverpool and Manchester trains, and by rapid connections. The spread of industry from the great cities is recognized and catered for by stopping a number of trains at stations on the perimeters, as for example Runcorn, in the case of Liverpool, and Stockport in the case of Manchester. In the southbound direction the evening business trains will each call to set down at Watford Junction. [34]

To celebrate the scheme there was, as ever, a publicity brochure: *Your New Railway: London Midland Electrification*, priced at 2s 6d and dated April 1966.

An advert at the front of the brochure boasted that:

Electrification means
LONDON –
MANCHESTER
LIVERPOOL
In just 2 hours 40 minutes centre to centre
It's a great way to go.

At the bottom of the advert was the new Corporate Identity Symbol and beside that, the new logotype: British Rail. To the right of that there was another new logotype, in the italicised version of the new Rail font: Inter-City.

Inter-City was to be the new brand for British Rail long-distance services, and the WCML, with its new electric services, was to be its flagship line. The term 'Inter-City' had been used by Dr Beeching in the Reshaping Report but this had not been its first use by British Railways. As a title it had originally been given to a Paddington–Birmingham–Wolverhampton train in 1950; this train lost its title when it was decided to transfer it to the new West Coast Main Line service. This was ironic as the WCML was the traditional competitor with Western Region Paddington–Birmingham services. Another use of the term 'Inter-City' also came about when it was applied to the DMUs built by Swindon for the Scottish Region.

In its report and accounts for 1964 BR had stated that: 'A planned national pattern of inter-city [sic] services between major centres, providing regular high-speed passenger services on all main routes, was an important objective in 1964.' In the 1965 report 'Inter-City' was capitalised – it had become a *brand*. The central advertised principles of the new services entitled Inter-City were speed and regularity. The BTC's policy of speeding up the schedules of entire lines was beginning to bear fruit.[35]

On the WCML there were now to be regular-interval services to the north taking under three hours. As O.S. Nock enthused:

> It has not been considered sufficient to provide a small number of fast 'prestige' trains; everything is fast, and the service between London and Liverpool and London and Manchester in its frequency and regular interval departures, savours much of the highly competitive services operated before World War I between Liverpool and Manchester themselves, by the onetime L.N.W.R., L.Y.R., and Cheshire Lines routes.[36]

A leaflet entitled *Your Guide To The Greater London Network* of 1 April 1966 stated:

> London is the centre of the British Rail Inter-City network. Inter-City trains run from one city-centre straight to another. They're fast and frequent. Run round the clock and through the calendar. They get you to your destination prompter, fresher and happier than any other form of inland transport.

And beneath were maps showing the networks run by Sleeper services and Pullman services.

Such was the notion behind Inter-City; it was a new brand conjoined with the new identity and very much part of the Beeching revolution in terms of image. But in operation it was nothing other than a fulfilment of the modernisation plan. In the first edition of *British Railways Today and Tomorrow*, published in 1959, G. Freeman Allen had commented that: 'In recent years there has been a noticeable trend towards even-time services on British Railways, though it has so far been more pronounced on local than main line, long-distance workings.'[37] He gave the example of the Western Region services to South Wales, operated on never less than a two-hour interval between 7.55 a.m. and 8.55 p.m. on a weekday, and also of trains from King's Cross to Newcastle, at close on hourly intervals each weekday. He contrasted this with services on the Continent, where, due to their arrangement of leaving spaces in the timetable for freight trains, there are often large gaps in the middle of the morning.

To advertise the new electric service BR turned to television for the first time in British railway history and the next year BR commissioned adverts for the whole Inter-City network.[38] The adverts for Inter-City were aimed at a wide spectrum of the population, intending to reach out beyond the railways' traditional market base and to encourage people to travel for leisure. An early icon developed for the adverts was 'Monica', a fashionable young woman who was chosen clearly as a method of reinforcing the idea that rail travel was for the young, and also for the glamorous. Down the years the slogans changed: 'City to City – Heart to Heart', 'Have a good trip!', 'This is the age of the train', and 'We're getting there'. But an attempt at mass appeal was always a common factor to all of them.

From the start Inter-City was to be available to everyone, first and second class, without supplementary fare. Inter-City was also, inevitably, aimed at the traditional business market – customers likely to have an expense account that could even run to first-class travel. The 1967 *Southern Travellers Handbook* informs us under the heading 'business travel' that 'Today's businessman cannot afford to be deskbound. In this bustling competitive age he must get up and go and he is increasingly looking to British Rail's Inter-City services to help him to do this.'[39]

The West Coast Main Line electrification proved to be a resounding success. By September 1966 it was reported that total passenger numbers on the route were up 65 per cent, with takings up 55 per cent. *Modern Railways* trumpeted that 'One airline has probably lost half its business to BR's new service.'[40] Those who had doubted the value of speed were now silenced and BR's ambition to raise the average speed of principal Inter-City services to 75mph was seen to be vindicated. On the East Coast similar triumphs were reported as the Deltics did battle with the airlines. One airline terminated its Heathrow–Teesside service due to railway competition, and a firm of aviation consultants recommended against the building of an airport at Sheffield due to BR services – principally the Eastern Region Pullmans.[41]

Speed came to be seen as the crucial means to compete with the internal airlines and much work continued to be done to upgrade the rail network to enable higher speeds. A 1970 booklet for drivers detailing faster speeds on the East Coast Main Line (ECML) had a statement pasted on the inside of the front cover:

The speed improvements shown in this booklet are proof of British Railways' belief that if a good enough railway service is provided it can hold its own against road and air competition. A considerable sum of money has been spent on these track improvements, and it is hoped that all concerned will back the effort to provide the best possible service.

Another pleasing issue for the accountants was that with the speed the time-interval style of service could make much better, intensive use of stock. This had already been well-proven on the Midland Main Line where 113 carriages had been saved, mostly due to a timetable speed up.[42] Similar results had been achieved on the Eastern Region.[43] Carriages that reached their destinations more quickly could complete more journeys. The carriages on the electrified main line were not to lead the leisurely lives of their predecessors but were to be diagrammed to get the most out of them, as quickly and as often as possible. They were to be used in 'fixed sets' with none of the coupling and uncoupling of through portions that their predecessors had seen. Fixed sets also enabled more economic maintenance systems to be put in place. This was to be the future of passenger service operation on BR.

Despite the egalitarian vision of Inter-City, BR still sought to cater for the premium service market with a new range of Pullman trains on the WMCL. Initially the plan was for a single service from Euston to proceed to Crewe and for it to be divided there, four coaches going to Liverpool and six to Manchester. This clearly breached the new orthodoxy of keeping fixed sets together and eliminating through portions, so eventually the plan was revised so that eight coach trains ran straight between Euston and Manchester and sets consisting of four Pullmans together with second-class ordinary stock would make up direct services to Liverpool. The Pullman cars were air conditioned and all first class, meaning that for many years the Manchester Pullman was the only all-first-class train on British Rail. The Liverpool cars were not a success, but the Manchester Pullman brought in much business and even gained some customer loyalty. It lasted twenty years in service, the cars being finally withdrawn in 1986.

The introduction of the Manchester Pullman from Euston meant the withdrawal of the Blue Pullman service to Manchester from St Pancras. The spare diesel Pullmans were offered to the Eastern Region, who didn't want them, and ended up on the Western Region with their kin.

Another attempt to cater for the premium market was the 'lounge first'. These coaches featured three normal first-class compartments and two large compartments in which four swivel chairs were organised in the middle, with banks of normal, fixed first-class seats against the bulkheads. There was plenty of leg room for the swivel chairs, as was demonstrated by a young model in a miniscule mini skirt in the 1968 BTF film *The New Tradition*.[44] Only three of these carriages were constructed, as prototypes, by converting three Mk1 1962 'corridor firsts'. They had in fact been ordered two years earlier after a mock-up was shown at a trade fair in 1964. By 1967 the decision had come firmly down on speed and, thus, minimum weight per passenger as the important factors. The large amount of space per passenger in the lounge compartment didn't fit into this strategy.[45]

Elsewhere on BR the business market was also being pursued in the traditional fashion with luxury and titled trains. A February 1963 booklet entitled *Named Trains On The Western (Your Business Means Travel. Travel Is Our Business)* advertised titled trains for the Western Region's business passengers from South Wales, the West of England and the Midlands. This campaign, of course, was halted in the great cull of Western Region named trains in the mid-1960s. Not all names were abolished though. In 1964 a special service for businessmen from Plymouth was inaugurated, titled the *Golden Hind*. The up service started at 7.05 a.m. from Plymouth and took just three hours and fifty-five minutes to reach Paddington with stops at Newton Abbot (for passengers from the Torbay branch) and then at Exeter, finally arriving at Paddington at 10.55 a.m. This was all enabled by special measures – the keeping of a 'Golden Stud' of six of the region's D1000 series,

2,700hp Western diesel-hydraulics in top nick for the service. Customer appreciation was good: all seats were reserved, but even so within three months BR was
selling 70 per cent of them. As I have said, crack trains with special locos was not
what Inter-City was meant to be about, but nevertheless the *Golden Hind* survived, fitting into the time-interval services and also into the 125 era.[46]

BR was to turn away from the pursuit of premium services only to revisit the
idea in the 1980s. Meanwhile it worked on speed, air conditioning as standard,
and high-density seating as its primary tactic in pursuit of revenue.

BR may have been beating the internal airlines but its principal rival remained
the car and the nascent motorway network. Since the 1950s BR followed a strategy not of directly competing with the car but of accommodating the motorist.

One idea that was already being operated on the Eastern Region of BR was
based on a fairly simple notion. You travelled by train and your car did too. This
was something the airlines couldn't possibly do, and it was a BR idea that was
later to spread to Europe. It started in 1955 with the Anglo-Scottish Car Carrier.
This was to be the first of many services which offered sleeper accommodation
on a train which also carried the passengers' own cars. As the leaflets said: 'park
your car on a night train … and sleep the miles away.'

The old practice of the pioneer days, where gentlefolk's carriages were loaded
onto flat trucks behind the train, was reborn. The services grew in popularity and
the number of loading facilities in London expanded to include King's Cross,
Holloway and Marylebone. Different types of car carrier service were developed.
Another brochure read:

> Like thousands of other carefree motorists begin your 1961 holiday at a railway
> station. Make for the open road – by train. Climb into your sleeping berth and
> arrive fresh as a daisy to pick up your car at your destination the next morning.
>
> There are three kinds of car-carrying services operated by British Railways.
> With the CAR-SLEEPER and CAR-CARRIER service passenger and car
> travel by the same train. With the CAR-TOURIST service passenger and car
> travel by separate trains, the car through the night and the passenger by day
> or night …[47]

By the mid-1960s it was clear that the services from London required their
own designated station and specialised loading facility. The place chosen was
Kensington Olympia. It was completely rebuilt with four lines and three wide
platforms under a new train shed with new buildings for a reception, waiting
room and refreshments. It was unveiled on 24 May 1966, unveiled together with
a new name for the service; it was now branded 'Motorail'. Motorail was to be
one of BR's big success stories and, with the growing frustration of long-distance
motoring coupled with the petrol price hikes of the 1970s, was to be very well
patronised for more than a decade.

A delicious irony for the railwayman and the rail enthusiast is that BR found another way to cash in on the car-boom. A gigantic car crusher, named after its inventors, the Proler Steel Corporation of Houston, Texas, was set up at Mitre bridge, Willesden, on the site of some old carriage sheds. It was claimed that the Proler could crush 15,000 cars a day and they were delivered by rail. With the railway already in place, a siding for thirty-four, 16-ton wagons was built and the site serviced by two trains per day.

Motorail was not the only way that BR was adjusting to cater for the car owner, trying to entice her or him from behind the wheel and onto the rails. The closure of so many small goods yards adjacent to stations came with something of a bonanza, in that BR could use the land as parking for passengers. In the mid-1960s this idea was taken a stage further when the first of a new breed of stations, designed with the motorist in mind, was opened at New Pudsey.[48] This was the beginning of what was to become the Parkway concept – stations built and designed with the specific object of allowing the motorist to park with ease and use the train.

The trouble with parking your car and using the train is that you don't have the use of your car at the other end. British Railways had come up with an idea to cover this and that too pre-dated the Inter-City era. A leaflet from 1957 assured you that you could arrive fresh and relaxed then drive on your way – in a latest model car. This was due to the:

BRITISH RAILWAYS AUTOBRITN PLAN

Evolved and operated in association with the Victor Britain Rent-A-Car system. When travelling to any of the cities and towns shown on the facing page you can now book a new Victor Britain self-drive car to meet you. When buying your rail ticket at any of the 200 stations listed overleaf … ask for a new self-drive car to be reserved at your destination … pay the reservation fee of 5/- … and British Railways will ensure by 'phone or wire that a Victor Britain representative meets you on your arrival. In the unlikely event of no car being available your 5/- will be refunded.

The tariff scale was arranged according to the size of the car: small (e.g. Ford Prefect or Morris Minor), medium (e.g. Morris Oxford, Austin A55 or Ford Consul) or large (e.g. Ford Zephyr Automatic). Later on the service was taken over by Godfrey Davis.

Another mode of transport that the railways embraced was the airliner. Whilst the internal air services represented real competition, international air travel represented an opportunity for rail. When British railways had been nationalised they were still serving the ports with boat trains, the ocean liner being the dominant mode of overseas travel. Within a couple of decades that situation had changed completely; the transatlantic liners had been converted to cruise ships whilst the

jet age took off. BR was to lose out to the tube – the Piccadilly Line – in providing a direct rail access to Heathrow. British Rail was stuck with offering links by
bus from 'convenient' stations such as Woking. BR did succeed in developing
a rail link to Gatwick. This was based on the old racecourse station which was
rebuilt in 1967–68 as a proper rail-air interchange. There was also Birmingham
International, a massive £5.9 million investment opened in 1976 that served both
the airport and the National Exhibition Centre.

There was one form of transport to which the railways became less accommodating, and that was the bike. Up until 1966 a bicycle went free but from that
point on a charge of half fare was made to carry them. In 1977 this decision was
reversed, but by that time the guard's vans of new coaches and units were much
smaller than those built in the 1950s. As a result in December 1979 BR banned
bikes from all trains within a 30-mile radius of London. In the 1980s the *British
Rail Guide to Better Biking*, supposedly intended to encourage rail travel by cyclists
with their cycles, contained a range of restrictions and warnings that on any journey; trains, particularly those formed of the new Pacer and Sprinter units (see
Chapter 11) and also the IC125s, may not be able to accommodate cycles due to
their small van space. There was supposed to be information available to indicate
the most likely chances of getting space for a bike, but in practice those trying to
find this out didn't get far. There were also other restrictions and charges, particularly at the London termini, to catch the unwary. What should have been a logical
pairing – the bike and the train – fell foul of cost accounting and the need for as
many seats as possible.[49]

The early 1960s was a period of cuts, but also of significant progress in developing the modern railway. But it is for the cuts that most people remember
this period – as well as for the demise of steam, of course. Did the Beeching
remedy work? The figures are startling. In 1965, the year of Beeching's departure, the deficit rose again by £11.5 million to £132.4 million per annum.[50]
The British Railways Board (BRB) blamed the delay in implementing closure
procedures for much of the loss.[51] According to D.L. Munby, between 1961–66
costs declined by 3 per cent, but revenue also fell by 2 per cent, leaving the situation more or less the same. The railways were restricted from raising their prices
by government intervention, while an increase in their own costs – particularly
for labour – wiped out any good work that the cuts might have done.[52] Of course,
without the cuts things might have been worse.

Meanwhile, changes were afoot as a consequence of the change in government
in 1964. The first impact felt by the railways was partly negative – Terry Gourvish
states that the consequences of the Labour government's prices and incomes policy
was to cost BR £3.9 million, although that was offset by a £3.5 million saving in
wages.[53] In 1968 a positive development was the introduction of selective pricing on
the railways, at last exploiting the freedoms brought in by the 1962 Act to price high
or low depending on the competition and the quality of service offered.[54]

In March 1967 the Network for Development Plan mentioned above was to usher in a complete change in the way the railways were financed. This new vision for the railways was to be laid out in legislation via the 1968 Transport Act. The Development Plan had stated that around 11,000 miles of railway would be retained. All that was needed now was for someone to pay for it.

6

In Search of an Identity

In modern transport management no detail is too trivial to be brought under the discipline of visual order and good taste.

Christian Barman[1]

We must recognise that this is an age of presentation.

Stanley Raymond[2]

In 1965 the British Railways Board undertook one of the biggest corporate makeovers in history. It discarded the crests and emblems, totems and typefaces of its predecessors and adopted a striking modern symbol. It truncated its name, calling itself 'British Rail' and adopted a modern typeface and a bold new livery. It was a move which drew criticism from some conservative quarters, but it was at last to give British Rail a strong, coherent public image.

British Rail had struggled with its identity ever since its inception in 1948. The issue was of course bedevilled at the start by the fact that it was owned by one organisation (the British Transport Commission, or BTC) and run by another (the Railway Executive).

Perhaps it is hardly surprising that the choice of a symbol to represent the new organisation was the source of controversy between the Executive and the Commission. The Executive produced a symbol that came to be known as 'the hot dog' or 'the flying sausage', which did indeed look like an over-sized sausage in an undersized, rip-off bun. It was an obvious imitation of the London Transport logo, stretched out horizontally. It was tried out on the side of an ex-Southern locomotive's tender and looked a bit odd, to say the least. Meanwhile, the Commission had come up with something more traditional: a badge designed by sculptor Cecil Thomas to represent the Commission and its activities as a whole. The image was of a wheel with a lion stretched out above, and around, the upper part. Across the wheel was a bar which bore wording appropriate to each Executive and its transport mode, thus for railway purposes it read 'BRITISH RAILWAYS'.

In essence the Thomas design was another rather obvious derivation of the LT symbol with a bit of wildlife added in for good measure. This wasn't such a big hit either. The fact that the lion was stretched out over the top of the wheel gave its body an exaggerated yet thin look and the fact that it had its mouth open made it look like a vomiting anorexic. At some point it gained the nickname 'ferret and dartboard', which stuck. After some trials and disagreements it was finally settled that the BTC lion and wheel should grace the sides of locomotives and the power cars of multiple-units, while the Executive's 'hot dog' would be the symbol used at stations. In an interesting concession to regional identity the station signs were colour coded for regions. On the Eastern Region they were Oxford blue; on the North Eastern, tangerine; on the London Midland, crimson; on the Scottish, Cambridge blue; on the Southern, 'middle green'; and on the Western, light chocolate. It was an interesting idea, but it did tend to disrupt the unity being strived for and involved some unfortunate colour choices, since those chosen rendered some signs difficult to read.

As befitted his character, when Brian Robertson took over he wanted something rather grander to represent his command. In 1956 the British Transport Commission was granted an 'achievement' by both the College of Arms and the Lord Lyon of Scotland. This meant that it had its own 'Coat of Arms' which had been designed in consultation with armorial expert C.A.H. Franklyn.[3] To traditionalists, such as the founder of the Historical Model Railway Society, George Dow, it was a very pleasing design. To others with a more modern taste in things it did not sit well; a *Modern Railways* editorial called it a 'heraldic abortion'.[4]

To this author it looks like a lion holding a wheel whilst springing out of a mess of ribbons, like a bimbo out of a birthday cake. Beneath it is a shield with three wheels, some blue wavy lines and a portcullis being propped up by what look like two *Star Trek* aliens, both with wheels pinned to their chests. They are standing on a grassy knoll across which the words *velociter securiter* – swift and sure – are emblazoned. Above the whole unwieldy assemblage is the word 'Forward', which Dow interpreted as a salute to the previous generations of railwaymen. He was clearly impressed with the whole assemblage. The 1960s generation must have thought that the designer had found acid earlier than they did.[5]

The full heraldic device was not used on vehicles. Instead a truncated version with the bimbo lion and crown was produced. It was placed in a circle with the word 'British' on one side and 'Railways' on the other. Another badge was produced for main-line coaches and multiple-unit driving vehicles with the lion and crown on a light background with the words 'British Railways' circled around it.

Even internal reaction to the new logo was snotty. The August 1956 in-house *British Railways Magazine* relegated the news of the new emblem to page three. The front page was taken by a picture of ticket clerks busily giving advice on holiday journeys.

Unfortunately after having gone to all that trouble to get it done properly they messed it up. The crest of the Arms featured a lion facing left, and this was copied to make two badges for the sides of locomotives and carriages with the lion facing both left and right. It was only after a few months that someone pointed out that the BTC had no authority to reverse a heraldic device in that way. It was only authorised to use it with the lion facing left (even the picture in the magazine referred to above had shown it facing right). The livery scheme had to be revised to allow for the lion to face left (backwards) on the right-hand side of locomotives (this is why on modellers' transfer sheets, such as HMRS sheet 14, there are more left-facing crests provided than right facing ones). Ultimately, as most of the new diesels had cabs at both ends, it didn't seem to matter that much. The emblem was also used as a cap badge and as such can be seen being worn by staff in the late 1960s in pictures and films.

Heraldic devices were getting very near their sell-by date in 1956. It was however an interesting nod to a railway tradition which must not go unnoted. Doubtless they had seemed far more appropriate in their time, when the railways really had been supreme in transport and trade. All of them had something like it in the Victorian era and Dow's wonderful book *Railway Heraldry* is a fascinating cornucopia of how the old private railways had aggrandised themselves with such decorations. Only the Great Central, LNER and the Southern had previously gone as far as being granted an achievement (anyone can design a fancy pattern and paint it on their own property).

There had been moves before the war to get away from the heraldic and its decorative traits. The LNER had commissioned Eric Gill, sculptor and typographer and a former pupil of Edward Johnston, to produce a version of his 'Gill Sans' font for them. He also produced a totem, looking like the outline of an 'Egyptian eye' with the letters LNER in the middle. This was very effective and modern and appeared on some rail vehicles, although the only locos to feature it were tank engines built in the 1940s. The GWR had sought to copy this and produced a circular monogram, popularly known as the shirt button, which was a neat piece of graphic design. It seems that the shirt button did not go down too well with the traditionalists at Swindon and its time was comparatively brief, lasting only about eight years.

The heraldic motif was not universal on BR in the Robertson era. For the Glasgow electrification, opened in 1960, a new motif was created by the highly respected designer F.H.K. Henrion, who was already an OBE. The motif was two arrows, in fact Vees, one blue, and the other yellow. These were on their sides pointing right and left, the blue one imposed over the yellow. This matched the

Caledonian Blue with black and yellow stripes which the new power units were painted in. Sadly though, the power cars bore the heraldic lion and not the new motif, which was used only for publicity material and station signage. It was a toe in the water into the world of modern corporate design, though.[6]

For the West Coast Main Line electrification itself the blue was continued for the locomotives (not blending terribly well with the carriages which were still dismal Midland maroon). The crest was treated differently, however. Milner Gray of Design Research Unit redrew it as a casting, together with stainless steel numerals for the new locomotives.[7]

When Dr Beeching took over he eschewed the aggrandisement of Robertson's regime. The grand boardroom of the Commission went unused and it was only a question of time before he turned his attention to getting rid of the heraldry. Dr Beeching was to demand an image that broke entirely with the past and which represented his vision of a modern, businesslike and efficient railway. In the spring of 1964 he had written in *The Financial Times* of the need for a powerful new symbol to represent the railway. There was also to be a new name, new letter styling and new house colours.

As I related in Chapter 4, Beeching already had at his disposal an in-house Design Panel set up by Brian Robertson at the start of the modernisation plan. Whereas the Panel had not been able to make much headway in forming a coherent design policy in the 1950s, Beeching ensured that it assumed a new authority. In 1963 John Ratter took over as chairman of the Design Panel, replacing T.H. Summerson, who retired. George Williams was given a newly created post of Director of Industrial Design, and two new design officers were appointed, one for industrial and graphic design and the other for research. From this point on the Panel met four times a year rather than twice annually to cope with the amount of new work. A working party was appointed to oversee the development of the new corporate identity and this was chaired by Milner Gray of Design Research Unit.[8]

The new corporate identity was specified in a manual[9] – the *Corporate Identity Manual* – which was issued throughout the organisation to the appropriate staff. It specified the look and position of all wording, signs and symbols, on all posters, leaflets, documents, stationery, buildings, vehicles (road and rail), and ships. It even specified such details as clock faces and antimacassars. It was in full colour and illustrated throughout, in modern form in a folder with the parts numbered. Pages were reissued as elements of livery were changed over time. This document, and BR's entire corporate design programme, was to become a benchmark in industrial design the world over and is another reason to celebrate BR as a world-beating company that attracted overseas attention for the right reasons. In 1986 a book on BR design was published by the Danish Design Council. Written by the then head of BR Design, James Cousins, it was in the Danish language as well as in English.

At the epicentre of the new corporate identity was a new symbol – or perhaps in fact an ideogram. BR must have been continually casting an envious eye at the London Transport logo. It is no wonder as it is a masterpiece of simple, iconic design that is recognised and admired the world over. But the London Transport symbol had been a product of evolution coupled with trial and error. BR was in need of something that equalled it but that could be conjured up right – sorry for this – out of the blue.

Several ideas were put forward. One consisted of the letters BR but struck through with white stripes, to give the appearance of the union flag. Another attempt was a representation of the union flag with a strange five-pronged fork hung on the left-hand side. A further attempt was basically a noughts-and-crosses framework with an arrow going off top right and bottom left. It was similar to the successful design and may have been a step on the path to the symbol that was chosen. This, as we all know, consists of two arrows, one on top of the other, the bottom one facing left and the top one right, the upper and lower arms joined as one. This deceptively simple design was the work of Gerald Barney. It became what British Rail was pleased to call the 'Corporate Identity Symbol'.

The Corporate Identity Symbol, or CIS, is not as simple as it appears. The arms at top and bottom both widen in the outward direction, otherwise, the designers found, they would appear to taper. This is one reason why it is so difficult to draw the symbol freehand. Another point is that the light on dark version has slightly narrower lines, otherwise it would look too 'fat'.

The CIS first appeared on the Class 47 locomotive placed at the head of the XP64 set (see Chapter 7). At this point the logo was white on a red panel. This was removed before the locomotive went into traffic as the CIS wasn't yet authorised. It started to appear for real in 1965.

At first public reaction to the CIS was mixed, with critics likening it to a piece of barbed wire or a bolt of lightning[10] (although one would have thought that with the new WCML electrification coming on stream lightning was extremely appropriate). George Dow voiced the criticism that contemporary designers only seemed to be able to produce arrows in different forms and saw it as the result of sterility in design.[11]

BR research found that after just a couple of years the CIS was as recognisable to many people as the Michelin Man.[12] Given the immediate recognisability of the CIS and its now well established longevity that may well have been true. Certainly the words 'railway station' are now redundant on British signage; the CIS *still* does the job of those words, more succinctly, and more comprehensibly. The BR symbol was to outlast the corporation which devised it, surely proof that it achieved its ultimate purpose – it became the symbol not of a company but of a national service, used on road signs and station signs to this very day.

Just as with the LT symbol, there have been attempts by railways the world over to copy the CIS with their own version – none that I have seen are anything like as successful as the original. At some point a sceptic – most likely a BR insider – provided a subversive interpretation of the sign when they called it 'the arrow of indecision'.[13]

As said above, the Corporate Identity Symbol was just one part of the package that was unleashed in 1965. There was of course also the name – the truncating of British Railways to British Rail. This was only for publicity purposes; the *Corporate Identity Manual* stressed at the beginning that for all legal and official purposes the name of the organisation was still British Railways: 'British Rail' was only for public consumption. It was claimed that the name British Rail was 'more forceful, simple to read and comprehend'.[14] Whatever the critics may have thought it did catch on and was to remain the public name of the nationalised railway until its demise. Perhaps it is not surprising, for the new name successfully truncated something of a mouthful whilst remaining self-explanatory. It had all the virtues of a colloquial shortening as well as having visual impact. When British Airways was formed in the 1970s as a result of the merger of BEA and BOAC it did not choose to go down the same route by calling itself 'British Air'. Doubtless the fact that it is not quite so self-explanatory had something to do with it: 'British Air' sounds rather vacuous and rather suggests that it might be the parent company of British Oxygen, British Hydrogen, or British Carbon Monoxide. On the other hand, when the Post Office telecommunications separated they chose to call themselves British Telecom – a shortening of telecommunications. That name too has the virtue of being self-explanatory.

Then maybe it is necessary to mention what is surely the silliest and most unnecessary corporate rebranding in British history, when the Royal Mail decided to rebrand itself 'Consignia'. Surely this tells us something about why 'British Rail' was a success. Consignia says nothing about what the company does, and does not relate in any way to its older identity – there is no continuity with the past. This was, at its worst, a deliberate jettisoning of all public customer goodwill. Royal Mail is already a short, brief name that says it all – like British Rail. Trying to change 'Royal Mail' was perverse.

Another thing that undoubtedly helped the new name was that it appeared in a new font called 'Rail'. This was the work of the already established design team of Jock Kinneir and Margaret Calvert. Ms Calvert had been a pupil of Kinneir's when he was a visiting teacher at Chelsea Art School. Impressed with her talent he gave her a job, as he had just started his own design firm. Kinneir then struck lucky when he started chatting to a man at a bus stop. The man just happened to be an architect on the new Gatwick Airport. As a consequence of this chance meeting Kinneir and Calvert got the job of designing the signs for Gatwick. One person who noticed the excellence of their work was Colin Anderson, the Chairman of P&O and Orient, who employed the pair to design luggage labels so that people's cases wouldn't be lost by 'illiterate' porters. Anderson was also appointed as chairman of the committee to advise on motorway signs.

Again he hired Kinneir and Calvert. Ignoring an injunction not to do anything new, they set about investigating the readability of fonts for road use. One font they looked at was 'Akzidenz-Grotesk', as well as Johnston's 'London Underground' font. From these influences they created 'Transport' – a modern sans serif font which they tested out in Hyde Park and then on the Preston bypass. Kinneir and Calvert also designed many of the modern road signs, including the 'children crossing' sign which is based on a photograph of Margaret Calvert as a child.[15]

Soon after Kinneir and Calvert were asked to design a new font for the NHS, and this was later adapted for British Rail, becoming the 'Rail alphabet'.[16]

All part of the new corporate identity package was a new colour scheme; as with the symbols, this was not the first new scheme since 1948. The Executive had experimented with various colours for locomotives before, settling on dark green for passenger locomotives with orange and black lining (the black sandwiched in between two stripes of orange) whilst mixed traffic locos were black with white and red lining. The early diesels were black. Coaches were quite bright, a livery called carmine and cream being finally chosen (often referred to as 'blood and custard'). The Southern Region was allowed to retain green as the colour for its electric multiple-unit fleet.

With the abolition of the Executive and greater freedom being granted to the regions the Southern Region gained permission to paint its loco-hauled coaches in green livery. The Western Region gained permission to paint some stock chocolate and cream for its titled trains, and, it is said, added more titled trains to the rosters to excuse more chocolate-and-cream coaches. The London Midland reverted to a maroon colour for its coaching stock and the Eastern Region used this as well, presumably because reverting to the LNER varnished teak would have been too difficult in the era of metal-sheeted coaches.

Loco colours and lining stayed the same in the second era except that diesels started being turned out in green, and, later on, together with multiple-units, gained yellow panels on the cab ends.

There were some odd exceptions. The Clacton Electrics were originally and uniquely painted maroon. Experiments with a new livery were tried out on some of the Western Region diesel-hydraulics. Sand and golden ochre were tried on the D1000 Western series before maroon was settled on for the whole fleet. Some of the Warships were also painted maroon.

With the new corporate identity the dull greens and maroons were to be discarded for bright new colours. These were 'monastral', also known as 'rail blue', 'pearl grey', and 'flame red'. It seems there was some doubt about the wisdom of using these colours on locos and carriages in early 1965 as they had yet to be approved in January of that year.[17] Perhaps this is hardly surprising, since BR had in fact gone to a great deal of trouble to investigate the durability of colour schemes throughout its existence. Documents in the HMRS archive reveal that previously BR had concluded that blue and white-grey were colours 'totally unsuitable' for railway use. The investigators had concluded that the best weathering was the Southern multiple-unit green, although the varnished teak of Gresley's coaches was found to be very hardwearing. Nevertheless, the decision was finally taken to go ahead with the blue for locomotives and the pearl grey/blue livery for main-line carriages. Probably with an eye to not showing the dirt, provincial and suburban carriages (including MUs) were painted an all-over blue livery that was not actually prescribed by the manual. In later years the decision was taken to paint all passenger coaches in blue/grey, except for those DMUs that were already porting the refurbished livery (see Chapter 8). The pearl and blue came to be associated with Inter-City but there is no ready evidence that this livery was intended specifically for that brand. It was something of a coincidence that it arrived at the same time as the West Coast electrification and the new Mk2 carriages.

As well as the three colours specified in the manual a fourth colour became a distinctive feature on BR locomotives and multiple-units. For safety reasons BR had experimented with painting the fronts of trains in a highly visible yellow colour. In the green era this was restricted to a panel on the front, but with the new corporate identity the yellow was extended to the whole front end, and in some cases to the cab-side windows. (For those locomotives which had a bonnet, only the front of the bonnet was painted – to my knowledge there is no evidence of any experiments trying out yellow on the window frames of these locos.)

It took a very long time to implement all this. Railway rolling stock does not get repainted overnight and for much of the 1960s there was a bewildering variety of liveries, with the old colours running alongside the new corporate livery. Locomotives, too, took a while to be sorted out and one diesel, 40 106, was never painted blue. It survived in green until 1978[18] albeit in a truly shabby condition. Later that year it was repainted green as a 'heritage' livery.[19]

On the whole, with the new corporate image, BR had achieved a bright and modern-looking identity that left the past behind and pointedly suited a 'modern' railway. It was just what BR needed. It proved to be a successful makeover that caught the public mood. Modernity was *in* in 1965. Alec Issigonis's Mini motor car and Mary Quant's miniskirt were riding high. Just a year before, Terence Conran had launched the first store of his Habitat chain – selling modernist furniture and lifestyle aspirations to ordinary people. The 1960s were now 'swinging' and BR looked like it was joining in. Sadly, George Williams was not to see the completion of the programme he had worked so hard to create, as he died at his home in November 1965.[20]

Heraldic crests weren't the only victims of the new identity scheme. On 7 December 1964 the board decided that the naming of locomotives was a 'remnant of the steam era' and 'not in accordance with a forward thinking railway system'.[21] Naming locomotives was of course a very ancient tradition on British Railways. Indeed, maybe to the shock of many train spotters, locomotives had borne names long before they bore numbers.

Soon after it was formed the BTC set up a three-man committee to oversee the naming of railway traction and also produced guidelines regarding names. The committee was headed by George Dow. One of Dow's first ideas was that the names of the passenger locos on the Woodhead route should be those of characters from Greek mythology. During the 1950s the naming committee was kept busy, first with the new steam locomotives and then with the new diesels, the early Type 4 and 5 classes being given names. Class theme naming broke down in the case of the Deltics which were assigned to three regions – Scottish, North Eastern and Eastern – and ended up being given the names of Scottish regiments, northern English regiments and racehorses respectively. The Western Region got permission to name the smattering of Brush Type 4s that it gained to haul main-line trains. There were too few of these for a theme to make sense and the names were drawn from ones previously used by the GWR. In the early 1960s the responsibility for locomotive naming was delegated to regional level, almost certainly an early indication of the lack of importance placed upon it by the Beeching regime. Then, of course, came the infamous ban.[22]

To many it was a sign of further sterility and lack of imagination on the part of the railway, a retreat from glamour into banality. Perhaps it is worth considering just why a self-propelling metal box is worthy of a name. Because it brightens the lives of those involved with it? Perhaps that is reason enough. Those names that had been agreed before the embargo were applied, meaning that the last loco to be named in the 1960s was D68 *Royal Fusilier* (45 046) on 21 January 1967.

The banning of names was unpopular with staff, but pressure to return to naming was not heeded. In 1975 the board came under pressure from the Stephenson Society to commemorate 150 years of the Stockton and Darlington by naming a locomotive *Stephenson*. At first this was refused but after an offer to pay for the nameplates the board reconsidered. Nevertheless, the suggestion that the name be applied to the new thyristor-controlled 87 101 was turned down, and it was applied to 87 001 on 14 January 1976, somewhat after the anniversary it had originally been intended to commemorate. The naming of 87 001 was supposed to have been a one-off but such was the reception that there was a change of policy. In May 1977 the BRB's head of public relations, Henry Sanderson, announced that naming would return to some classes of main-line locos to brighten up the railway and to encourage railway enthusiasm. On 11 July that same year 87 001 was officially named – or renamed – *Royal Scot*[23] and the *Stephenson* name transferred to 87 101 after all.

Apart from on Sodor, the tradition of naming coaches really belonged to the Pullman Car Company whose first-class parlours traditionally sported names. They were usually taken from Greek mythology or were female first names or names that were both. The last Pullman cars to be named when built were the Mk1s. The diesel and the Mk2 Pullmans all bore numbers only. In their last years the Brighton Pullman cars lost their names when they acquired rail blue. But in the 1980s, with the advent of the ersatz MkIIIB Pullman, names made a comeback. Improbably, some of the names were even of working-class heroes – Sir Stanley Matthews and John Lennon (people in the Pullman seats, rattle your jewellery?).

From its inception BR had followed the group companies in using train names for publicity purposes – previous to the grouping, train titles had rarely been recognised 'officially' and headboards were all but unknown.

During the Second World War most trains lost their titles in accordance with the general spirit of austerity, but by 1946 many of the pre-war names were restored and some new ones added to the list. In that year the first edition of C.J. Allen's *Titled Trains* contained entries on seventy trains; the second edition in 1947 was expanded to seventy-nine. In 1953, when British Railways had been in operation some four-plus years, the third edition of Allen's book described as many as 108 titled trains, whilst the fifth edition in 1967 described 120, although by that time sixty-nine were no longer borne by any train in current use and the services that once bore them had ceased to run. This was partly because together with the policy on locomotive names BR also changed its policy on titled trains. There was a widespread cull, particularly on the Western Region where named trains had previously proliferated. By 1978 there were just twenty-two titled trains running on the British Rail network. The vast majority were on the Eastern Region and most of those on the East Coast Main Line out of and into King's Cross. The others were on the Midland Region and two – the *Cornish Riviera* and the *Golden Hind* remained on the Western Region. Only the *Night Ferry* remained on the Southern.[24]

Four of those on the ECML were named 'Executives', prefixed by town names, respectively: Hull, Newcastle, Leeds and Bradford. These trains had begun their careers in 1968 as Deltic-hauled eight-carriage trains designated high speed, scheduled to run at times convenient to business people. It was an unusual initiative coming as it did straight after the imposition of corporate identity and shows how keen BR was to gain the business *business*. In the 1980s the East Coast Executives formed the basis for the abortive Inter-City Executive initiative to capture more of the business travel market. From 1970 the London Midland Region had its own venture trying to entice businessmen from the Midlands to travel to Scotland via *The Midland Scot*. This title, together with others, was executed in the 1975 cull to purge titled trains that did not meet the 'Inter-City standard'.

The Midland Scot featured entrance door destination boards, described as 'new-style' by *Modern Railways* at the time.[25] Traditionally, destination boards had been on the roof, where no one could see them. The BR standard coach brought them down to below cantrail (gutter) level and originally had fittings for them to be hung. In the 1960s the Western Region had experimented with waist-level destination boards, which tended to be obscured by crowds.[26] Now, at last, BR was moving to put the destination where the passengers were most likely to look – on the doors.

Following its Executive initiative from October 1972 the Eastern Region adopted a policy of not just running named trains but actually publicising them in timetables. The trains were now to feature outward-facing door labels with the train title, destinations and carriage letter as well as staff with lapel badges with the service name and menus bearing the title. Travelogues would give the history of the service (the format of these is unspecified). Barrier boards at stations would bear the train's name before departure. It was all intended to brighten up an otherwise dull rail scene, according to the publicity. The complexities of modern rostering prevented the one thing that many would think makes a titled train: the headboard.[27] This initiative seems to have been the beginning of the modern era of door destination labels; paper and tacky they may be, but they serve a useful purpose. Plus, if (no, when) they are stolen by souvenir hunters they are much cheaper to replace.

But the mere paper label slapped on a door does raise the question as to what is a titled train. Does it have to have a headboard? Should its name appear in the timetable? There are purists who maintain that it is only a titled train if it is 'officially' recognised, presumably meaning it is a hard case to prove that even the most famous titled train – the *Flying Scotsman* – was featured, or not featured, in timetables at any given point (the general consensus is that it was unofficial until the 1920s).

Headboards were not a universal feature of the pre-nationalisation scene. Only the LNER used them extensively; the LMS never did. On the GWR only one train bore a headboard; in the timetable it was known as the *Cheltenham Spa Express* but perversely the headboard read *Cheltenham Flyer*. The Southern only started using headboards after the Second World War. BR went to town with headboards and had several different designs. Doubtless the impetus was an attempt to show it was recapturing something of the glory days before the war. There were too many titled trains – and too many headboards, some would say. Dave Peel, author of an excellent history of British train headboards, would probably disagree wholeheartedly![28]

BR tried out new train titles from time to time and one of them certainly stuck – *The Highland Chieftain* service which has run to and from Inverness and King's Cross via Edinburgh since 1984.

There had been variations of the corporate identity livery from the start – the new Mk2 Pullmans had found themselves in a reversed livery where the body was painted in the grey and the window band in blue. The prototype High Speed Train (HST) and the experimental Advanced Passenger Train (APT-E) found themselves so decorated. For the DMU refurbishments in the 1970s a similar livery but with the blue as a band below the windows was adopted.[29] Neither of these liveries could have been terribly practical as they must have been hard to keep clean.

A further break from the corporate livery came with the production HST – by then known as the Inter-City 125. Instead of the warning yellow covering the entire front of the power cars it was split by a band of corporate blue enclosing the driver's window. The yellow ran down the lower sides, just over halfway along where it ended in a diagonal edge. This was matched by another diagonal edge where the grey band enclosing the side windows began at the rear end of the power car. Although often unnoticed this diagonal cleverly matched the angle of the crosspieces within the radiator vents in the rail blue area between the ends of the bands.

A new version of the 'Rail' font was devised for the logotype and the numbers 125 with the characters in outline – white with rail blue centres.

Up to this time all variations at least used the same colours. In 1978 the first serious break with the Corporate Identity Livery occurred with the launch of the new Advanced Passenger Train (APT-P). The APT was an in-house design and sported a livery of grey, red and dark blue – the blue being a shade that was not in the original manual. This blue was used on the main area around the windows. The lower parts were white grey with a red stripe cutting through it at waist level. Another stripe of white sat on top of the blue up to cantrail level. The bands created by this were swept up behind the cabs of the APT-P where they met the warning yellow. The cab windscreen had dark blue surrounds.

For a few years the APT-P was unique in this livery, but when Inter-City was looking for a new image it chose this livery and in 1983 it was relaunched, together with a new logotype which now spelt 'InterCity' without the hyphen. The logotype was also nudged up closer to the CIS, abandoning the rule of the original manual regarding the distancing. A BR brochure of the time claimed that in this form it 'began to look like a service in which British Rail had confidence'. Thankfully, the tile spacing of the alphabet was – quite rightly – maintained for all informational signs.[30]

Meanwhile, things had happened to the CIS. It had grown up – or at least it had grown much bigger. In 1978 Class 56 locomotives started appearing with the CIS writ huge.[31] It extended from the cantrail right down the bodyside. Now the entire cab sides, not just the window frames, were yellow. BR was proclaiming its corporate symbol with the fullest pride. The remarkable thing was that it worked in this new livery – although it had its critics, some describing the size of the logo as being for the myopic. It was nevertheless a bold statement of corporate pride that seemed to fit in with the new era of the 1980s, with its increasing confidence and brashness.

The IC125 and the large logo were just the start of a system-wide set of image changes and by the mid-1980s unified corporate identity was being broken down.

The newly empowered sectors (see Chapter 2) each sought to assert different identities. The Scottish Region also assumed its own identity – ScotRail – and adopted a logotype using the rail alphabet but in a distinctive light blue. The new Pacers and Sprinters (see Chapter 11) were delivered in new liveries involving light and dark blue stripes. On the Southern Region a curious but unsuccessful livery of brown upper panels, beige lower panels separated by an orange stripe was broken out in 1985. The livery understandably earned itself the sobriquet 'Jaffa cake' and was short-lived, quickly discarded.[32] This was due to one of the most startling breakaways from the Corporate Identity Scheme. In 1986 Chris Green launched Network SouthEast – the new name for the London and South East Sector.

Green set out a brief that was sent to a dozen design companies. This stated that the identity should convey the impression of a 'modern efficient, professional and innovate' railway. A list of adjectives which should be applicable to the new design was supplied: bright, cheerful, pleasant, imaginative, dynamic, creative, striking, smart. It should say: value for money, reasonable quality, well-informed staff, visible local managers, local individuality, and suburban express service. All that was supposed to be summed up in a design image – but hey, this was the 1980s: creatives ruled!

James Cousins, Director of Industrial Design for the BRB, was joined by the then head of advertising, John Cimelli, and the Director of Public Affairs, Grant Woodruff, and three senior LSE sector managers to judge the entries. The winners were the advertising agency J. Walter Thompson and the Jordan Williams Design Agency.

The choice of a new name seems to have been easy – the suggestion of Network SouthEast was the straightaway favourite. Network embodied the suggestion of frequent service, and the SouthEast part was a clear geographical statement. The gut feeling was borne out by market research.

Other alternatives were considered: SouthRail, CentralRail, LondonRail, CapitalRail, City, and Coast and Country. In addition were a couple with science fiction connotations: LASER (London and South East Railway) and StarTrack.

The colours chosen for the new livery were patriotic and consciously so: red, white and blue. Robin Jordan of Jordan Williams pointed out at the time that due to these colours being adopted in the flag of the union in 1606 Britain could claim precedence for their use over other countries such as the Netherlands (1630) the USA (1776) and France (1789).

For the train liveries the colours were formed into longitudinal stripes of blue, red, white and grey. The logotypes were placed on the white stripe. The most characteristic feature was at the cab ends, where the stripes were swept upwards. It was very effective on multiple-units and served to give them a definitive middle and end; it was less effective on locos and later was amended so the sweep was abolished on them. It certainly smartened up the look of the old Southern slam doors as well as the fleet of Class 50 diesels – although it was a case of old wine in new skins. With all the emphasis on horizontal stripes the era of NSE is probably best remembered for the red lamp posts. NSE brought a new blaze of colour to a region which had been dismal for far too long.

One of the issues regarding the new livery was that its bright colours were much more likely to show the dirt. This was seen as a positive by its designers, in that it would give staff an incentive to wash them more regularly! Another thing that factored into the thinking was the still extant regional rivalries – green was avoided due to its association with the Southern and the new livery had to be acceptable to the other regions.[33]

Not everyone was madly enthusiastic about the new livery. Railway design expert and critic Brian Haresnape (fellow of the Royal Society of Arts) who had welcomed in the Corporate Identity Livery over twenty years before[34] castigated the new NSE identity as a 'visual disaster', remarking that 'advertising agents and graphic designers with no railway interest have been let loose on machinery in a way that recalls Coca Cola tins and tubes of toothpaste, rather than durable and efficient rolling stock' and that 'locos in Network SouthEast livery look like they are wearing too much make-up'.[35]

In 1986 Jane Priestman was appointed Director of Architecture, Design and Environment, bringing together in one authority elements that had traditionally been distributed throughout the railway under different heads of department.[36] Priestman came to BR having previously been General Manager in Architecture and Design for the British Airports Authority for eleven years. She was to over-see InterCity and Regional – formerly Provincial Railways – gaining distinctive identities. There was also the rebranding of the freight businesses, with a co-ordinated set of large symbols representing each of the freight sub-sectors. According to Tony Howard, Executive Design Manager at that time, the Corporate Identity Manual came to fill ten filing cabinets, whilst the design department employed forty people who could be dealing with 1,200 projects at any one time – from new trains and their interiors to logos right down to socks.[37]

In 1987 InterCity was 21 years old. To mark its majority it hired the design consultancy Newell and Sorrell to give it a distinctive brand. The logotype *InterCity* was now borne by a serifed font, and a new logo – a swallow – was used in place of the Corporate Identity Symbol, which was no longer borne on *InterCity* locomotives or stock.[38]

With such an anarchic situation the design organisation was restructured in acceptance of the new power given to the sectors in the devolution. In 1989 the Design Panel was disbanded to be replaced by two new panels, an Architectural Panel and a new Design Panel. Design decisions had now become Executive pre-rogatives and both the panels were now merely advisory. The new Design Panel's concern was with the 'quality of BR's policy of design'.

The purpose of the Architectural Panel reflected BR's 'new found' love of its old buildings. 'In the past we have neglected and undervalued our architectural heritage,' Priestman confessed. As I have mentioned, BR had done rather more than just neglected its buildings; it had taken a wrecking ball to some of them, yet Priestman must have come across as sincere, and *Modern Railways* reported that: 'One of her passions is the integration of modern and historic architecture. She describes Liverpool Street as the "Jewel in the crown" and Paddington as "the great hope for the future".' Such a challenge must have been a change for someone coming from an airport authority. As I said earlier, Victorian airports are rather rare.[39]

The main change this new regime undertook was the creation of a new image for what had been known as the Provincial Sector. The term 'Provincial' had long been used by BR as a catch-all for its services that couldn't be described in any other way. It had originated as the title of a column in an account book and had inadvertently become a brand name. It took more than a while for someone to notice the more deprecating connotations of the word. One really wonders what other alternatives could have been contemplated in the same spirit – Parochial Railways? Rustic Rail? Yokel Rail?

In December 1990 Provincial changed its name to 'Regional Railways' in England. In Scotland the name ScotRail was already established and incorporated into the new sector identity, meaning that ScotRail was the only one of Regional's five profit centres to have its own identity.

Under the sector's managing director, Gordon Pettitt, a 'new, strong but sympathetic corporate identity scheme' was adopted. The logotypes were drawn in the serifed 'Joanna' typeface, although all information continued to be printed in the sans serif 'Helvetica' derived font. There was also a 'fleximark' – a set of horizontal lines which, the brochure said, 'will, little by little, stamp itself indelibly on the mind of the customer'. Frightening stuff. The range of house colours chosen were those that had already appeared on the new Sprinters and Pacers: light blue, dark blue, dark grey and silver grey.[40]

By this time many of the trains run by Regional Railways were financed by the Passenger Transport Executives and thus carried the PTE's own brand. The unified corporate identity had truly broken down. It was just a foretaste of the variety that was to come when the system was shattered by privatisation.

But the corporate identity had done its job. BR had come to be seen as a unified whole and as a modern railway whilst it shrugged off the reminiscences of the group companies. By the 1980s variety had returned, but people now knew that BR was a unified company.

I have said that BR had embraced television advertising from the mid-1960s, but since 1949 the Commission had had an organisation working at improving its image by making original documentaries. This was known as British Transport Films (BTF). The Southern Railway and the LMS both had their own film units prior to nationalisation and these were amalgamated into the new organisation headed by Edgar Anstey.

Anstey's background in documentary making lay in the pre-war period. He had joined the Empire Marketing Board film unit prior to it being moved to the General Post Office and becoming the GPO film unit. At Empire he had become a protégé of John Grierson and had worked as an editor on the film *Industrial Britain*, now regarded as a watershed in British documentary making. At this time the Empire/GPO unit was gaining a strong reputation for socialist realist documentary making. Later Anstey had moved to the Shell film unit.

Initially the focus of the BTF unit was on all modes of transport operated by the Commission but when the British Railways Board took over in 1962 the unit came under their control and from that point on was mostly a railway film unit. It was to document the changing railway scene for more than thirty years, until it was disbanded as part of the economy drive in the mid-1980s. The unit was also to win many film awards, particularly for John Schlesinger's legendary documentary about a day at Waterloo, entitled *Terminus*.

In a lecture to the British Railways Western Region Debating Society in December 1960[41] Anstey laid out three categories of film produced by the unit. Firstly there were those 'for the instruction and education of staff'. The second category of film was for 'informing the public about the achievements in our field, the difficulties we are running up against and how we are trying to overcome them'. Lastly there was the 'selling' type of film, 'the film in which we endeavour – sometimes directly, sometimes less directly – to put before the public what we have to offer in the way of passenger and freight facilities'.

Anstey's lecture also gives us an insight into the working methods at the time. This began with a script. The writer 'writes down all the facts he can find, takes the advice of the experts and gets a reservoir of raw material. Then it is his, or some other writer's, job to compose this material on paper into the shape of a successful film.' With a satisfactory script it was then time for the director and his film crew to go to work. Anstey went on: 'he plans with his camera crew how to get the maximum feeling of participation from the audience by the way in which he photographs the events written down in the script.'[42]

Of course, this differs very much from the modern TV documentary approach, which is to film what is there and then to organise it. From our perspective the BTF's approach to documentary making has a touch of playing God, of manipulating reality to suit the constructed truth of the authors; a methodology that was to be discarded, in effect discredited, by the later generation of fly-on-the wall documentary makers.

The method employed does raise the question, of course, as to whether those appearing in BTF films were staff doing their real jobs or effectively serving as actors performing a role. This question was in fact raised at the Western Region Society lecture by a Mr Watson of the Establishment and Staff Office. He recalled that when working in the staff office at BTC headquarters he had had a claim from a dining car attendant for appearance in a BTC film. The attendant claimed payment at the rate of £2 15s a day 'that being said to be the minimum rate recognised by the British Film Artistes association'.

Anstey answered that this had 'become a rather academic fight, or skirmish renewed from time to time with very good feeling on both sides'. The principle of the BTF was:

> ... if the chap is doing his ordinary job and being photographed doing it we can see no case for payment and we will never pay anybody the film artistes rate. But in the case of somebody who is putting himself to special inconvenience out of hours, or is asked to do something which is not normally part of his job, we find a way of compensating him and this seems to have left everybody happy. I hope it will always be like that.

Anstey was in a lot more trouble with the next questioner, a Mr Crute from South Lambeth, who lambasted the conditions under which commercial customers were shown BTF films:

> I remember some two or three years ago great play was made from one of the offices and there was a film put out and the public and the trader were encouraged to come along to the local stations and depots and see the film. This film came to certain depots up and down the country. Cameramen [did he mean projectionists?] attended and sheets were put up and traders came along sometimes thirty or thirty five. They were all given a cup of tea and a biscuit. They sat down and watched the film and after the film was over, they said 'Cheerio – thanks for the film.' I do not know if that is selling business. Quite frankly I think it is disgusting. And that is what did happen with one of your British Transport Commission Films, and that is a fact.

Mr Crute questioned what sort of impression it gave to the customers. He then went on to say: 'We are trying to buy business by this means but we are telling a lot of fabrications when we are saying we can deal with that, when up and down the country we have got stops on and goodness knows what. Are we not jumping a little ahead?'

When faced with professional railwaymen like Mr Crute, Anstey must have known he was a long way from Cannes. He was not going to be drawn on the issue but there is no doubt that there are fabrications in the BTF films. They are not just falsely posed; the real issues which the railways were dealing with are not addressed in anything like a critical way.

In the case of the film *Just Like the Rest of Us* (1983) there is outright and purposeful distortion. Victorian architecture is shown as being inaccessible to the disabled whilst modern buildings are purported as being accessible. The stairs at the side of St Pancras station are shown as if they are the main entrance – which is actually on the flat, up a sloping cab road where there was some parking space. Euston is shown as the new model of accessibility, whereas in fact the contemporary RADAR guides to British Rail for the disabled state that the entrance to Euston is by stairs and there is 'no convenient parking'.[43]

Whatever its faults, the closing of the BTF in the 1980s was not just an artistic issue but a sign that the public service ethos of the railway system was now being discarded.

7

Speed with Comfort:
A Technological Revolution

With the West Coast Main Line electrification in progress and the Deltics running, BR could now haul trains at 100mph, but could it do so safely and maintain passenger comfort?

In 1963 G. Freeman Allen commented that: 'No vehicle has changed less in the previous thirty years than the British long-distance passenger coach.'[1] The mainline carriage was a liability; speed was necessary to have any chance of competing with the internal airlines or the new motorways, and the carriage produced by the Executive at the start of the 1950s wasn't up to that job. British Rail needed an entirely new design.

Unfortunately, the development of the new coach occurred in a piecemeal fashion which resulted in duplication of effort, false starts and the need to continually rework the design during production in order to fit the bits together.

The first piece to be developed was the much needed new standard bogie. As mentioned in Chapter 3 the standard bogie originally designed for the Mk1 carriage was far from satisfactory, and was finally proven so when used under the Southern Region's South Eastern division express multiple-units. The bogie was of a very traditional type that had served the British railway system well since the turn of the twentieth century, but design details of the British Railways version, coupled with modern running conditions – particularly on continuous welded rail – had meant that they had failed to live up to expectations. It was hoped that it would be capable of 100mph running but this had to be limited to 90mph when rough riding was frequently reported. In its traditional form the British bogie had reached the end of its useful life and alternatives were sought. Many off-the-peg bogie designs were tried out in the middle 1950s in order to select one to become the mainstay express passenger bogie until something new could be designed by BR. The design chosen was the Commonwealth bogie, named after the US Commonwealth Steel Corporation. This bogie consisted of two steel castings and was very heavy but it did the job. It went under the first fleet of Mk1 Pullmans as well as catering vehicles and many other express coaches, giving the result of much improved riding and comfort.[2]

Meanwhile, BR engineers worked on a new bogie. This was developed at Swindon – which was rather ironic as the Mk1 bogie had been based on GWR practice. The new 'B4 bogie', as it became known, was tested extensively for several years – doubtless because BR was now very reluctant to invest in another failure. Eventually it was adopted as the standard bogie from 1963.[3] It was of lightweight construction, fabricated of channel sections by welding. It had coil springs, practically a novelty for a British-designed bogie. It also had traction bars to prevent the bolster (on which the carriage itself rides) from rubbing against the transoms. It was a thoroughly modern bogie, for its time, and the first serious technological innovation embraced by BR rolling stock engineers.[4]

The new coach that would eventually ride on these bogies began as two different projects, one championed by Swindon works and one by the Design Panel working with engineers at Derby. The trick was to get these two projects to mate up.

In May 1958 the Western Region's carriage and wagon engineer, J.W. Innes, commissioned a document entitled 'Report on Proposed Standard Carriage', which laid down the principle of an integral loco-hauled carriage. The basics of this were approved by Innes and detailed drawings and a portable model were made. The design was refined until a full sized prototype was authorised by the BTC. Construction began at Swindon works in 1960.[5]

Meanwhile, under the Design Panel, an entirely separate project had been ongoing since the Battersea prototypes of 1957. The Design Panel had set about responding to the views expressed in this exercise and by 1959 had worked up their own concept carriage.

By 1961 this project had gained the title of 'Carriage of the Future'. At this stage there was antagonism between Harrison, the CME leading the body shell development, and Williams the designer, who was leading the development of the design project,[6] but in July 1961 the decision was made to proceed with both projects and to incorporate the new elements from the Design Panel's ideas when they were tried and proven.[7]

From August 1962 the Swindon design went into production, a new integral carriage with many antique internal features. Meanwhile, the Design Panel's project resulted in the commissioning of an eight-coach experimental train, to be constructed at Derby using the Mk1 as its basis but with the new features such as wider doors.[8] This led to the Mk2 having by far the most complicated development history of any mark of BR coach design. There had been a wish to have far fewer body types[9] (there had been fourteen different body types of Mk1, for different purposes, on two different underframes) and this was fulfilled, but the economies of that work must surely have been undone as the Mk2 was repeatedly redesigned to incorporate new features as they came along.

Production started at Derby. The first built were forty-six 'corridor firsts', with vacuum braking and steam heating, except for the twenty that went to the Southern, which had electric and steam train heating and were converted to air braking. From the very first the Mk2 was to form the basis of a non-standard fleet.

By 1965 there were enough Mk2s to run the prestige services at the west coast electric switch-on, thus BR was able to sport a thoroughly modern carriage – in structural terms – with *some* modern fixtures and fittings right at the start of its 'new railway'. The Mk2 won its spurs: it was now the carriage that launched Inter-City.

In 1961 Dr Beeching had taken over the BTC, and later became the first head of the board. As I have said, he put a much greater emphasis on the importance of good design and it seems very likely that he banged heads together. From 1964 all of the involved parties met together and were collectively known as the Rolling Stock Design and Development Panel.[10] The design of a successful passenger coach catering to current and future public tastes was clearly of paramount importance in the development of profitable railway services, and it was too important to allow squabbles between departments to obstruct it.

In 1963 the Design Panel's ideas were exhibited at the Design of British Railways exhibition and a full twelve-coach train was commissioned to test them. Although the Mk2 body shell was already in production it was deemed much easier to use the Mk1 as the basis to try out the new features rather than go to the expense of redesigning the Mk2 body shell, only to have to change it again later on. So it was that eight new carriages were constructed at Derby to the Mk1 design, but with the new design features. All were mounted on the new B4 bogie. A further four Mk1 coaches were converted to include the new features. In 1964 the twelve-coach concept train was unveiled, now known as 'XP64'. It featured forced air heating and ventilation, improved soundproofing, panoramic windows, better lighting, scientifically designed seats and wider entrances enabled by folding doors. The lavatory was said to be compact and hygienic. It also featured airline-style face-to-back seating.[11]

In the review in *Modern Railways*, G. Freeman Allen's wife, Mary, pointed out the more significant defects. The folding doors were hard to move, and why did the door handles always have to be so far down the outside of the doors? There were no handles on the inside for safety reasons, but anyone shorter than 5ft 6in barely had arms long enough to reach out and over the open window, and the top of the window cut painfully into the armpit.

Then there was the loo – medically approved it may have been, but Mrs Freeman Allen considered it impossibly cramped for mothers with toddlers, the elderly or the disabled.

The set was put into service in summer 1964 on the Talisman and later on the West Riding. In spring 1965 it had moved to the London Midland on the Heysham–Euston trains and then onto trains for South Wales on the Western Region. It was trialled behind two of the English Electric Type 3s, regeared for 100mph running on Paddington–Bristol services. During these trials on three of the five regions (Scottish and Southern excluded) the views of passengers and staff were recorded. Passengers reaction must have been generally favourable as many of the advanced features found their way into the production Mk2s – eventually. objections were raised to the doors that Mary Allen had found so difficult and the design was abandoned.

As said in Chapter 5, the new Mk2s were also built as Pullmans. Overseeing the new Pullmans was industrial design consultant Jack Howe, who had previously worked on the Blue Pullman trains. Bafflingly, the acclaimed fixtures and fittings of the Blue Pullmans were not continued and Howe went on the record as saying that the best of the Blue Pullman interior design was being eroded and replaced by railway features.[12] Amongst other things the airline-style seats of the Blue Pullmans were replaced with a Derby design. Howe also envisaged that the new Pullmans would have the same Nanking Blue and white paintwork as the diesel Pullmans, but the new rigour of corporate identity meant that the new exterior had to conform; eventually the Pullmans were finished in a not unattractive reversal of the standard corporate identity coach livery; the body sides were predominantly white-grey with a rail blue band enclosing the windows with semi-matt finish. As with the Blue Pullmans none of the cars bore names but only the Pullman crest and the same serifed font as the Blue Pullmans. The bodysides of these cars were flatter than those of the other Mk2s and they retained the definitive Pullman inward-opening doors and transverse vestibules at the ends.

The electric Pullman services started on 18 April 1966 but were not considered successful enough to justify further construction of Pullman vehicles. Despite air conditioning they were not significantly different enough from the first-class Mk2s for passengers to prefer them. Consequently these were to be the very last purpose-built Pullman cars for the British railway system, but, as will be explained, the Pullman brand itself was far from finished.[13]

The Mk2 story developed slowly. In 1967 the Mk2as were the first to be all air-braked. In 1968 the Mk2b was produced with 3ft entrance wraparound doors – a reworking of the wide door idea that had been trialled on XP64. These doors were one-piece though. The centre entrance doors were also abolished. Unfortunately the redesign involved compromises in body shell strength, which led to the early retirement of these coaches. It was one of the prices paid for amending a design as it went along.[14]

For a long time the marketing department had been pressing for air conditioning as an essential for all *Inter-City* services in order to compete with the airlines.

Experience with the carriages in traffic also showed that something needed to be done. The double glazing fitted to all the non-moving windows kept noise out, but on a hot day, when the sliding windows at the top were open, it was a different story. At speeds of 100mph the noise could be quite enervating and defeated all attempts to provide a comfortable passenger environment. Market research bore out the notion that passengers themselves place a high priority on air conditioning.[15]

The Mk2b had been made longer – extended to 64ft – to accommodate an air-conditioning unit which was never installed.[16] The Mk2cs had a redesigned ceiling installed to accommodate air-conditioning equipment at a later stage – this was never installed either. BR was waiting upon the development of its own air-conditioning system to be developed in order not to have to pay to use the Stones patent, as it did with the Pullmans. In 1969 the CM&EE department finally conceded its inability to develop a system cheaper than the one patented by Stones,[17] so in that year the board finally decided on a policy of air condition-ing for all new stock and later contracted with Stone-Platt for the equipment. This led to the Mk2d rolling out in 1970. Although structurally similar to the 2cs, the 2ds had an entirely new look. The sliding ventilator windows were gone, and with them the last vestiges of the pre-war LMS appearance of BR stock. The windows were now sealed and their dimensions gave the new carriages a sleek look that was enhanced by the corporate livery. The coaches looked dif-ferent from all their previous brethren, and not like any other carriage on BR metals. The modern carriage had arrived in earnest. British Rail was the first railway in Europe to provide air conditioning for ordinary passengers.[18]

Together with air conditioning the Mk2ds also featured a newfangled public address system, the Ripper Robots Audio Navigator Mk5, with the 'train talk' system – developed by Ripper Robots Ltd of Cranfield, Bedford. This system took more than six years to develop and test. It delivered pre-recorded voice announcements relevant to the place the train was passing. The system worked by a pulse generator on the axle which transmitted the distance travelled in digital form that the on-board computer could understand. This was sophisticated stuff for 1970. Train staff had to do no more than feed a rather bulky cassette into the unit.[19] The new system was of course for the public's convenience but was also beneficial for the railways, since by keeping passengers informed it speeded up de-training and thus helped to accelerate the whole process of station stops. It also enabled adverts to be slipped in for the buffet cars and other amenities.

As has been shown, the outstanding success of the West Coast Main Line elec-trification was a clear lesson to BR that speed sells tickets. It led to the obvious demand for yet more speed. The title of an article in the December 1966 edi-tion of *Modern Railways* screamed 'BR should plan 125mph coaches now [*sic*]'.[20] It went on to point out the obvious frailties of existing stock regarding the bogies, as well as the fact that the Mk2 coaches were not an optimal design in terms of their weight. It stated that there was a case for a 75ft-long coach which would be able to carry more passengers for the overall weight, and proved this with an alarming mathematical equation, which is excluded from this volume on grounds of health, taste and decency. It does make sense though; a longer coach means more passengers per bogie and also enables more to be served by the same on-board equipment, reducing machinery and thus weight.

Consideration of such a vehicle was already taking place within BR circles – as the source for the above-mentioned article probably knew full well. The first proposal was for an 80ft coach, but this was in fact downsized to 75ft with a maximum body width of 9ft. With so many of the basic design requirements resolved via the development of the Mk2, the Mk3 could be planned as a high tech vehicle from scratch. It was designed from the start for air conditioning as well as to be able to use the minimum number of body shells for the maximum number of vehicle types. Again the construction was integral. Underframe equipment was modular – air-conditioning units, batteries and motor alternators could all be switched out with ease, enabling maintenance on them without the carriage being withdrawn from service. Interior fittings were also modular and designed for easy removal and replacement in case of damage or simply changes of fashion. Much use was again made of glass fibre for its weight saving and easily mouldable properties.

One of the most important features of the Mk3 was its bogies; these were the result of research conducted by BR from the early 1960s and this is a story in itself.

BR had inherited research facilities from the LMS at Derby. All of the group era railways conducted scientific research, but the LMS had been the only one to set up a separate department specifically for this purpose, following in the footsteps of its great constituent, the LNWR, who had had research facilities at Crewe. The LMS research unit took a holistic approach, looking at the interaction of rolling stock with the track. A particular focus was passenger comfort, as well as eliminating such effects as hunting: this is when the wheels start to move from side to side in a rhythmic motion. Cine cameras were used to record the effects of using different tyre treads at speed.[21] Relations with the CME's department were reportedly strained, although eased by the good nature of the CME, William Stanier.

The 1947 Transport Act empowered the BTC to engage in research, but also required it to obtain approval from the minister. A Transport Research Council was established and a chief research officer appointed. When Brian Robertson took over and the modernisation plan was being effected research gained a new status – at least amongst those at the top. The existing facilities for research were recognised as inadequate and plans were put in place for an entirely new laboratory. This was much delayed by the Commission's financial position and not actually opened until 14 May 1964. New equipment included a digital computer, originally housed in a temporary building until the permanent one was complete.

One area of research, undertaken by Dr Alan Wickens, was the problem of traditional wagon and bogie designs on continuous welded rail (CWR). This was becoming an increasing problem as freight wagons were derailing at speed due to the interaction. CWR was a major advance in improving passenger comfort at speed as well as preventing the metal fatigue associated with traditional rail joints. It was important to get it right. Research found that the problems lay in the very smoothness of continuous rail, which lacked the breaks that had disrupted the oscillations, particularly when modern steel vehicles with traditional suspension were worked at high speeds. This research led to the development of the ground-breaking High Speed Freight Vehicle 1 (HSFV1), which eliminated many of the problems. By 1967 work was under way to derive the appropriate specifications for new passenger bogies for both high-speed and commuter trains. This was to result in the excellent BT10 and BT15 bogies that were to be placed beneath the Mk3 carriage and the BT13 that was placed beneath the Great Northern four-car outer-suburban units.

Not everyone welcomed the intervention of the research department. In their book *British Railways Engineering* John Johnson and Robert Long point to a deep division between the research and engineering departments. At that time Harrison, in charge of rationalising the diesel fleet, was having to deal with the mess created by the 'modernisation' plan while the Chief Engineer (Way and Works), A.N. Butland, didn't welcome anything that didn't fit in with his own views.[22] But in 1965 the head of the research department, Dr Sydney Jones, had been given a seat on the British Railways Board, making it clear that research was on the agenda and giving it a voice at the top table.

In Japan and France new railway lines were built enabling very high speeds, but Britain is a tightly packed country where building new lines is likely to be highly controversial (as HS2 shows!) so making the best use of the existing infrastructure is at least an arguable solution. Due to the chaotic planning procedures of the nineteenth century, curves make up 50 per cent of the total rail lines in Britain.[23] In the mid-1960s the view was taken that curve realignment costing £20,000 to £200,000 (in contemporary money) for each operation was not worth doing simply to shave a few seconds off of a journey.[24] BR had to find a novel way to overcome the basic inadequacies of the existing network. One idea that was proposed was for a train that could take passengers safely and comfortably around curves at high speed by tilting. At first British Rail was unwilling to pay for such an experimental project but Sydney Jones went straight to the minister and sought funding.

The government was sold on the potential export possibilities and in 1968 it was agreed that funding would be split between the Ministry of Transport and the British Railways Board.[25] In 1969 the BRB approved the construction of the APT-E – an experimental train that would provide a test bed for the new technology. The APT is more commonly referred to as the tilting train, together with a rider like 'the one that didn't work', but tilting was only the most visible and most obvious of a number of design innovations it incorporated. Essential to its high-speed mandate it was designed to minimise the amount of unsprung weight upon the track – particularly with the Class 86 fiasco in mind (previously known as AL6, see p. 70). For that reason the traction motors were incorporated into the body rather than bearing upon the axles or being mounted within the bogies. They were separated from the track by both the primary and secondary suspension.

The weight of the train was drastically reduced by employing aerospace technology to construct an aluminium frame; this enabled the number of wheels to be reduced, thus minimising friction, without raising the axle weight too high. Conventional brakes on a train travelling at such a speed would not be effective or reliable, so a form of hydraulic brake was designed. This involved two axles, one inside the other. The outer axle had blades on its inside face, the inner axle having blades on its outer face. Normally the cavity between the inner and outer axles was empty but when brake force was required it was flooded with fluid. This was churned by the blades which acted against each other and turned the movement energy into kinetic energy by heating the water, which was then removed from the cavity and cooled. Conventional friction brakes were also fitted, as hydrokinetic brakes are not so effective at low speeds. The brakes were to prove one of the Achilles' heels of the design prototype.

Most remarkable of all, though conventional, was the tilt mechanism. Other tilting trains had been developed previously but they had been of the so-called 'passive tilt' variety – these tilted from a high point at the top of the carriages and used the train's own weight to swing itself into curves. This was fine if you had a capacious loading gauge to play with, but as ever the restrictions within the British system didn't allow for such an uncontrolled movement. Thus an 'active tilt mechanism', using jacks, was developed with a very low tilting point.[26] The original experimental APT was powered by gas turbines, although electricity was another option. A diesel engine of the necessary power would be twice the size of a gas turbine propulsion system – with a need to keep weight down it was ruled out.[27]

In July 1972 the APT-E completed its first test run. Unfortunately at that point an industrial dispute broke out over the fact that there was no extra seat in the APT-E and the prototype HST for a second driver (see Chapter 9) and it was not until September 1973 that tests could be resumed. In August 1975 the APT-E achieved a British speed record with a 254.4km/h (152.4mph) run between Swindon and Reading. In April 1976 it was retired to the National Railway Museum at York. The experimental phase was over.

Whilst the APT remained experimental, or theoretical, however you may view it, another project took shape in parallel. In 1967 Walter Jowett, formerly of English Electric, joined BR as Director of Design. One of his tasks was to look at BR's traction requirements for the 1970s and he produced two so-called

'Black Books', the first titled *Locomotives for the Seventies*. His view was that conventional locomotives could achieve 150mph and he clashed openly with the research department at one meeting, where he disputed that the APT was the only way to achieve higher speeds. This was to lead BR to take a two-pronged approach, pursuing the APT as a long-term goal but also looking at an evolution of existing technologies.

A primary requirement for a high-speed train was, of course, a power plant. For some time the idea of a 4,000hp Deltic had been mooted, but as Terry Miller had become the CME in mid-1968 that idea was unlikely to prevail. As referred to in Chapter 4, Miller was hostile to the Deltic engine, having had first-hand experience of it on the Eastern Region.

BR was already trying out a locomotive that was designed with a view to 125mph running. This was the Hawker Siddeley Brush HS4000, also known as *Kestrel*. This project had been initiated by Brush in 1966 with a view to sales to BR as well as abroad. Doubtless the realisation of the importance of speed had much to do with it. However, BR engineers had severe doubts about it functioning at 125mph, because of its 133 tonnes weight, albeit that they spread this over two three-axle bogies. In 1968 *Kestrel* was handed over to the BR at Marylebone for testing and it went into service pulling freights. In 1969 Brush yielded to the weight concerns and placed it on bogies from their successful type 4 design. The locomotive underwent further trials, this time on passenger trains, recording over 100mph on several occasions. BR was not buying though and in March 1971 *Kestrel* was withdrawn from BR service and shipped, unloved, to Russia, with whom Brush were in negotiations. Sadly for Brush, the Russians also found it unsuitable.[28]

BR thinking was already moving in another direction. The second of Jowett's Black Books: *Diesel Electric Multiple Unit Trains* pointed to an answer for the power problem. This proposed the use of the proven Ruston Davey Paxman Ventura diesel power plant in two power cars, one at each end of the train. This distribution of weight and power would enable the power cars to be light enough to satisfy the track engineers whilst giving the machine enough power. In Jowett's original vision, the engines were to be powered by a sixteen-cylinder version of the engine, generating 3,000hp to a combined total for both cars of 6,000hp – enough to haul a ten-coach train. In the end the twelve-cylinder version of 2,250hp was adopted, limiting the capability to 125mph with seven carriages in between the powered cars.[29] This project was initially called the High Speed Diesel Train, or HSDT, but later this was shortened to HST. When marketed it became, of course, the Inter-City 125. During development stages the Mark 3 version of the Ventura engine used was renamed the Valenta.[30]

As mentioned above, one thing that had become clear in the years of running the Class 86 locomotive, with axle-hung, nose-suspended traction motors, was that the design was unsuitable for 100mph plus running. The prototype locomotives, without axle-hung, nose-suspended traction motors (AH-NS) (AL1–AL5 81–85), performed very much better than the later 86s. The resting of so much of the weight of the motor on the axle resulted in an unsprung weight of 4.25 tons – this translated into a dynamic sleeper load of 75 tons at 100mph rising to 98 tons at 125mph. The Deltics, too, had axle-hung, nose-suspended traction motors but they were smaller, only 3.3 tons per axle, the result of the Deltics being Co-Co[31] machines with six traction motors sharing the work as opposed to four. The HST power cars were planned as Bo-Bo machines, so clearly AH-NS traction motors were out of the question.[32] The answer was to mount the traction motors in the bogie frames and to transfer the drive from them via cardan shafts.

With the engine/locomotive format decided it was only sensible that it should be married with the newly conceived Mk3 carriage project, and this is what did happen – clearly some joined-up thinking was taking place. The first prototypes of the Mk3 would now be built in conjunction with the HSDT project. Meanwhile, the research at Derby had borne fruit in the form of a new type of bogie to go under the power cars and the Mk3 carriages. This utilised – watch out, here comes the technical bit – radial arms to connect the axle boxes to the bogie frame. Only one spring and one damper provided the primary suspension for each wheel. These bogies represented a further revolution in maintaining passenger comfort at speed.

In August 1970 authority was given to design and build a prototype HST. With the APT also in its design and development phases there was, inevitably, some sense of competition between the two teams; it was the HST that won, but then it did have some advantages because of its traditional technology, as well as some help from the other side.

Apart from all the technical stuff there was, of course, the most important question of what the machine should look like. The emphasis placed on good and modern-looking design by Robertson's Commission had not gone away. James Cousins, the current head of BR design, asked respected designer Kenneth Grange to have a look at the HST concept and 'decorate' it.[33] Grange had previously worked for a number of well-known household brands including Kodak, Ronson, Kenwood and Morphy Richards. He was presented with a model of the existing design, which he described as 'lumpish and brutish'.[34] Fortunately Grange rebelled against his limiting brief and carried out his own wind tunnel tests at Imperial College to discover an optimum aerodynamic shape. What he produced laid the foundations for an iconic design.

The prototype HST was completed as early as June 1972. Unfortunately industrial action (see above) delayed its testing for many months but when it finally took to the main line the prototype flew, logging a new record speed for a diesel train of 143mph between Darlington and York.

The HST could do it.

Now came the task of turning the prototype into a working production machine. The industrial action over the HST (and APT-E) had in part centred on the fact that it had originally been designed for single manning. The agreement reached with the unions required a redesign so that a second man could sit in the cab beside the driver. This meant a wider windscreen so that both men could look forwards with the correct angle of vision. The glass was of a special type, tough enough to withstand a brick at 225mph in order for the driver to be protected from vandalism.[35] At first it looked as if the windscreen would have to be produced in two pieces with a central support bar down the middle, but the manufacturers then announced that they had the technology to make it in one piece. But the increase in the windscreen size meant that the meeting with the cab sides was sharper and less aerodynamic than the original design – a problem that may have gone unresolved but for a single, impertinent question. Grange chanced to ask the chief engineer whether the train needed buffers at the ends. The answer was that in this train there was much less need than normal. The High Speed Train was to be exempt from shunting; it would be permanently coupled up as a complete train and was unlikely to meet another train end to end. That was the breakthrough. The buffers were dispensed with and as a consequence the airflow was now enabled to pass from the front of the unit over the top instead of around the sides. This produced a much better looking front end; in fact once the livery was applied it was an iconic image.[36]

As the HST went from prototype to production run, the APT project was progressing slowly. In 1971 the BR report *Inter-City Passenger Business: A Strategy For High Speed* had advocated the development of APT and the board had given approval for an electric version. With rising fuel costs, in 1973 British Leyland ceased production of the turbine engines and the idea of a fossil-fuel powered APT was abandoned. The APT was now to be electric and the focus was to be on getting it onto BR's main route – the electrified WCML. Also in 1973 the APT project was transferred to the Chief Mechanical and Electrical Engineer's (CM&EE) traction and rolling stock department. The first brief from BR's Passenger Business Management outlined a twelve- to fourteen-coach train and in September 1974 three prototypes were commissioned. The development of these prototypes, however, was fraught with difficulties. To get sufficient traction for such a long train two power cars would be required. It was impossible to use two pantographs to take the power from the overhead wires because at the speed the train would be travelling the wires would be disturbed and contact between the pantographs and the wires disrupted. Running power lines over or through the train was also ruled out on safety grounds. Although this is done on other trains, such as the TGV, it was realised that the tilt on the APT would stress the cables as each car would have its own tilt mechanism, operating independently. The stressing of cables carrying 25,000 volts was considered inadvisable. There was nothing for it but to marshal the two power cars together. It would have been best if this could have been done at one end, but the carriages would not have taken the force of both cars pushing the whole train, so the power cars ended up in the middle with the train split in two, as passengers could not pass through them. It was in effect two trains running as one, but given the length of it, two sets of catering and guard's vehicles would probably have been needed anyway.

The position of the power cars was the least of the APT-P's problems. The restriction in the wiring mentioned above also meant that the control wiring connections between each carriage were limited. As the trigger for the tilt on each coach was from the coach that preceded it along the track, this was an essential feature for the tilt to work and originally there had been a backup for the system. This came to be overlooked in the production version with the consequence that one stressed set of connections bore the whole responsibility for triggering the tilt. These often failed and when one coach tilt mechanism failed the whole train had to be slowed and taken out of tilt mode for the sake of the comfort of passengers. Another problem was the binding of the conventional brakes, something which should have been easy to fix given more time and effort.

The plan had been to have eighty production APTs in service by 1980 but the proving trials of the first production version did not even begin until May 1979.[37] It was scheduled to enter passenger service in 1980 but it had to be postponed due to the reliability problems. Finally on 7 December 1981 it did enter passenger service, only to have problems due to driver error on the return trip when a bend was taken too fast. Two attempts to run the train were thwarted by heavy snow. Highly embarrassed by these failures, BR withdrew it from service. It was supposed to return in the summer of 1982 but never did. In September of that year the idea of the trains entering service as a squadron was abandoned.

The APT was certainly BR's most embarrassing failure, and one which attracts much comment. But why did it fail? In his book *On The Right Lines* Stephen Potter outlines several reasons why. One was simply the clash of cultures whereby new technological innovation sat uneasily with railway engineering, where a cautious, evolutionary approach, slowly building on the tried and tested, was the accepted method of technological development. Potter points out that the concept of a project team sat uneasily within the CM&EE department, where it was isolated to its own detriment. With more input from other engineers experienced in railway maintenance the design team would have been informed that the troublesome brakes required a level of maintenance beyond what was available on BR.[38] They would have been told that an operating maintenance depot was not the right place to debug the prototypes.[39] At the top the Chief Mechanical Engineer was on the whole supportive of the project but Potter points to a lack of support and even obstruction at lower levels, with work for the APT given the lowest level of priority. Kit Spackman, Tilt System Development Engineer of the E train project, comments that the APT-E train project team were essentially isolated from the rest of the railway world, but were faced with a bad attitude now and then when they met such colleagues professionally. David Halfpenny talks of 'withering scorn, often expressed in macho blue ribaldry', although co-operation was available to anyone who wasn't 'too prickly or up themselves'. Given all this, Potter regarded the progress that was made on the APT as 'remarkable'.

There was one issue that he points to as the main stumbling block that brought all progress to a grinding halt. This was our old friend reorganisation, this time of the CM&EE department, beginning in 1976 and taking four years. It mirrors the reorganisation in all other parts of BR in this period and was intended to restructure the CM&EE department to be in line with the commercial demands of the railway. During this time members of the APT project group found themselves dispersed throughout the new organisation as it was divided into the three product groups: freight, Inter-City and suburban. The APT project now came under the control of the 'Inter-City Engineer', a post to which the APT design engineer was promoted. What with the reorganisation and the hostility to the project in other parts of the department many of the best and brightest members of the team left for other posts just at the time when BR should have been keeping together those staff that knew the project and were the best to perfect it and see it through to completion. On 14 July 1980 the APT project group 'officially' ceased to exist, but it had plainly taken a long time dying, with its work disrupted since 1977.[40] Yet again reorganisation crippled BR's efforts at a crucial time, in a crucial project.

Having reviewed BR's most high-profile failure, it is important to remember that BR did have many successes, and some of them were small but fundamental and of immense importance. It developed, sometimes nurtured, some of the best ideas used on the railway system to this day.

A good example is the Pandrol clip, now a practically universal device. They are on most railway sleepers in the world, and their excellence should be sung more loudly, for a short while.

The Elastic Spike Company had successfully developed the eponymous elastic spike, a device that gripped flat bottom rail in a much more effective way than the traditional steel spike. They were also more efficient to install, particularly compared to installations of bullhead rail. But Leopold Stewart Sanson, Managing director of the Elastic Spike Company, was not satisfied with the firm's product and began to scour the world for the next generation of rail clips. This quest took him to Oslo, where he had an appointment to meet the Chief Permanent Way Engineer of the Norwegian State Railways (NSR). This man was the co-inventor of a new rail clip. Sanson was offered the chance to sell this worldwide, but he refused this opportunity.

During his time in Oslo he had already met an employee of the NSR called Per Pande-Rolfsen who worked on the Chief Permanent Way Engineer's staff. He had his own design of clip which his boss had not been impressed with –

possibly because he was trying to sell his own. As someone employed to work on such matters, Pande-Rolfsen was obliged to offer his employers the first chance of taking up the design but had now waited the legally required six months for them to consider the proposal. He was now free to sell it to anyone. He had taken the opportunity to show it to Sanson, who immediately saw its genius and bought the worldwide rights straightaway. It was a simple, paper-clip-like design where a bar of steel was twisted in such a way that it placed an elbow on the top surface of the rail base. The brilliance lay not just in the simplicity by which it could be produced, but also the ease by which it could be installed, simply by being slid into a hole in the base plate. Once properly installed it actually tightened its grip on the rail when the assembly came under stress. It was genius, and it still is.

Sanson took the design back to Britain and straight to BR, where the research department at Derby played a substantial role in developing and testing the clip. In 1965 it was accepted as British Rail's standard rail clip.[41] Along with the IC125 and the huge advance made by other projects at Derby and on BR elsewhere, it is a major contribution to today's high-speed, comfortable and extremely safe railways worldwide.

In the late 1960s BR made another investment that is still with us today. This was the computer system known as TOPS – Total Operations Processing System – which permitted the ability to track trains and individual vehicles around the system. Licensed from the Southern Pacific Railroad, it used a central on-line computer regularly updated from terminals at depots around the country. The first priority was the freight vehicles, and once they were accounted for, and traffic patterns studied, it led to a considerable reduction in the fleet. Locomotive and passenger carriages were also entered on to TOPS, giving for the first time a clear pattern of where they were, when they were there, for how long, as well as much other information.[42]

8

The Social Railway and the Commercial Railway

The 1968 Transport Act changed the game plan for British Rail. No longer was it stuck in the fix of having to fund unprofitable yet socially necessary services out of its own revenue – what there was of it. It was the end of what Terry Gourvish has referred to as 'one of the great charades' of the post-nationalisation railways, BR being forced to seek the closure of un-remunerative services in order to meet the requirement to break even, only to have those attempts blocked by the minister.[1] In truth it only ended half the charade – BR was still to be required to provide a range of services on a business basis while political pressure forced it to restrain price increases.

The act effectively divided the railway. From an economic point of view it was now to be divided into two: the social railway and the commercial railway.

The social railway was, of course, to be those lines supported by the government through the mechanisms in the legislation – as the Commuters Charter of 1981 described it, 'the railway which provides a lifeline to rural areas and performs the major task in the conurbations and London and the South East, in particular, of getting people to and from work.'[2] The commercial railway was to be the freight business and the Inter-City network. This was of course theoretical, as neither freight nor Inter-City was as yet showing a profit. Their commercial status was an expectation rather than a reality.

The social railway was itself split in two by the legislation: firstly those lines initially subsidised under Section 39 of the 1968 Act, then later under the Public Service Obligation grants of the 1974 Act, and secondly those subsidised via the Passenger Transport Executives (PTEs) under Section 20 of the 1968 Act.

In 1967 British Rail, in anticipation of the 1968 Act, submitted 469 cases for consideration for the new subsidies. In 1969, 302 lines were subsidised to a total sum of £61 million (in contemporary money).[3] These included loss-making main lines and some commuter lines. Closures were not stopped entirely. The minister had the final say over which lines were subsidised and, if subsidy was refused, closure loomed – and British Rail no doubt got the stick for it. Dr Beeching was long gone when the Alton–Winchester line got the axe in February 1973, but most people probably still blame him.

The first Passenger Transport Authority (PTA) to be formed, together with its executive, was the West Midlands, on 1 October 1969. South East Lancashire North East Cheshire (SELNEC), Merseyside and Tyneside PTAs and PTEs were then created at monthly intervals. In 1973 the Greater Glasgow PTA and PTE was created. In 1974 two new PTEs were created: South Yorkshire and West Yorkshire.[4] With this there were no more conurbations considered of sufficient size to involve BR in further negotiations with yet another such body.[5]

The metropolitan counties continued the role of the PTAs until their abolition by the Thatcher government in 1986.

The PTEs had the power to integrate transport services and to contract with BR to provide services under what were termed 'Section 20 grants' – named from the relevant part of the act. One of the PTEs went further – in the case of the Tyne and Wear Metro a wholesale takeover of the existing rail system in the area came about, turning it into a pioneer light rail system.

In 1904 the North Eastern Railway had installed a third-rail electric system on Tyneside. In January 1963 Beeching's dislike of electrification asserted itself and it was dismantled. The claim was that it was cheaper to run DMUs on the line, although that is doubtful – it was more likely a shot across the bows of the electricity companies regarding their prices.[6]

The low-quality DMU service was resented by the locals, so when the PTE was established it planned a new electrified rapid transit system – to be run by the PTE itself. Initially there was some resistance to this idea from BR, but an unnamed spokesperson for the PTE was reported as saying: 'we will grow mushrooms in the tunnels rather than pay through the nose to have the Metro run BR's way.'[7]

In 1974 work started to turn the 27 miles of existing BR line into a rapid transit system working with overhead electrification at 1,500 volts DC (Direct Current). To these 8 miles, half underground and partly under the Tyne, were added an extension of the line to Newcastle and Gateshead. In 1984 it was extended to South Shields and to Newcastle Airport in 1991. Latterly it has been extended to Sunderland.

For the original service a total of ninety six-axle articulated units were ordered from Metropolitan-Cammel. These provided services every ten minutes to the stations on the route and were manually operated on a driver-only basis. They were painted white from waist to roof level and yellow below the waist.[8]

British Rail and the PTEs often co-operated a lot better than was the case on Tyneside. On Merseyside BR worked with the PTE to bring about a new integrated rapid transport system involving new tunnels beneath the city. The story began in the late 1950s, when local officials had been horrified by the proposed costs of new road schemes. BR proposed a less costly solution to Liverpool's transport problems: a circular, 2-mile tunnel under the city which linked up key stations – including the extremely busy James Street, one of the busiest outside London. Part of this tunnel was formed from 800m of the former Mersey Railway, but the rest was new. The trains running around this loop are those that come from the Wirral Line which are turned by the effect of going around the loop and then head back out onto the Wirral, having completed the circuit. The powers to build came from the Mersey Railway Extensions Act of 1968 and Merseyside PTE gained further powers for a link to the Southport/Ormskirk lines in 1970. The line was electrified, being an extension of the Wirral Line's electrification of the LMS. At the same time the electrification was extended to Kirkby. The line finally opened in sections from 2 May 1977. Originally the services were operated by BR using existing multiple-units of LMS design, before being replaced by new BR units.[9]

In Manchester the PTE brought about improvements on the Manchester–Bury route including the lengthening of platforms to allow for six-car trains. On 17 March 1980 a new interchange at Bury replaced Bolton Street as the terminus. Bus services were co-ordinated with the trains and the traffic on the rail service increased considerably.

Another scheme was abandoned on grounds of cost, not to be reinstated. This was the cross-city underground line intended to connect Piccadilly and Victoria stations, providing a through link from Bury to Alderley Edge.[10]

It was not until the 1980s that two major historic flaws in the Manchester railway network were corrected with the Hazel Grove chord and the Windsor link. The Hazel Grove chord, completed it 1986, allowed trains from Sheffield, via the South Pennine route, to reach Piccadilly from Stockport. With the Windsor link, completed for the May 1989 timetable, the Bolton line and Manchester–Victoria lines were connected to the line from Manchester Piccadilly and Oxford Road.[11]

Meanwhile, like so many other places, Manchester had caught the light rail/tramway bug. In 1984 the PTE submitted its light rail plan to parliament. This was to involve the takeover of the Manchester–Bury line from BR in August 1991 and its inclusion in a new light rail system known as Metrolink. In 1992 the line was extended to Piccadilly.[12]

The West Midland PTE also did much to improve services. In December 1976 it signed £460,000 contracts to build, rebuild or reopen four stations as part of the Birmingham Cross City line. It also involved the remodelling of junctions and re-signalling, all carried out over an eighteen-month period on intensively used lines.

An early image of the new nationalised railway system on the front cover of a publicity booklet published in 1951 – 'Festival of Britain' year. The picture is very socialist realist, somewhat in contrast with the title which is in the Wild West 'Playbill' typeface – yeehah, comrade? (Author's collection/ photograph Paul Lund. Permission granted from the National Railway Museum/Science & Society Picture Library to include images of BR material)

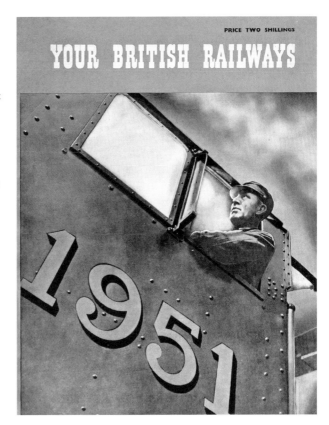

PRICE TWO SHILLINGS

YOUR BRITISH RAILWAYS

1951

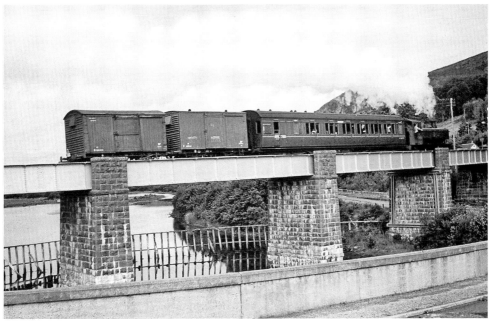

The railway as it was; this is a train on the Dornoch line, Scotland in 1959. It consists of an old LMS brake composite together with a couple of vans. The locomotive is pannier tank 1649; a Great Western design but actually built by BR in 1951. The Dornoch branch was closed less than a year after this photo was taken. (D. Twibell/The Transport Treasury)

This picture is so redolent of the traditional British railway compartment that it is hard to believe that it was taken as recently as 2010 on the Keighley and Worth Valley Railway. The black and white helps, as does the steam rising near the window. This is in a suburban loco-hauled carriage, but once closed compartments – with no connecting corridors – were the rule in all British carriages. (Alan Crawshaw)

The original BR standard carriage – subsequently designated Mk1 – is here represented by a corridor composite preserved on the Bluebell Railway. On this example bogies are of original pattern with leaf springs and static, white metal bearings. Note the swing links in the middle supporting the bolster via coil springs. Beneath the floor of the carriage a vacuum brake cylinder, a battery box and the vehicle's belt-driven dynamo are visible. (John Lewis)

The LNER was the pioneer of camping coaches, old carriages that were life-expired as far as travel use went but were converted into holiday homes. Most of the original camping coaches were scrapped in the Second World War, but BR converted a new generation that operated up until the late 1960s/early 1970s. (Author's collection, photograph Paul Lund. Permission granted from the National Railway Museum/Science & Society Picture Library to include images of BR material)

BRITISH RAILWAYS

CAMPING COACHES
for delightful inexpensive holidays
1955

LIVING ROOM
SCOTTISH REGION
COACH

Camping Coaches provide

- Holidays in specially selected places in England, Scotland and Wales
- Out of doors camping holiday with the comfort of well-appointed living accommodation at reasonable cost
- A cheap and ideal holiday for the family

Apply to the addresses shown under "Location of Coaches and Rental Charges"

A WESTERN REGION
CAMPING COACH

The 'Britannias' were intended to be the top of the line of the standard classes designed by R.A. Riddles (the single 8P *Duke of Gloucester* was a one-off to replace an 8P loco lost in the Harrow and Wealdstone disaster). The 'Britannias' were good, simple machines and did sterling work. Like many of the steam classes, their demise came prematurely. (Ray Vincent/The Transport Treasury)

George Williams objected to the 1956 badge believing that 'debased heraldry' had no place on the side of a modern locomotive. Given that, its presence on the side of this English Electric Type 4 invites the question as to exactly what was modern about the early Type 4s. D208 is seen at Noel Park Goods Depot, Wood Green. (Ray Vincent/The Transport Treasury)

The final main-line hydraulic design for the Western Region were these 2,700hp twin-engine machines built by BR at Swindon and Crewe with Maybach engines and Voith transmissions. The noteworthy body styling was by Misha Black and J. Beresford Evans. D1012 is on the 12 noon to Swansea at Reading, on 18 April 1964. (D. Twibell/The Transport Treasury)

One of the recommendations accepted by the Railway Executive was for the development of lightweight diesel multiple-units for branch lines. For their time they were a radically new design involving integral construction, that is with a load bearing body. This picture, taken at Leith, pre-dates the fitting of window strengthening bars. (J. Robertson/The Transport Treasury)

Dieselisation, particularly the use of diesel multiple-units, was considered as an answer to the problem of uneconomic passenger services, but it proved to be a false hope in many cases. For the modernisation plan large numbers of vehicles were ordered from a number of builders. Here a brand new three-car unit, constructed by Metropolitan-Cammell, is seen at Dundee on 30 May 1959. (George C. Bett/The Transport Treasury)

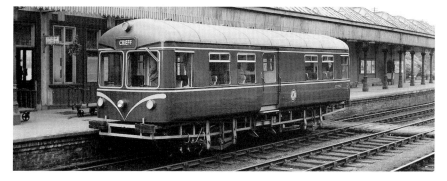

Lightweight railbuses were already in use in Germany, where they also hauled trailers. Many of those built in Britain, like this example, lacked the coupling and buffing gear, and probably the horsepower as well, for hauling either a passenger trailer or a van. This wasn't much use when the railways were still having to service the 1854 Act's requirements to carry goods, but why weren't the railbuses fitted to do the job that was needed? (George C. Bett/The Transport Treasury)

A bit of inspiration from Sir Edmund Hilary (because it's there!) was undoubtedly useful to those trying to board the railbuses from lineside halts. As well as the railbus' own steps – an idea taken from GWR autocoach practice – there is also a spare set of steps available. Clearly, it wouldn't pass the test of being accessible to the disabled. (GNSRA Norris Forrest/The Transport Treasury)

Number 27003 *Diana* at Manchester London Road on 31 May 1966. The early electrifications carried out by BR were leftovers from the LNER schemes aborted due to the war. The 1,500-volt DC system used was abandoned when the 25,000V system was adopted in preference. Photographic evidence suggests that Gresley carriages were regularly used on this, secondary, route, but in this photo the train consists of Mk1 stock in BR maroon. (D. Twibell/ The Transport Treasury)

E3023 on the 2.05 p.m. to Glasgow at Euston on 28 May 1966. For the WCML electrification the BTC commissioned five different prototypes, each produced in batches of ten or more locomotives. The first delivered were from the Birmingham Railway Carriage and Wagon Works and designated AL1, later Class 81. Although the five different designs differed fundamentally in engineering terms they all conformed to the same body styling by Sir Misha Black. (D. Twibell/The Transport Treasury)

The Blue Pullmans were the Design Panel's first real chance to shape a project from the start and they did a very good job with renowned designer Jack Howe creating both the body styling and many of the fixtures and fittings in the passenger compartments. This is one of the Western Region units seen departing Paddington on 22 July 1964. (D. Lindsay/The Transport Treasury)

'Blue Train' at Motherwell on 18 August 1966. The Glasgow Blue Trains were the second project on which the Design Panel had significant influence. It is obvious by the wraparound windows, so beloved of designers of that era. These proved to be a serious liability, being expensive to replace, and in later years were replaced by flat glass and side pillars. (D. Twibell/The Transport Treasury)

D9012 on the up *Tyne-Tees Pullman* at Doncaster on 15 May 1964. The Deltics were the saviours of the East Coast Main Line in lieu of electrification. They were the result of the English Electric Company's purchase of the Napier Company which developed the Deltic engine. There were only twenty-two Deltics and it wasn't really enough. (D. Twibell/The Transport Treasury)

Number 1712 at Paddington on 26 February 1969. This is the diesel that did it – the Type 4 that was finally up to scratch. The Class 47, as it became known under the TOPS classification, became a mainstay of main-line passenger trains and freights from the 1960s onwards. Styling was by E.G.M. Wilkes and followed BR's new preference, set by J.F. Harrison, for flat-fronted locos. (D. Twibell/The Transport Treasury)

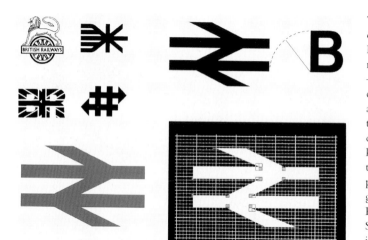

The Corporate Identity Symbol, designed by Gerald Barney of Design Research Unit. The negative version – light-on-dark – is slightly fatter than the dark-on-light version. The top and bottom arms are also flared at the ends. A number of ideas were considered before the CIS as we know it was settled on, as shown top left. (Author's collection/ photograph Paul Lund. Permission granted from the National Railway Museum/Science & Society Picture Library to include images of BR material)

The Rail alphabet, designed by Jock Kinneir and Margaret Calvert, was governed by specific rules relating to the spacing of the letters, each one having its own 'tile'. These were shown in the manual for both upper and lower case. This is the page for the latter, which also shows symbols. (Peter Stanton collection/photograph Paul Lund. Permission granted from the National Railway Museum/Science & Society Picture Library to include images of BR material)

Rail alphabet
Combined sheet - lowercase

| sheet no. | 1/12/1 |
| issued | Sept 1965 |

This sheet must be used for all lettering applications in preference to sheets 1/11 and 1/12

Number 50002 is at Hereford on 9 February 1986. The large logo livery rather suited the Class 50s, but on smaller locomotives it could look a bit unwieldy. The fifty Class 50s were the last diesel locomotives to be built by BR with passenger duty in mind. In fact they were the last true locomotives (defined as producing their own power) built to haul passenger trains by a British railway. (L. Nicolson/The Transport Treasury)

Early Mk2s were not air conditioned and had windows very much like the earlier Mk1s. Mk2A, FK 13462, of 1968 vintage is in NSE livery at Waterloo in 1992. (John Lewis)

The air-conditioned Mk2s are represented by BR Mk2D FO 3188 in InterCity blue/grey livery at Liverpool Street on an unrecorded date. The difference in appearance between this and the earlier Mk2s is all too obvious. It is only the shorter length that enables them to be distinguished from the Mk3s. (John Lewis)

The Mk3 was conceived initially as a loco-hauled coach, yet the first examples into traffic were to be in IC125 sets. The IC125 version was incompatible with loco-hauled coaches due to their special electrics, meaning that they were a somewhat inflexible resource. Number 11922 is an open composite converted from a First open and is on Edinburgh–Glasgow push-pull services. It is in ScotRail livery at Glasgow Queen Street, in July 1990. (John Lewis)

Before there was a prototype APT there was an experimental APT – the APT-E, seen here in graceful retirement at the National Railway Museum at Shildon. At Shildon the APT-E is being restored by a team of volunteers, including some of those who originally worked on the project. (Author's collection/ photograph Paul Lund. Permission granted from the National Railway Museum/Science & Society Picture Library to include images of BR material)

The prototype HST/IC125 seen at York, *circa* April 1973. The design had to be revised due to union objections that there was only a single driving seat. In the end it turned out to be a redesign very much for the better. (53A Models of Hull Collection. D.R. Vickers)

A speciality of the Western Region was mystery tours, starting in the mid-1960s. See the colour section for further images of excursion leaflets and other BR ephemera for recreational journeys. (Author's collection/photograph Paul Lund. Permission granted from the National Railway Museum/Science & Society Picture Library to include images of BR material)

MYSTERY TOUR

BY DIESEL TRAIN ON SUNDAY MAY 30
Over 250 mystery miles ⚡ British Rail Western Region

A magnificent train at a magnificent station; this picture shows newly built power car E43059 at the head of a test train at York prior to the introduction of scheduled services on the ECML. This was Kenneth Grange's final design of the IC125, allowing for two-man crews and eliminating the buffers. This allowed for restyling that causes the air to pass over the top rather than around the sides. (53A Models of Hull Collection. D.R.Vickers)

" Cheerful obedience "

For many years BR published a booklet entitled *British Railways Welcomes You* for new recruits. Different editions differed considerably in tone, varying from Missenden's cosy allusions to BR as a 'family', with cartoons, through to rather more robust, businesslike language. This cartoon is from the early phase. (Author's collection/photograph Paul Lund. Permission granted from the National Railway Museum/Science & Society Picture Library to include images of BR material)

By the 1980s the amount of literature the ticket clerks had to process just to sell a ticket was quite large. The racks of Edmondson tickets may have been abolished but in some ways things were just as complicated. (Author's collection/photograph Paul Lund. Permission granted from the National Railway Museum/Science & Society Picture Library to include images of BR material)

" *Ingenuity* "

Another jolly cartoon from the *British Railways Welcomes You* booklet from the Missenden era. This is very much of the old railway, before things got serious; and when there were still porters to carry your bags. (Author's collection/photograph Paul Lund. Permission granted from the National Railway Museum/Science & Society Picture Library to include images of BR material)

This is the front cover of a 1958 BTC booklet for telephone switchboard operators, covering such matters as the equipment, how to speak properly and standard expressions to be used. Most – if not all – telephone switchboard operators would have been women but nevertheless a man is seen here on the front cover. (Author's collection/photograph Paul Lund. Permission granted from the National Railway Museum/Science & Society Picture Library to include images of BR material)

BR's first essay in Southern commuter stock was the 4-EPB (electro-pneumatic brakes). Essentially this was a continuation of the 4-SUB construction programme but with BR control gear and a slightly different front end. This version of the EPB was a hybrid from the start, also featuring a mix of open and compartment carriages. In the 1980s units were re-formed to eliminate the compartments; 5486 is of the new number series that resulted. (John Lewis)

Shame of the Southern electric system was the Mk1 EMU stock built as late as 1974 and which lasted into the twenty-first century. Nevertheless, the 4-VEPs particularly did sturdy work as the region's backbone semi-fast vehicle. Some of us still remember them with fondness. In Network SouthEast livery at Wandsworth Road, 4-VEP 423 3570 is seen in January 1995. (John Lewis)

With the 455 the Southern Region at last got some decent inner-suburban units of its very own – to keep (albeit that they were bolstered by some left behind trailers from the 508s). Many of the old timers from the 1950s were still going strong at privatisation, though. (John Lewis)

Number 142 023 shows off the Regional Railways branding at Rochdale on
3 November 1993. A BR internal document said that the 'fleximark' (the thin blue
stripes visible on the side of the cab) would 'stamp itself indelibly on the mind of
the customer'. (John Lewis)

The Express Cross-Country Sprinters were initially troublesome but settled down
to provide high-quality cross-country services with air conditioning – a far cry
from their rattling predecessors, whether multiple-units or loco-hauled coaches.
(John Lewis)

Traditionally the railways had aimed prestige services at the business market. The leaflet
on the left, advertising named trains on the Western Region and dating from 1963,
is a continuation of that policy. The advent of Inter-City and time-interval services
necessitated an appeal to a wider market – Inter-City was for everyone. By the 1980s
pressure to make a profit led to renewed efforts to sell premium services. (Author's
collection/photograph Paul Lund. Permission granted from the National Railway
Museum/Science & Society Picture Library to include images of BR material)

Not a locomotive, despite the appearance, but the Mk4 driving trailer brake van of an IC225. On the East Coast Main Line British Rail implemented a push-pull system with a locomotive hauling the carriages in one direction and propelling them in the other – being driven in 'reverse' from unpowered vehicles. Picture taken at King's Cross in 1991. (John Lewis)

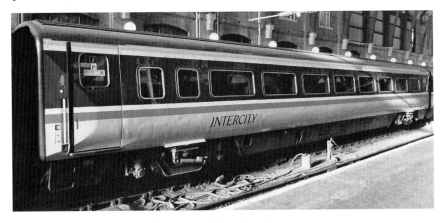

The Mk4s were built specifically for the ECML electrification and were the last loco-hauled coaches to be designed and built by BR. In fact they were the last loco-hauled coaches built for use within the British mainland. Now the multiple-unit's dominance is all but total. This Mk4 is a First Open, seen in *InterCity* livery at King's Cross in 1991. (John Lewis)

'Bring Back British Rail' is a campaign group whose stated aims are to restore the railways to public ownership so that they will be run for the benefit of the public and without public funds subsidising private profits. Demo at Waterloo in August 2011. (Robin Prime)

One of the stations, 'University', was completely new and serves Birmingham University and Queen Elizabeth Hospital. The line was opened by William Rodgers, Minister of Transport, on 8 May 1978.[13] Given that the line crossed the West Coast Main Line it made sense that it should be electrified. This did not happen until the 1990s, though, with the final switch-on happening on 12 July 1992. Even then it was not a total triumph. The planned new 323 EMUs had such serious teething troubles that older units had to operate the service until the problems with the new ones could be ironed out.[14]

In Strathclyde the PTE began with big plans for the region's railway system. There was, of course, the modernisation of the Glasgow Underground which had already been approved in principle before the creation of the PTE, but which it was to oversee. Glasgow is the only city in the UK apart from London to have its own Underground – this is outside the scope of this book, since the system was never operated by BR, but the information is worth noting.

Under the agreement struck with British Rail, the Greater Glasgow PTE funded all of the BR electrified services even where they extended beyond the boundaries of the PTE. This was done entirely from local funds and revenue, but a transitional grant to ease in the PTE was made by the government. This was reduced by degrees during the period 1975 to 1979, whereupon the PTE was in for a bit of a shock – a matter I will return to in Chapter 11.[15]

The partnership with BR meant that the GG logo was applied to the sides of the trains in addition to the CIS. It was also in addition to the original Glasgow electrification symbol and resulted in an untidy confusion of identities. The logo 'Trans-Clyde' was also adopted for use on the sides of multiple-units adjacent to the 'GG' (Greater Glasgow) symbol.

In autumn 1973 Greater Glasgow Transportation Study and British Rail published the *Clyderail Plan*, which outlined further electrifications and reopening of lines. This included the opening of two cross-city link lines: the Central Low Level connecting Rutherglen with Stobcross, and a Shields Road–St Johns link. Only one of these has so far been completed, that between Rutherglen and Stobcross, brought into use in November 1981.[16]

The West Yorkshire PTE (WYPTE) assumed financial responsibility for the rail services in its area from 1976 but it wasn't until 29 November 1978 that a formal signing for a Section 20 agreement took place.[17] This event, attended by Peter Parker himself, marked the end of a period of evaluation and negotiation between the two sides and culminated in a plan for major improvements to rail services in the area, including integration with the PTE's bus services. WYPTE accepted responsibility for all the local rail services in its area with the exception of the line through Pontefract and Moorthorpe – primarily part of the Sheffield–York line – and the single branch to Clayton West, subsequently closed to passengers in January 1983.[18]

New timetables planned by the PTE now placed an emphasis on even-time services and integration with its own bus as well as Inter-City services. Stations were given a makeover and the DMU fleet refurbished.[19]

Previous cuts in services had left no-go areas for trains in even populous areas of West Yorkshire and, like other PTEs, WYPTE began a programme of reopening stations and building completely new ones for areas that had not had a rail service before. One of the major successes of the PTE was to be the electrification of Leeds/Bradford–Ilkley/Skipton services. This was completed in 1995 and funded by both the PTE and BR.[20]

In March 1978 the South Yorkshire Passenger Transport Executive (SYPTE) signed a Section 20 agreement to run the lines between Sheffield and Barnsley/Darton, Rotherham, Doncaster/Thorne and to Kiveton Park. The agreement included the rebranding of South Yorkshire rail services as 'Link-Line'.[21] Railways were a smaller proportion of this PTE's activities compared with the other PTEs and it has been known largely as a bus PTE. The creation of the Sheffield Supertram might be regarded as them hedging their bets. This was first suggested in the early 1970s and finally opened in stages from 1994 – partially along the alignment of a freight railway line.[22] Two other significant developments were the Swinton and Meadowhall interchanges. The construction of the four-platform Swinton Interchange was accompanied by the construction of a £6.4 million curve linking the previously separate Dearne Valley and Doncaster lines. The new station enabled passengers to change from one line to another and, with a fifty-space park-and-ride car park, enabled road users to join the rail network. The Meadowhall Interchange was part of a new retail complex that was built on a former steelworks, 3 miles from Sheffield city centre. The station lay on the routes to Doncaster and Barnsley and was built at a cost of £7.5 million.[23]

BR might not always have got on with the PTEs but the relationship between WYPTE and SYPTE also provides a classic example of PTEs not co-operating.

When BR closed the Woodhead route in 1981 it left WYPTE and SYPTE in a quandary. The route was used by services funded by both the PTEs as it ran from Huddersfield in the WYPTE area to Sheffield in the SYPTE area. It was against BR policy to use its PSO grant to subsidise infrastructure within PTE areas, meaning that the whole cost of running the line fell to the two PTEs. But at a TUCC inquiry a bright idea was suggested: to route services through Barnsley instead. It was a longer journey but it would avoid the costs of subsidising a route for just one set of services. An experimental period was agreed, scheduled to end in May 1984. At this point WYPTE got cold feet, though, fearing that it would be left funding the stub of the old Woodhead route if things went awry. In May 1983 it issued a one-year notice of its intention to withdraw its funding for services to Denby Dale, right at the border. Fortunately this wrangle was resolved and the experiment proved successful, even increasing the ridership of the route.[24]

Ever since they were set up the PTEs have done excellent work in integrating and improving the lives of the people who travel within their areas. The proof of this surely lies in the fact that the youngest ones are now heading for their fiftieth birthdays, despite many political changes in local government. The PTEs themselves have been retained by successive governments of different political persuasions.

Outside of the PTE areas BR's unremunerative services were funded directly from government. From 1968 to 1974 this was done as a tedious, route-by-route business, with the secretary of state deciding which line was worthy or not. After 1974, when the law was brought into line with EU legislation, BR was refunded for running such services with a general Public Service Grant. This led to some confusion as to how was BR to follow the injunction to break even, and then to be compensated for running services. It didn't make sense. Not surprisingly, there were not too many big projects outside of the PTE areas. Most major changes were simplification – in other words cheapening of infrastructure. Members of staff were withdrawn from many stations as the use of Pay-Trains increased.

One issue that was to confront BR and the PTEs was that of the age of the DMU fleet. Yes, it may have seemed like five minutes ago since the modernisation plan but by 1975 it had been twenty years since its inception, and some of the DMUs resulting from the RE's plan had been in service since that time or earlier. The age of the DMU fleet was of concern to the PTEs. As we have seen, it deterred the Tyneside PTE from investing in the BR option and encouraged them to go it alone.

In 1974 British Rail unveiled a plan to refurbish the existing DMU fleet. One of the 1959 Metro-Cammell units was given a full overhaul at Doncaster works and was then subjected to to alternative treatments, termed 'low cost' and 'medium cost' options (it is not quite clear what the high-cost option would have been – a new DMU perhaps?). The low-cost option involved new seat covers, new linoleum for the floors, new carpets and curtains in first class, and replacing old-style lighting with fluorescent lights.

The medium-cost option included the above and in addition the replacing of first-class seats with Inter-City 70 seats, replacing wall panels with melamine ones and the addition of new features to upgrade the carriage, as well as water heating.

In July 1974 the refurbished unit set out on a three-month tour to gauge the views of the PTEs and other interested groups. It was decked out in the new, but rather impractical, white with blue band livery.[25]

In 1975 the board ordered a full programme of refurbishment for DMUs and spent £13 million in renovating 1,600 vehicles.[26] In 1976 the decision was taken to re-engine the facelifted DMUs as well, because spares were no longer available for the original ones.[27]

Such was the nature of the social railway.

As said previously, the passenger parts of the commercial railway were the trunk route services that had been branded as Inter-City in the 1960s. The trouble with

Inter-City was that by the 1970s it was increasingly difficult to pin down what it was, apart from being a regular service from city centre to city centre. In some places, particularly the South East, that was nothing particularly new. The quality of rolling stock provided was the most variable aspect. The latest air-conditioned top-of-the-line Mk2 carriages on the WCML were substantially different in quality from the rattling electric multiple-units that served the South Coast from terminals like Waterloo, yet all had come into the Inter-City brand in the attempt to capitalise on it and establish it as a network. In truth, much of it was the same old railway, old wine in new wine skins, trying to provide what service it could with what it had. As we have seen, even where the latest carriages were on offer, they had to run with old Mk1 catering carriages. There were also some mysteries: for instance the boundary of the Inter-City network stopped at Plymouth, so did services on the West of England Main Line miraculously change into normal ones, like Cinderella at the stroke of midnight, when passing onwards to Penzance?[28]

Of course, Inter-City was, in the 1960s and 1970s, just a brand. It had no separate management and no separate control of rolling stock or fares. Fares were fixed at board level but the regions had some discretion on fare offers. This led to a variety of different publicity initiatives from the regions to sell different products under a number of brands, such as Merrymaker and Awayday.

To add to the confusion there was of course also the old Pullman brand. This had been continued under the IC brand through the Pullman carriages introduced on the West Coast Main Line in the 1960s. By the 1970s, however, there was much less difference between a Pullman carriage and the later versions of the Mk2 carriage that now offered air conditioning to first- and standard-class passengers alike. There were of course still Pullmans rattling around the network that didn't even have air conditioning, but their days were to be numbered.

The Mk2 Pullmans were to be the very last purpose-built Pullmans. The WCML electrification was to prove the economic value of intensively used, standardised sets and the Pullmans were in conflict with this plan. Although they were profitable, they were not as profitable as the standard sets and a recommendation was made that they were only to be used at peak time. This, of course, diminished their earnings value.[29] There were enough problems finding a one-size-fits-all solution with the ordinary stock as morning, daytime and evening services vary in their make-up regarding class. There had been cases when there was a shortage of first-class seats that had left business passengers standing.[30]

In the early 1970s the showpiece diesel Pullmans of the modernisation era were withdrawn after just fourteen years of life. The worn out electric multiple-units of the *Brighton Belle*, much older at forty years, were also withdrawn in 1972 and replaced in service by ordinary Mk1 multiple-units.

As stated earlier, the introduction of the Mk2 air-conditioned units was a serious upgrading of quality for British Rail. Britain was now in the vanguard of passenger comfort with the first non-supplement, all-classes, air-conditioned trains in Europe. Of course, they were just the start in a decade which saw BR regain the laurels for excellence in high speed and passenger comfort due to the HST – or, as it was branded when launched, the Inter-City 125.

The first public service by a production Inter-City 125 was made on 4 October 1976. It made the television news that day and the passengers shown being interviewed were enthusiastic and complimentary.[31] There were not yet enough sets for a full 125 service – that had to wait until the next year – but from then nowhere outside of Japan had a superior railway service to that running from Paddington to Bristol, and what was more, BR had managed to do it on a railway that was approaching its 140th birthday.

As passenger appreciation became evident through ticket sales, a new term was coined for the effect of the IC125. After the 'sparks' effect of the WCML, there was now the 'nose-cone effect'.

Interestingly, BR had had some qualms about marketing the 125. A major concern had been that ordinary passengers might think that the 125 was too luxurious for them. High speed had always been sold as a premium product, often with a supplement, but now it was to be for the masses and people had to be convinced that it was just an ordinary train.[32] A brochure for the 125 once more emphasised the Inter-City ethos stating under the heading 'Value for Money': 'British Rail decided that money for replacement and improvement should not be spent on a few crack trains, but should instead be used in such a way as to provide improvements in speed and comfort for all customers on its main services.'[33]

When it was launched on the ECML, BR released an information pack for its staff which included an amusing set of dos and don'ts. Representatives were urged to think of the type of passenger and how the 125 might meet their individual needs. For example:

Don't sell speed regardless of your customer. Not every 70-year-old granny likes the idea of travelling at 125mph. But she will benefit from the 125 because it's quicker, smoother and less tiring.

Don't sell features in technical detail unless you're sure you're talking to a railway enthusiast.

Do 'sell the three Cs' of the 125.

More comfort, better catering. More care for our customers.

Most importantly:

Do take the opportunity to sell extras connected with the 125. Like hotels, car hire, Inter-City travel goods.

Don't always settle for just selling a ticket.

The need to provide the fast, high-frequency, regular-interval service experience meant that BR needed HSTs in squadron numbers if the timetable was to be entirely speeded up. But despite their excellence and initial success the IC125s were slow coming online. Originally BR had wanted as many as 161 sets being built at a rate of thirty to forty a year, but its 1972 Report and Accounts were more restrained, projecting a mere seventy. At some point the number coalesced into a projected requirement for 105, of which only ninety-five were actually built. In May 1978 the East Coast Main Line got its first taste of IC125 running; at this point there were not enough to make up a full schedule and conventional trains filled in. This showed up the desirability of the new trains with the public though, as people were prepared to stand on the new trains whereas there were seats to spare in the older ones. The next proposal was for the long-neglected cross-country north-east to south-west services between Cardiff, Bristol and Leeds, York, Newcastle and Edinburgh. These units were not to come online until 1981, with a full service not until May 1982.[34]

Another thing that the HSTs brought with them was a new generation of catering vehicles. Apart from the Mk2 Pullman vehicles the construction of new catering stock had skipped the second generation of BR coaches entirely; incorporating old Mk1 catering cars into the HST sets was simply not an option.

The choice of open saloons for both first and second class meant that there was no longer a need to marshal specific open vehicles next to the catering cars to serve as restaurants. Now the passengers could eat at the seats they would occupy throughout the entire journey, only leaving them to purchase food or use the loo. The first catering vehicles within the HST sets were classed as 'TRUKs' – standing for trailer restaurant unclassified kitchen. They had twenty-four seats in a single saloon which was laid out as first class with first-class-style seats, but were in fact for both classes – hence unclassified. Microwave and 'Microaire' ovens were installed as well as the famous griddle in the buffet. They were also the first catering vehicle in Britain to provide *draught* beer and lager.

According to the staff information pack: 'Prices are reasonable – toasted steaklet costs about 28p, sausage egg and chips about 60p, a pizza about 55p. A cup of tea is 12p … '

Very reasonable!

The blurb continued: 'The buffet car has its own "pub", a bright social area where passengers can drink and talk. The buffet car also has a separate microphone into the public address system, enabling the Chief Steward to advise passengers of the range of Travellers' (sic) Fare facilities available … ' The pack also promised a trolley service, but that was still a fraught issue with the unions and would have to wait for a later date.

Until 1973 on-board catering did not have a snappy brand name, but in that year customers were asked to choose one from a range of names presented to them by a management consultant. The one that they chose was 'Travellers-Fare'[35] (which really should have an apostrophe either before or after the 's', depending on whether it refers to single or multiple travellers). Despite the grammatical flaw, the name was to grace the catering services of BR for much of the rest of its existence. The newly named Travellers-Fare organisation was already in the middle of spending a £5 million grant from the board to refurbish some of its facilities.[36]

The nature of British catering had changed since the 1950s. The days of 'meat and two veg' followed by stodgy pudding and a slice of custard, washed down by tea tasting of dishwater were fast disappearing. New waves of immigrants were bringing a culture of more palatable food with them, while membership of the European Community also meant a more adventurous cuisine was sought. In the face of this, railway catering needed to change. One example of this was at Liverpool Street, where in 1973 two of the old tearooms were knocked into one and turned into a bistro serving Continental dishes. This was a big hit and attracted diners from the city offices. As had long been the case on the Continent, railway cuisine wasn't just for travellers, any more than foreign food was just for posh restaurants. It was competing with the local restaurant trade – but hopefully some of those who got a look at the station were then tempted to risk the trains too.[37] Meanwhile, BR was to improve the quality of the beer available at its station buffets. The 'real ale' movement led to the bars of forty stations providing it throughout the country by 1978. Twenty of these were in London. The licensing trade were dismayed to find BR offering coupons for 2p off a pint, and this provoked an 'angry reaction'.[38]

One solution to the difficulty of making hot drinks quickly and efficiently was to buy in a range of instant drinks of the 'just-add-water' variety. As a solution BR switched to serving the Max-Pax range of instant drinks on its trains. There were regular complaints over these from travellers and the bodies who represented them, but at the same time they did increase sales – in 1977, 13.2 million cups of tea and coffee sold over the previous best-ever figure of 5 million. The total takings were £1.17 million. It is not clear whether the drinks were cheaper or whether they enabled greater throughput of custom or simply availability, but improved stock control was said to have been obtained.[39]

Being an even-time service with many scheduled services throughout the day, Inter-City had many seats to fill; regularity was a selling point but also required utilisation to justify it. Thus BR turned to the traditional schemes to try to encourage people to travel off-peak by special offers, promotions and excursions. Now, though, there was to be a focus on brands and marketing techniques. Television advertising was often used, but there were also more mundane options such as leaflets at stations and even door-to-door leafleting. In 1981 Hugh Jenkins, Divisional Manager at Stoke, and his Passenger Manager Ian Brown took to the streets of the town, clad in sandwich boards to advertise the £9 'London Saver'.[40]

One experiment launched in 1977 was the Big City Saver. Initially these were tickets sold for return travel between London and Glasgow for just £15. In the first six months of the offer over 50,000 such tickets were sold, marketing research indicating that over half that number were sold to people who would have chosen other transport modes but for the offer. With this influx of new business due to the scheme, it was extended from 2 October to Edinburgh–King's Cross and also to a number of points in between London and the Scottish cities.[41]

Surely the most iconic BR brand was the Awayday. This had its origins on the Southern Region in 1972.[42] Originally it offered savings of up to 35 per cent in the pound. Colour TV commercials featuring a cartoon family were broadcast on the London ITV channel and Southern Television, supported, of course, by the usual paraphernalia of press advertising, posters and leaflets. Awayday was really just a new name for the old cheap day return but it was less of a mouthful and suggested – well, an enjoyable day rather than a cheap and possibly nasty day. It was a good piece of rebranding. In 1976 more than 93 million Awayday return tickets were sold.[43]

BR also started teaming up with a number of commercial organisations to pro-mote rail travel. The first and most long-running of these relationships was with Kellogg's, the breakfast cereal manufacturer. The first offer, valid until 14 June 1975, saw two million special cereal packets distributed in Wales and the south-west. By collecting six tokens a free ticket could be obtained for a child accompanied by a paying passenger. The offer was repeated with national availability in 1976. This offer led to 800,000 applications for free tickets. In 1977 it was repeated, with over 1.2 million vouchers being issued via the scheme.[44] Given this success it is not surprising that others wanted to get in on the act.

From October 1976 to June 1977 a voucher – obtained by redemption of cer-tain Co-op product labels – enabled a child to travel free with an adult with certain restrictions. In July–August 1976 the *Daily Mirror* contained tokens that could be exchanged for up to two accompanied children to travel free on any Awayday or weekend journey. In 1978 prospective travellers could exchange Heinz labels for a travel voucher worth £1 which, with £4 cash added, could be used to purchase an exchange voucher worth £5. There was no refund if a ticket worth less than £5 was purchased with the voucher; however, there was no limit to the number of vouchers that could be applied for.[45] Other big names involved in BR promotions were Lever Brothers with its Persil brand and, as late as 1991–92, Boots.[46]

For many the 1970s will be remembered as the last full decade in which the cheap excursion flourished. Indeed, it gained a new impetus in the late 1960s and 1970s, as well as new brand names. In 1965 the West of England division of the Western Region found there was a market for mystery tours by train. By 1969 they ran thirty in total. The Cardiff division joined in and started running its own mystery excursions. It led to a rethink on the whole excursion market within the divisions, resulting in the re-pricing of existing trips to traditional destinations such as the illuminations at Blackpool.[47]

On the London Midland they revamped the excursion with the launch of the Merrymaker. The Merrymaker was a by-product of the electrification of the West Coast Main Line in the 1960s that came from the recognition that the higher speeds now put many more places in range of a daily excursion. The idea was to encourage parties to book a whole coach in special excursion trains. Merrymakers were promoted by leaflets at stations, the traditional advertising having been dropped as costly and ineffectual. This meant that regular travellers were now being targeted to make further use of the railway they were already familiar with.

It all really took off in 1971, when fifty-five Merrymaker excursions were run from various parts of the London division carrying 22,000 passengers. Destinations included trips to Liverpool, Skegness, York, Canterbury, Windermere, Chester, Rhyl, Ryde on the Isle of Wight, and also a mystery trip. In 1973–74, 173 trains were run, but that represented a peak. As the paths of the WCML were increasingly filled as regular electric trains to Glasgow started, it became obvious that too many Merrymakers were being offered for the market. By 1980 there were only fifty-five, as in 1971. The emphasis was now placed on selling block bookings for excursions within existing timetabled trains but still, in 1981, 1,500 different Merrymaker products were on offer and it was estimated that 40,000 had travelled by Merrymakers in 1980 – 480,000 since the scheme began.

Soon advantage was being taken of the Awayday brand to offer excursions and inevitably there was going to be confusion between the Merrymaker and the Awayday outing; this was conceded on a 1974 leaflet which advertised 'Awayday Merry-makers [sic]'. Another Merrymaker leaflet of 1975 was overlaid with the strap 'Awayday Special Bargains'. The Eastern Region had also come up with its own brand of excursions – the 'Happy Wanderers'.

Another option was given the unfortunate name of The Britainshrinkers, operated by Road 'n' Rail Tours Ltd in co-operation with British Rail.

By now the vehicle commonly used for the special excursion trains was the veteran Mk1 coach. These would be non-refurbished vehicles of some twenty-five years' vintage and were passing their sell-by date by the early 1980s, particularly when compared with the new air-conditioned coaches, or with modern motor cars or road coaches.

Sports events had long had their own special excursions but in the 1970s and 1980s the so called 'Footex' trains became notorious for the amount of vandalism perpetrated. Television news carried images of wrecked carriages with smashed windows. Perhaps this is why BR provided football fans with their own train – the 'League Liner Train', which had at least one dedicated carriage. It had converted a Mk1 Second Open into a saloon discotheque called the 'Kick-off disco' for use in football excursions. It had the windows plated over and was equipped with disco lights and murals along the walls that looked like they had been done by a five-year-old with crayons. The legend 'Kick-off disco' was written in 1970s 'funky' letters on the side of the carriage rather than 'Rail' alphabet.[48]

Despite the trouble, BR was keen on the football business and in autumn 1978 launched a drive to attract more of it. By that time the bill for vandalism had dropped from £100,000 just three seasons before to a mere £1,000 the previous season. A booklet was sent out to supporters' clubs which focused mainly on the opportunities for charter trains, something that had not been taken up very much at that time. The booklet included the names of BR Special Football Liaison Officers. Measures to be taken to prevent further trouble included the assigning of the same group of police officers to the fans each time they travelled (to enable 'mutual respect' to be fostered) and the labelling of the carriages with the organisers' names – not that of the club – so as to avoid gatecrashers.[49]

By the early 1970s it had become plain that Beeching had been right to launch his cull of the holiday summer-relief services. The car and cheap package holidays abroad ate heavily into the holiday market and British Rail was having trouble filling the seats on the remaining holiday area services, particularly off-peak. In the late 1940s and early 1950s BR held around 50 per cent of the domestic holiday travel market, but by the late 1960s that had declined to a mere 11 per cent. It was mentioned in Chapter 3 that camping coaches were things of the past by 1971, but British Rail still appreciated that inclusive holidays – booking a package of rail travel and accommodation together – could be attractive, and offering this was a viable way to sell rail travel. Thus in 1971 Golden Rail was introduced to offer just that.[50]

The name Golden Rail undoubtedly indicates its primary target market as the over sixties. In its first year British Rail operated it in conjunction with SAGA. One fifth of Golden Rail travellers paid a supplement to travel first class, comparing well with the 10 per cent/90 per cent first-class/second-class split for BR's customers as a whole.

The basis of Golden Rail was that BR did not own the accommodation, which was at comparatively modest privately owned establishments such as small hotels and guest houses, although Golden Rail was eventually to branch out into self-catering flats and caravans. Originally accommodation was not booked in advance of sales and this led to some complaints about the slowness of confirming bookings compared to foreign packages, where hotels were pre-booked in blocks. Later on, with the brand established and the popularity proven, establishments pre-allocated accommodation for Golden Rail. It proved successful, and by 1973 was offering holidays by rail at thirty-three resorts and the service had, in BR's words, moved into 'full profitability'.[51] By 1975 the number of Golden Rail resorts had risen to forty-three, including Ayr, Fort William and the Lake District. In 1974, 90,000 people took Golden Rail holidays and many more bookings had to be refused due to a lack of accommodation.[52] In 1980 Golden Rail catered for 139,000 holidaymakers.[53]

As well as the corporate promotions, the 1970s was also the era of one of BR's greatest marketing strategies, a legacy that has outlived BR. This was the Railcard: a piece of identification that enabled discount travel through the course of a specified time period (usually one year). For this BR took a sum of money in advance, which it kept even if you never used a train. It was a good idea that doubtless encouraged many onto the rails, and to keep coming back, just to get their money's worth out of the card. The Student Railcard – later known as the Young Person Railcard – was the first of these, being introduced in January 1974. It followed a series of promotions in which young people were given discount travel on production of some proof of their age, such as an NUS card. This cost an incredible £1.65 in 1970s money. It was issued by National Union of Students' offices and featured a passport-sized photo of the purchaser. It allowed the holder to purchase a second-class single or an ordinary return at half price, subject to a minimum fare.[54]

Next came the Senior Citizen Railcard, introduced on 1 April 1975.[55] In the first year 206,000 were sold[56] and by 1979 there were 1 million, accounting for £60 million's worth of revenue for BR.[57] There were also 720,000 Student Railcards issued.[58]

With such a marketing success BR sought to extend the railcard concept to other areas and turned its attention to the family. The International Year of the Child in 1979 led BR to raise the minimum age at which children pay fares from 3 to 5 years old, and also to introduce a new club for 5- to 14-year-olds to encourage them to travel by rail – and doubtless to encourage (nag?) their parents to do so as well. This club was first known as the Great Rail Club – although the name was later changed to Railriders. Members received a regular magazine together with vouchers for reduced rail travel.[59]

It was recognised that while many wish to travel as a family group it could be prohibitively expensive to do so when individual fairs are totted up. Thus was born the idea of the Family Railcard. This was initially priced at £16[60] and by the end of October 1979 BR had sold 60,000[61] of them. In October 1980 BR reduced the price to £5, as the expiry date was fixed at the end of February 1981.

Compared to the Student and Senior Citizen railcards the uptake of the Family Railcard was slow and might have been seen as disappointing, but BR was determined to press on and it entered a second year, and then continued. In 1980 BR claimed that it was generating around £2.5 million worth of ticket sales and that 30 per cent of this represented new business.[62] The aim of the Family Railcard was to get families out of their cars and onto the railway, whereas the previous cards were aimed at people who habitually used rail but were probably encouraged to do so more by the possession of a discount card.

In 1981, the International Year of the Disabled, British Rail decided to introduce a Disabled Persons Railcard, although it wasn't until September of that year that it appeared. Apparently the delay was caused by BR needing to gain verification of the disabled status of applicants, finally organising for this to be provided by the Post Office. This was presumably because of some of the conditions of eligibility, which were: receiving Attendance or Mobility Allowance,

War Pensioners Mobility Supplement, Industrial Disablement Benefit, War or Service Disability Pension for 80 per cent or more disability, as well as users of a DHSS motor car or a three-wheel invalid car. Alternatively, British Rail could also check status with the Department of Health and Social Security (DHSS). Initially the railcard cost £10 and allowed the holder and a travelling companion half price on Awayday tickets, ordinary singles and returns. In 1983 the price was raised to £12.[63]

The MkIII was the first British Railway vehicle to have purpose-built accommodation for the wheelchair-bound as standard. At the end of each first-class saloon a removable seat and table meant that space could be provided for a wheelchair (advance notice was required). From 13 July 1975 the disabled passenger and their companion were charged only the price of the second-class single fare to travel on such trains, whilst those who still had to travel in the guard's van due to lack of accommodation were charged, along with their companion, only half the second-class single fare.[64] For some reason these arrangements only applied to non-motorised wheelchairs.

In 1975 BR had published, in conjunction with the Central Council for the Disabled, a guide for travelling on BR. It gave general information on travelling by rail and also contained details of 281 principal stations covering parking, refreshments and lavatory facilities. It was available free from the Central Council for the Disabled apart from a 25p fee for postage and packing. In 1979 a much expanded edition was published in conjunction with the Royal Association for Disability and Rehabilitation (RADAR), the successor organisation to the Central Council for the Disabled.

By the end of the 1970s BR had amassed a strong portfolio of marketing tools. It was going to need them as the new Conservative government, which swept into power in 1979, was going to press the case ever more strongly for BR to function as a commercial organisation. At the same time the deregulation of long-distance coaches and the expansion of the motorway network were to present a serious threat to BR's core Inter-City business.

9

Serving the Public Right

It was not many years after the Society [ASLEF] was formed that the idea of
nationalisation was first discussed. In those far off times it seemed an impossible
dream. Nationalisation, they believed, would be the Utopia where they would
work for themselves, and their fellow workers and their country; where they
would have some control over the way they worked, be paid a decent wage,
and all under first class conditions. Now, in 1948 it seemed as if that dream was
about to come true.[1]

The creation of the publicly owned railway by a supposedly socialist government
may have been welcomed by many ordinary railway workers but it was not to
bring an end to industrial strife on the railways. What is more, the unification,
then the rationalisation, of the transport system was to mean cuts in jobs – many
of them. British Railways was to oversee the biggest downsizing of the railway
workforce in the history of the British railway system, from almost 650,000 in
1948 to *circa* 121,000 in 1994. Meanwhile, the pay of railwaymen was to dip below
that of their private sector colleagues to the point where some were regarded
as living in poverty. Some of the jobs 'lost' were in divisions that were separated
out or sold, such as the National Freight Corporation; but that should not dis-
guise the fact that the majority were jobs on the railway itself. From the time of
Beeching staff were paid off with generous redundancy settlements, meaning that
there was little union opposition.[2]

The effect for passengers was a decline in overall service. There were fewer
members of staff around dedicated to helping the customers: fewer porters, fewer
booking clerks, and fewer people to help you with queries. Fewer with genuine
authority down on the ground to sort out customers' problems.

In this chapter I am going to look at some of the issues behind BR staff
policy, but it is important to remember that there were plenty of people doing
good jobs on the nationalised railway – in many aspects it was a success –

a fundamental contention of this book. It should also be firmly argued that there were plenty of employees who were capable of doing, and would have been willing to do, a good job for the public had they been properly supported, trained – and paid.

In terms of recruitment the nationalised railway was operating in a very different world to its predecessors. The war had disrupted the tradition of young people following family members into working for the railways, while the number of people available for work meant there was a genuine skills shortage. The railways were losing out due to poor pay, unsocial hours and the general poor image of railway workplaces, perceived as dark and dirty.[3] BR insiders were aware that they were being sent the dregs of the Labour Exchanges (Job Centres), which, in the view of Michael Bonavia, should not have been involved in railway recruitment at all.[4]

To remedy this the BTC commissioned a report from Stanley Raymond which was presented in March 1956.[5] Amongst his recommendations was the setting up of recruitment offices in each centre of population and the appointment of a recruitment officer for each region. He also wanted to see a General Railway Apprenticeship scheme. This would attract into the wages grades 'some of the best boys'[6] leaving the technical schools between the ages of 15 and 16. The apprenticeship would give them a thorough grounding in the railway business and a chance to experience work in various roles. After six months they would be given the opportunity to decide on their future course: whether to go into the motive power or the operating department. The scheme envisaged a planned career with a line of promotion out of the wages grades – ambitions that had not been encouraged or aided previously.[7]

Nothing came of the General Railway Apprenticeship scheme. According to Michael Bonavia this was because 'various difficulties arose' and he commented that 'if the scheme were confined to a fairly limited grouping of functions in the traffic field, it would be easier to administer and would probably arouse less opposition from the trade unions'.[8]

In the early 1970s a report on recruitment at Surbiton found very much the same procedures operating as had been in place twenty years before. Recruitment was still taking place on a local basis with applicants applying through the local Labour Exchange and being interviewed by the station master. Many of these applicants were found to be unsuitable. The report's author doubted that the station master had suitable training to carry out such interviews,[9] echoing the Raymond report from fourteen years earlier which had recognised that interviewing and recruitment were specialised skills.[10] At a higher level, the Southern Region had turned to a recruitment agency that had succeeded in finding more suitable applicants.[11] In the early 1980s the Equal Opportunities Commission (EOC) examined BR recruitment. Even this late the Commission was to find that whilst candidates were expected to work for a lifetime in the railways they were not expected to view it as a career. Although managers and supervisors were expected to start in the lowest grades, promotion was by seniority until the management grades were reached, when 'suitability' became more important. The EOC found that BR assessed its own recruitment policy as 'insufficiently professional'.[12]

If recruitment was poor, then training was equally haphazard. According to the EOC report, the amount and quality of training received depended on what role the individual had been recruited for; if for the footplate, train or signalling grades, there were a large number of courses and passing these was essential for entrants to get the job. Others, destined to be porters or ticket collectors, were simply shown around the station and/or given basic instructions by their supervisor. They might at some stage be sent on a course, but this clearly wasn't deemed essential.[13]

On the Scottish Region it was the habit to put new entrants straight on to answering telephone enquiries – surely an indicator as to the priority given to customers. This was stopped in the early 1980s as part of the 'ScotRail revolution'.[14]

The most damning critique of BR's recruitment came from Anthony Hidden, who saw BR's recruitment and industrial relations as the root cause of the Clapham accident. He singled out the fact that BR promoted from within its own workforce rather than recruiting from outside.[15] This was the result of an agreement with the NUR and Hidden was critical of both management and unions, not to mention the evident level of distrust between them.[16] Hidden was also critical of the small size of the workforce available to BR and the remuneration packages available to attract and retain good staff.[17]

One recommendation that was taken up early was for a management training scheme. BR had inherited such a scheme from the LNER which was very extensive. This took university graduates, and those with promise, from the railways ranks and gave them a three-year introduction into all the departments of the railway as traffic apprentices. The LNER scheme had been imitated, less enthusiastically, by the other pre-nationalisation companies.[18]

Following Raymond's recommendations the British Transport Staff College was set up at Woking in 1959. It was based in the former Southern Railway School at Gorse Hill, whose amenities were upgraded and a residential block added. Michael Bonavia was the first Director of Studies. The college had three main aims. Firstly to improve the performance of those sent there – they were young and of middle-manager status. Secondly it served to enable managers from different parts of the Commission's activities to get to know each other and to understand each other's problems. Finally, it acted as a 'goldfish bowl', where talent could be spotted and people put on a fast track to promotion.

The curriculum was based around visiting lecturers, reports, conferences and overseas visits rather than staff instructors. Bonavia records that there was resistance in some quarters to releasing promising individuals for up to three months, but Sir Brian Robertson expressed his wish that it could be twice as long.

Bonavia records that this was very much coloured by Sir Brian's 'Camberley' experience (presumably he meant Sandhurst) and that he wished that the letters PSC – meaning 'passed staff college' – on a staff history sheet would become an essential qualification for those wishing to move up in the organisation.[19]

For the most part management training was organised on a regional basis. How relevant was it to what the wannabe manager would find when he was finally unleashed on the real railway, you are tempted to wonder. Stephen Poole was one of those who had come up through the ranks to enter the Southern Region management training scheme in 1979. He thus already knew what the real railway was about. He describes the training scheme as 'chronically out of date' and, what was worse, it 'even had mechanisms built in to keep it that way'.[20] On the training scheme he found himself 'plunged into what was essentially the nineteen fifties', and was taught about traditional vacuum brake marshalling yards and old-fashioned parcels depots. New signal technology was mentioned briefly, while the trainees spent most of their time in old absolute block boxes. Poole comments that: 'The emphasis was all on learning how to operate the railway as we found it, not on the development of fresh thinking.'

He continues: 'The training scheme was carefully designed to make a protest (or even constructive criticism and suggestion) difficult and I often wondered whether the Regional management realised how cleverly this was engineered by the training people.' Poole states that means had been found to obstruct the way that senior managers reviewed the training by ensuring that the review panel focused on reports written by trainees, but which had nothing to do with the training. On other regions, he believed, things were rather different and the panels did get to ask trainees relevant questions.[21]

At least on the Southern Region old tradition was dying very hard and the 'Sergeant Majors' were making sure it stayed that way.

The whole of British Railways' recruitment and training was out of date virtually from the moment the nationalised railway was born – as Raymond had recognised. It was stratified on traditional class and education lines like a military organisation, and could only have prolonged the traditional separation of management and workers. There was a lack of expectation for those coming into the railway via the wages grades, and only those coming in as management trainees were encouraged to view the railway as a career. There was a 'them and us' culture that was more than just a perception. It was there from the very beginning, at the recruitment stage. This was something that could and should have been tackled early – it wasn't. The unions were often identified as the principal block to progress, yet there were historical reasons behind their obstinacy.

British Railways inherited a situation where the unions cherished, and stubbornly clung to, many hard-won rights. The background to these was a struggle that had seen railwaymen sent to prison for striking in the early days of the railways. Amongst the rights won was the eight-hour day and 'the Machinery of

Negotiation', by which management negotiated with the unions, who represented the men in what was referred to as 'collective bargaining'.

The eight-hour day had been granted to the railwaymen by the government after their sterling service and loyalty in the First World War. The unions had long campaigned for it, largely on the grounds of safety, as the hours that railwaymen were forced to work in Victorian times were a national disgrace.

The Machinery of Negotiation was also the result of a long battle for union recognition which had resulted in the first 'Conciliation' scheme of 1906, when the railways were pressured by the government to allow unions to represent the wages grades. It was an agreed set of procedures – a hierarchical structure of committees and boards – through which management and unions met at national and local levels. The form as inherited by BR originated from 1935. As it stood it was a clumsy hierarchy of committees regulated by bureaucratic language. In the time of BR it often failed to resolve the disputes it was set up to solve, resulting in the need for judicial inquiries and summits between the leaders of management and unions. Classic examples of this were the judicial inquiries set up to investigate railwaymen's pay in the 1950s and the Penzance and Windsor meetings/agreements in the 1960s.

It didn't help BR that it had three different unions to deal with, and that these did not have good working relations with one another. ASLEF represented drivers and – when they existed – firemen (stokers). The NUR represented other wages grades such as guards, signalmen and porters. The Railway Clerks' Association (from 1950 the Transport Salaried Staffs' Association) represented the white collar, salaried grades. ASLEF were very keen to maintain pay differentials over the other grades, and the 1955 strike by ASLEF members – the first national railway strike for thirty years – centred on just this issue.[22] In the BR period ASLEF members were to see their pay rise at the expense of other grades.

The principal issues throughout the British Railways era were pay, productivity and maintenance of differentials – particularly with reference to the footplate grades. The judicial inquiry of 1954 established the principle that railwaymen's pay should keep pace with that in private industry. This was reaffirmed by the Guillebaud pay commission of 1958. Meanwhile, under government pressure, management sought to keep pay increases connected with increases in productivity.

In the 1960s and 1970s public pay came under pressure through the prices and incomes policies of successive governments. One way to get around this was to offer pay rises for productivity, but this very much favoured footplate and other traincrew grades. Even so, by 1974 BR was having trouble recruiting enough drivers and guards in the London area, although it was better off than London Transport.[23] Perhaps it is hardly surprising that 1975 saw a 30 per cent increase for all grades.[24] In 1980 the Low Pay Unit found that around 38,000 BR employees were receiving incomes below the official poverty line for a family with two children.[25]

With this in mind, perhaps industrial action was inevitable, but when it came it tended to focus on the issues that concerned footplate grades and guards.

One of the supposed benefits of modern traction was that only a single person was needed on the footplate – or indeed, even to work the whole train – that is in theory.

Electrical multiple-units had come into operation before union activism was fully fledged so that they were already operated in this way. Locomotives were another matter though, and for a long time there was the issue of the so-called 'second man' – essentially the redundant fireman who was still there because it hadn't yet been agreed that he shouldn't be (although, as has been shown, in the era of steam heat he did have a purpose: maintaining the essential but unreliable train heating boilers).

There was also the issue of the guard. It had long been technically possible for freight trains fitted with continuous brakes to be operated by a single individual. It was likewise possible for passenger trains to be operated by one person, provided that the doors could be remotely opened and closed from the cab. (Were this not possible the driver would be involved in having to secure doors manually by walking along the train.)

ASLEF wished to keep two footplate personnel in the cab, but the NUR wished to retain guards on board the trains. Of course, the tempting solution of combining these two roles crossed the line of differentials between footplate and other grades. In essence this last issue was to be resolved through the 'Traincrew agreement' in the late 1980s, at the same time paving the way for a smoother promotion path from guard to driver and easing more flexible working. Such agreements took a very long time to reach, though, and many of the disturbances caused to the railways' customers – particularly during the strikes of the early 1980s – were over these issues.

The issue of driver-only passenger trains had surfaced as early as 1975 when the Class 313 EMUs were introduced for the Great Northern electrification and made driver-only operation (DOO) possible for the first time. It was not until 15 November 1979 that the British Railways Board raised the issue through the Machinery of Negotiation. From that point it took until October 1986 to reach an agreement to allow DOO, starting on 19 January 1987 – with conditions. The DOO issue can be seen as conjoined with the traincrew grade proposal – BR's wish to unify recruitment and promotion procedures for guards and drivers under a single classification, something that was strongly resisted by ASLEF due to their traditional stance on differentials.

The other big issue was flexible rostering – an attempt to break out of the straitjacket of the eight-hour day. This would allow employees to work more than eight hours one day, and less on another, but it did threaten a long-fought-for principle that ASLEF in particular were unwilling to let go lightly.

In many ways all these things boiled down to what was a single issue: BR's attempts to reduce the number of staff required to operate trains, and to use those that remained more frequently and for more roles during their shifts, while the unions sought to prevent further redundancies (and let us not forget there had already been very many) as well as stopping members being to forced to work excessive hours.

The result was to be a damaging series of strikes by ASLEF, some of the worst in the history of the railways. In early 1982 BR lost a total of seventeen days in strikes that were organised to be on Tuesdays and Thursdays – guaranteed to disrupt the schedules for the whole week due to the misplacing of stock that resulted. This caused massive disruption to passengers.

Another contentious issue was the 'closed shop' that was brought in as a result of the Windsor agreement. A closed shop is a situation where membership of a union recognised by the employer is a condition of employment and refusal to join a union is answered by dismissal. Although introduced in theory in 1970 the implementation was aborted due to Conservative legislation banning closed shops in 1971. This was repealed in 1974 by the Labour government. It was not to be the end of the matter, though, as three BR employees who had been dismissed for non-membership took matters to the European Court of Human Rights and succeeded in winning their case in 1981.[26]

Such was the nature of industrial relations under BR. Given low pay and continual industrial strife, perhaps it is no wonder that many employees felt embattled. There were other reasons for their disgruntled feelings too, as Stephen Poole explains:

> With the early eighties on the suburban south eastern being typified by long queues, slow service, lethargic platform staff, ancient rolling stock, badly washed trains, cancellations due to chronic shortages of train crews and delays nearly every day it was not surprising that passengers sometimes became abusive or even violent. Assaults were common and abuse was almost taken for granted. It resulted in staff adopting a carefree attitude to the job and towards passengers. If your job didn't allow you to rise to each insult or slur then you coped with it by shrugging everything off. Hence the notorious indifference shown by so many railway staff – the calculated way in which staff carried on walking by when being addressed by a passenger and would never meet the passenger's eye. If you didn't get involved, nothing could develop.

Poole points to the advent of Chris Green and Network SouthEast as breaking the mould, but contempt for staff is still very visible in the 1993 documentary *Old, Dirty and Late*[27] (BBC *Inside Story*) where staff are seen being abused and spat at.

Where had the railway of old gone to? When had it been abolished? Had there ever actually been a better age? In his book *London's Lost Railways* Charles Klapper tells of how he went to buy tickets on the North London Line of the LMS, *circa* 1930, only to be told by the ticket clerk: 'Why don't you get a bloody bus?' The clerk then banged down the shutter.[28]

It may seem to be a cynical comment, but at least there was someone *there* to be rude to him – at least the station was manned. Slowly and surely the BR era was to see the de-manning of many stations. One of the most significant of these losses was surely the end of a station master for every station. In his book *Life and Times of the Station Master* David Holmes dates the demise of the title 'station master' to the early 1970s, pointing out that it had already disappeared in some areas but clung on in others, such as what had been the North Eastern Region.[29] *Modern Railways* heralded the change in its April 1965 issue, under the title 'From Station Masters to Station Managers on BR'.[30] The text made it plain that the purpose was a culling of local management – for station manager, read local/area manager in the case of small stations.

There was something of the old-fashioned disciplinarian about the concept of a station master. His original purpose is explained by Harold Pollins's account of a railway workforce that, in the nineteenth century, was often created out of rural populations unused to the discipline required in industry.[31] There was a need for a responsible representative of the company at every location. In the BR era the new managers were to be comparatively remote, despite the hype surrounding them.

The 1967 *Southern Traveller's Handbook* tried to put a positive spin on the advent of the area manager and to downplay and denigrate the traditional station master:

A is for Area manager

Every passenger on the Southern should have one by the time this book appears. He's a new and powerful local administrator in civvies responsible for a group of stations who will be assisted by uniformed 'Station Managers'.

The days of the remote Station 'Master' have gone. This is a brass tacks re-organisation designed to decentralise control of the railway and ensure a quick, authoritative local response to local demands.

In order to find out what the ordinary passenger thinks of the services in his area and how they can best be improved, every Area Manager has been told to get out and about as much as possible.

The picture beside this text shows Mr Joe Russell, the Southern's first area manager, boldly going where no area manager has gone before, stepping off a train in his bowler hat in businesslike fashion. We are told in the caption that he is responsible for seventeen stations on the Oxted Line. With that many stations under his purview, it does make you wonder how local he could have been to any of them.[32]

Whether or not the area manager started out as 'a new and powerful local administrator' the power of those in charge of stations was on the decline.

In his book *The Crumbling Edge* Stephen Poole describes the station manager in the last years of BR as 'increasingly impotent'[33] and as a 'lounge suited salesperson that would be equally at home in charge of a department of Debenhams.'[34]

> At the same time as Station Managers had their objectives more clearly defined in the direction of retail management, so their overall control, authority and status were reduced. So while on the one hand they knew more clearly what they were meant to be doing and, importantly, why – and had more information with which to do it, on the other hand they became increasingly surrounded by a railway over which they had less control.[35]

As Poole points out, some elements of the station amenities, such as catering, were there as tenants and were thus, in themselves, effectively customers who need to be pleased. Today, after privatisation, the train operating companies and their managers are themselves just tenants at most stations.

It must have saved some money to get rid of station masters – it meant the elimination of a whole tranche of people from the management grades and reducing those in direct charge at stations to ticket-collecting janitors. But it was not really a good move for the customer, and you could see that workers took little pride in their jobs.

The demise of the station master was reflected in the changes to the Rule Book. Rule 17 of *The Rule Book* of 1950 sets out the responsibilities of station masters as being the security and protection of buildings and property at the station, supervising employees engaged at the station or within its limits – promptly reporting any neglect of duty, a daily cleanliness inspection (including closets and urinals) and promptly reporting all complaints by the public. None of the items quoted above were carried through into the new modular *Rule Book of 1972.*[36] The primary reason for this was that the new Rule Book focused on safety, and it ought to be said that the separation of general duties and public service matters from safety rules was well overdue and quite proper. The old Rule Book was cluttered, disorganised and its focus unclear. Nevertheless, the removal of the injunctions regarding public service from the Rule Book must have detracted from its authority, and is an indication of where things were heading.

In the new Rule Book the term 'Station Master' is replaced, as said, by 'Station Manager'. This role is defined, vaguely, tellingly, as an 'Area Manager, or any person in charge of a station'. It is no longer a specific position, tied to a specific location. The only reference to his or her authority is in rule 5.2:

Employees under station manager's authority
All employees working in the area under the control of the Station Manager
are subject to the station manager's authority and direction in the working of
the railway.

This rule was carried through into the 1982 version of the Rule Book.

With computerised and centralised pay bills, sectorisation and the 'retail culture' of the 1980s, even this authority was eroded. Section B of the Rule Book from June 1989 does not refer even to station managers but to area managers, defined in its glossary as:

> Area Manager: Includes Assistant Area Manager, Area Operations Manager, Station Manager, Traffic Manager or Traffic Assistant.

By this time there is no rule about employees in the area of a station being under the authority of the area manager, or any other such person. But in 1989 there was still a rule about staff dealing with the public:

1.8 Dealing with the public
Each employee must be courteous and helpful when dealing with the public and must give his name when asked …

The withdrawal of the station master must have been a morale sapping experience for staff. Doubtless initially some (many) cheered the passing of this antiquated overlord from the Victorian era – it is always a relief to find there's no one looking over your shoulder. The second thought that must have occurred to staff is that their place of work no longer warranted anyone of importance being assigned to it. The culmination of all this must have felt like the slow withdrawal of the Roman Empire. Many stations were left unmanned as guards increasingly took on the job as sole custodians of the revenue take on 'Paytrains', where they both issued and clipped the tickets. Other staff – mere ticket collectors – were left in isolation like lonely sentries at the last outpost. By the 1980s there was a general move to open stations, and even some of the larger ones lost their ticket collectors.

Traditional discipline had already been eroded long before the demise of the station master. In the past the Rule Book had been at the heart of railway discipline. Frank McKenna, in *The Railway Workers 1840-1870* traces three distinct phases in respect of its application.

The first of these was where the Rule Book was the absolute word of the company and once transgression had taken place no appeal was possible.

The second phase started with the implementation of the railway disciplinary procedure initiated in 1912. The stringent application of the rules was relaxed and now men accused of an offence under the rules were issued with charge sheets. Formal hearings could be held and they could call witnesses in their defence.

In the 1930s the so-called vigilance movement championed the form of industrial action known as 'working to rule'. This is where the Rule Book is strenuously applied down to every dot and comma to the point where, in fact, normal work becomes impossible. In this way the workers became the masters of their workplaces and gained a valuable bargaining tool.

The third phase is what McKenna views as the *popularisation* of the Rule Book; this is reflected in the need for a moderate, common-sense interpretation of its strictures which allow normal working life to go on.[37]

There were those, such as Gerry Fiennes, who were outspoken about the way in which the power of the unions undermined managerial authority.[38] G. Freeman Allen points to an excessively conciliatory attitude under the Robertson administration.[39] In June 1956 Sir Brian Robertson had appointed J.W. Watkins, then the Regional General Manager of the LMR, to the Commission, apparently to relieve Robertson of some of the burden of industrial relations.[40] Later that year Watkins gave his views on industrial relations in a talk to the Railway Students Association in which he emphasised the importance of happiness at work, discipline and consultation. Happiness, he believed, was of the utmost importance, and that men and women who could feel 'reasonably happy' did better work. He emphasised that the right conditions included: 'making a man [*sic*] feel there is someone who is taking a real personal interest in his well-being, giving him the opportunity to unburden his soul occasionally, encouraging him, and helping him possibly with his personal problems.'

When it came to discipline, Watkins emphasised the importance of self discipline:

Comprehensive as our industrial relations may be, it is the individual man or woman who really matters in the efficient running of the railways. By the imposition of self discipline it would rarely become necessary to take action under the disciplinary procedure ... How much better the railway would be if every man had a sense of discipline which made him feel that he has great moral responsibility to give absolutely of his best without having to be supervised all the time, and to take that pride in his work which is so necessary in the Railway world today if we are to survive the revolution in Transport which is taking place.

He also commented that in his varied career he had found that:

disciplinary action, and possibly more serious trouble, would have been avoided if a little more thought had been given to the issue of instructions and the giving of decisions ... The average man appreciates firmness and a high standard of discipline and has little time for a supervisor – whatever his position may be – who is lacking in decision ...[41]

So that's what the weary, seasoned railwayman needed – a firm and decisive hand backed up by a shoulder to cry on.

In the 1980s the applicability of the Rule Book with regard to customer relations came to be rejected by the new breed of managers, starting with Chris Green on

ScotRail. Whilst emphasising the importance for firm rules to instil caution in matters of safety, it came to be recognised that in the field of customer relations rules could be more of a hindrance than a help. They instilled caution where an entrepreneurial spirit was more appropriate.[42] Speaking of his time at Network SouthEast, Green emphasises the use of encouragement rather than disciplinary measures.[43]

Nevertheless, in the Monopolies and Mergers Commission report on Network SouthEast of 1987 the unions were reported as stating that there had recently been a stricter approach to disciplinary matters across all regions with many more formal disciplinary actions being instituted. They claimed that on NSE the number conducted under so-called 'summary procedures' had gone up from three in 1985 to fifty-one in 1986, with all resulting in dismissal, only being subsequently 'modified' in four cases.[44]

The age of Bob Reid I had arrived.

It seemed that one rule from the Rule Book was never, or rarely, enforced: the one about employees being 'courteous and helpful when dealing with the public'. It was, of course, a traditional injunction and simply a rewording of the 1950 Rule Book, which can also be found in that operating at the turn of the twentieth century:

> Employees must …
>
> (ii) be prompt, civil and obliging, afford every proper facility for the Railway Executive's business, give correct information, and, when asked, give their names and numbers without hesitation.

Staff on BR had a reputation for rudeness and surliness that was not wholly undeserved, as I experienced myself on several occasions. I was once travelling from my home station and intended to purchase a return ticket, but was unable to do so because the ticket office was shut. At the next station I needed to change trains so I went to the ticket office to purchase my ticket there and asked, 'Can I buy a return from x (the station I had come from) to y?'

'What's the point?' The booking clerk demanded to know.

I patiently explained to him that I had come from there, had not been able to purchase a ticket and wished to do so now. He swallowed it with some ill grace.

In the late 1980s there was one ticket inspector at a station I travelled from regularly who was extremely polite and conscientious. I remember arriving at the barrier with my train in front of me, handed him my ticket and he gracefully waved his hand towards it, saying, 'Your chariot awaits!'

Later he was promoted to the ticket office and quite rightly so, but some time after he disappeared. I assumed that he had got fed up with the railways and moved on, but later, by chance, I met him socially and found out then that he had been promoted again. Something *was* working and the right people were being advanced. Unfortunately, it would seem that those with valuable customer service skills were having to accept promotion if they wanted a pay rise.

In the 1970s *Modern Railways* launched a campaign against what it termed 'BR storm-troopers' – BR employees who used their limited power and authority to intimidate passengers and as an excuse for surly behaviour.[45]

BR knew it had a problem. In the Southern's brochure *Want To Run a Railway* of 1962 it confessed: 'The public meet the odd wrong 'un on the staff, caught in a bad moment, offhand or rude. (Or just plain inexperienced. Labour shortages mean that some of the chaps you see in uniform have just arrived from the Labour Exchange.)'

It's no fresh young recruit who is the subject of the 1978 British Transport Films' (BTF) training film entitled *It Takes all Sorts*,[46] a very good, in fact a hilarious piece of work which attempted to persuade BR staff to treat their customers as if they were other human beings. It features Fred, a cantankerous, middle-aged ticket inspector who is a perfect, inglorious incarnation of a type all too familiar to rail travellers of the period. The similarity between Fred and some real BR staff was certainly not coincidental and is, to this day, positively horrifying. There are probably ex-BR managers who still have nightmares about Fred.

Fred's day gets off to a bad start when he gets his toes run over by a kid on a skateboard – just after giving his wife her final orders upon leaving his home for work. From there it's all downhill as he bullies and berates the very people who pay his wages. In the mess room Fred shares his corrosive philosophy with his colleagues, saying: 'Your travelling public couldn't care less how we treats 'em … All they cares about is catching them bloody trains.'

'Sorry, Fred,' says the commentary, 'but that's where you're wrong …'

The film makes a point of stressing that passengers and rail staff are all human beings, and that passengers are under pressure and confused by a strange and bewildering environment. It also stresses that passengers have a choice between rail and road, and that the way they are treated can make a difference to the choice they make. Got that, Fred?

In the 1980s BR bought in off-the-peg leaflets from the company Scriptographic Publications Limited. They were custom printed with the Corporate Identity Symbol on the front. One was entitled *Your Attitude and You*, another *About Courtesy at Work*. They consisted of simple cartoons and although superficially simplistic they did make some rather good points. One of these would definitely have had Fred spewing his coffee. It read: 'Start with the belief that the customer may [sic] be right!'

The Eastern Region's 1956 report on competition with the airlines, referred to in Chapter 4, had compared the staff on board trains unfavourably with those on board aircraft and had seen the need for train attendants paid at a higher rate and selected with the same care as airline personnel. Extensive training was also emphasised. It was considered that 'properly trained females' would give a higher standard of service as they would be better at dealing with enquiries from female passengers and are generally better at tidying up.[47] Nothing came of these proposals but both the LMR and the Western Region did employ women as travel advisers and hostesses, standing around on platforms all day in high heels handing out leaflets. The primary qualification for the job was physical attractiveness.[48]

In the 1950s and early 1960s the primary focus regarding work practices and training was on Work Study, which was the analysis of working practices with a view to increasing efficiency. As indicated by the illustrations on the 1958 Commission pamphlet *Work Study and You*, a primary focus of Work Study was the expensive sundries and single wagon freight business, something that was soon to be eliminated from the railway repertoire altogether. The pamphlet sought to reassure workers that they would be consulted and included in Work Study programmes, and also said 'no one is trying to put a fast one over on you'.[49] There was a British Railways Productivity Council on which both unions and management were represented in order to smooth out any problems.

It was not to be until the 1980s that customer-focused staff training was to start making its mark on the BR workforce. It began on the Eastern Region following the disastrous journey of a young woman travelling from Newcastle to Winchester who had effectively been stranded in London as a result of poor information. This was compounded by an outright denial from BR staff that they had any responsibility to make sure she got to where she had paid to get to. Frank Paterson, the general manager, had passed the complaint on to Valerie Stewart to investigate just how BR had managed so fundamentally to let a customer down.[50] This led to a fundamental change which involved customer care training for all staff, starting with those involved in contact with the customers, but involving all staff including managers, as well as management policy.

In 1983 Chris Green asked for customer-care training for his own staff at ScotRail. This customer-care focus became identified as an important part of the 'ScotRail revolution' but it was being rolled out, to different extents, in all regions of BR at that time. As I relate in the next chapter, staff for Pullman services were specially selected and groomed from the mid-1980s.

A universal, centrally co-ordinated policy of recruitment and training had to wait until the 'Organising for Quality' initiative and what was arguably its most important component: Quality Through People, designated as a 'Total Quality Management' initiative. It had its own director, Brian Bursdall.[51] It happily coincided with the implementation of the long-negotiated 'Traincrew agreement' on 3 October 1988.[52]

The key to the Traincrew concept was to offer a clear line of promotion from trainman or trainwoman to either driver or conductor and senior conductor (introduced as from May 1989).[53] The recruiters themselves decided who was to be passed on to become a driver and until the applicant qualified as a driver they would be trained as ordinary traincrew. Now guards or drivers' assistants who had been aged 45 or older on 3 October automatically qualified to be considered for promotion to driver. Traincrew were now recruited on a much more rigorous basis with customer skills at the fore; there were five recruitment centres at London, York, Manchester, Glasgow and Bristol. At last, by 1989, BR had in place a professional recruitment system of the type that Raymond had envisaged in his 1956 report. It had only taken thirty-three years to implement.

As always happens in a large organisation BR didn't get it entirely right. In 1991 eight guards from Asian backgrounds based at Paddington claimed that they had been discriminated against when they had applied to be drivers and turned down; it was found that BR discriminated against them by using tests that inadvertently excluded people from cultural backgrounds other than British. It was a sad reflection of the fact that BR still wasn't a multi-cultural organisation by the late 1980s, despite the fact that immigrants and their British descendants had contributed so much to the organisation.

Like the London Underground, British Railways had actively recruited from the West Indies in the 1950s and there was a racist backlash amongst some staff. In 1957 some King's Cross NUR members had stopped work to protest at the promotion of some black cleaners to shunters. Meanwhile the racist attitude of some firemen and drivers was blocking the prospects of promotion for black workers. According to Herman 'Harry' Robinson, an immigrant from Jamaica who started work at King's Cross in 1954, the solidarity shown by black workers during the 1955 strike went a long way to relieving tensions and making black people welcome in the railway workplace.[54]

The increasing use of immigrant – especially racial minority – labour was debated on numerous occasions in the 1960s and 1970s at the NUR's AGM. In the mid and late 1970s the rise of the National Front penetrated the railway workforce. In 1977–78 the National Front Railwaymen's Association started to produce its own newsletter, making what Philip Bagwell calls 'scurrilous attacks' on NUR and ASLEF personnel.

At the NUR's 1978 AGM a resolution 'condemning that organisation's activities and pledging the NUR's wholehearted opposition to all forms of racism' was carried unanimously.[55] At the same time King's Cross ASLEF gave support to the Anti Nazi League and was at the forefront in setting up the Rail Against the Nazis organisation.[56] According to the union histories, National Front activity on the railways declined after this date.[57]

Things were not so positive for women on the railways. Until 1967 female railway workers had no pension entitlement[58] and the road to equal pay for equal work was a long one. In October 1955 – two years after it was introduced into the civil service – the BTC announced that equal pay would apply to those women working for the railway in technical and clerical grades. Campaigners initially celebrated, only to suddenly realise that there was a catch. The small print specifically excluded those roles in which women were in the majority – to have the right to equal pay a woman had to have a job that was predominantly done by men. The Transport Salaried Staffs' Association took matters to the Railway Staff National Tribunal and won a ruling that female clerks should have equal pay to their male colleagues. Other grades were still excluded. Women were in the position of having to fight for equal opportunities grade by grade, and debates came to focus on issues regarding the suitability of certain posts for 'ladies', such as working in a yard after dark. It may seem amusing now but in the 1950s the signal box at Bletchley on the LMR was run entirely by four women who were trusted with all normal traffic, but when the Royal Train passed through a senior signalman had to take over. In 1970 the Equal Pay Act ensured that all women in all grades had to be paid the same as their male counterparts, although employers were given five years' notice before it came into force.

In 1974 the Sex Discrimination Act was passed and came into force in 1975.

In her book *Railwaywomen* Helena Wojtczak states that on BR the Sex Discrimination Act came into force 'inconspicuously'.[59] Overt discrimination now turned into covert discrimination, with women being purposefully discouraged and obstructed, or even intimidated:

> Typically, women were quizzed about their domestic responsibilities and intentions to have children, were sternly warned to expect 'no special treatment' and were told that, if they wanted a man's job, they would be treated 'as men', an expression that was often said in slightly menacing tones but always left undefined. Complaining about this treatment was simply not possible. Potential new entrants to an industry would hardly wish to jeopardise their chances of a job by complaining and being branded a 'troublemaker'.

Then, of course, there was always the old fall-back excuse of the toilets – for example 'we don't have any facilities for *ladies* here.'

BR did not have a female train driver until 17 February 1983.[60]

In the 1990s manager Caroline Stephens was employed to introduce a sexual harassment policy on a BR training programme. Her boss, who was always commenting on her clothes and tapping her on the head with his pen, pinched her bottom while she was bending over the photocopier and told her: 'Let me sexually harass you.' When she complained to the Divisional Director he asked: 'what do you want me to do?' He must have told her boss as he later said to her, 'you badmouthed me', and didn't speak to her for over a year after that.[61]

In terms of sexual equality, as in so much else, the personnel department on the railway still had a way to go.

10

The London Problem

If the chairmen and general managers of the nationalised industries are not getting the requisite capital to do the job and provide the services which the public and the Government wish them to undertake, they should say so, so that we may know where to apportion the blame. It has always seemed to me that the person who hollers the loudest is likely to get the greatest capital allocation. Capital has been available and it has been spent. It has been a matter of choice by the Government, and they have not allocated sufficient for this purpose.[1]

Margaret Thatcher, Shadow Minister for Transport, in a debate on commuters,
29 November 1968

No one can doubt that the task faced daily by London's public transport is colossal.

In the 1980s the number of passenger kilometres travelled on the London and South East Sector and Network SouthEast each year was nearly three times that of the entire Provincial sector – in other words three times that of the non-main-line rail services in all the other major metropolitan centres in the UK, and the rural services as well. Revenue per annum was more than twice that of Provincial.[2] Each day over a million journeys were made on the London and South East Sector.[3]

Inevitably there have always been great problems in servicing this demand. There is the complexity of many stations and lines that came about through private enterprise as the city itself expanded. There is maintaining the infrastructure within the tight windows offered by the demand – requiring expensive night-time and weekend working. There is the need to service and clean trains promptly within a few minutes and to keep them serviced. There is the small matter of timetabling many services which converge from many points on the system on just a very few central termini.

Then there is the enormous cost of all this. Who should pay so that hundreds of thousands of middle-class commuters can live in the Home Counties and travel in and out of London each day? This is what Peter Parker called, in his inimitable way, 'the combustible issue'[4] – the matter of pricing: whether the London commuters should pay the full whack of what it costs to take them from their suburban dormitory to their workplace and back again, or whether such people are really deserving of public subsidy. This is a matter that is still not resolved in 2013 and which privatisation, doubtless to the relief of the politicians, has helped to cloak.

To understand the problems BR and its successors have faced it is necessary to introduce a bit of history.

London's railway network – if it can be viewed as a single network – did not originate as a suburban network. The suburbs as they are now simply did not exist in the nineteenth century. Most of the main-line termini were initially built to serve trunk routes and some still reflect this in their cramped and unsuitable nature. In one respect they are well suited for their current purposes; they are at the heart of the areas they serve, although this is often because the city has grown outwards to meet them. Initially stations like Euston, Paddington and King's Cross were placed at the outskirts of the urban area at the insistence of the local authorities.

Not all the railways that built termini in the capital wanted the business of commuters. Railways such as the GWR and the LNWR continued to see themselves as major trunk routes and the running of inner city services was certainly not a priority. Eventually all those companies that entered or ran in London took to the running of commuter trains, but there is a distinction between those who saw it as worth their while to service the inner area and those who served the outer suburbs. Some of those built to service the inner urban area – such as the District or the Metropolitan – are now part of the Underground system.

The GWR changed its mind to some extent when it built the Hammersmith branch to link in with the City extension from Paddington but this was small beer. That too is now part of the Underground. The LNWR used Broad Street of the North London Railway (of which it owned two-thirds) as the terminus for its outer-suburban traffic, thus gaining direct access to the City and avoiding cluttering Euston with such traffic.

Unlike their northern and western counterparts the southern and eastern companies lacked a significant length of trunk route and their thoughts turned to exploiting the traffic from within and around London itself. Figures can mislead but they can also be revealing; in this case they tell a tale. Of the six companies obliged to run workmen's trains in the London district prior to 1883 the Great Eastern had the greatest obligation – it was required to run five, but in fact ran twenty-three trains. The LCDR was required to run one, but in fact ran thirteen.

Of those that had no statutory obligation, the LB&SCR ran fifteen; it also ran trains on the East London Line, where it had an obligation to provide just one, and in fact provided seventeen. The LSWR ran twelve and the GNR provided two. The GWR, LNWR and the Midland ran precisely none.[5]

In his book *The Railway System of London*, F. McDermott found that by 1881 the GER had opened sixty-eight stations within 12 miles of St Paul's, whereas the LNWR had opened fifteen stations and the GWR merely seven.[6] By the 1880s, 34,000 passengers were using the GE's new Liverpool Street terminus each morning, many of them workmen.[7]

By the 1880s London was already growing mightily. An essentially 'new' class of traveller was emerging, the middle classes, who bought property a short distance outside of the city but used the transport system to get to their daily place of work. There had always been some – wealthy people – who had done this, but the growth of suburban housing estates in the latter part of the Victorian period was a new trend.

In *London's Railways* Dr Edwin Course[8] lays out five phases of London's suburban growth which can be described as follows.

Phase one is that of 'Suburban Villas' constructed in the outlying villages by people with sufficient money and time to travel to and from the inner area. These were intended to be staffed by five to six servants and were situated in their own grounds. These are the kind of suburban houses featured in Sherlock Holmes stories.

Phase two had its climax in the 1880s. This involved the construction of two-storey houses. There was no provision for servants and they were often built in terraces. These developments started to ring the inner-urban area.

Phase three reached its busiest time at around 1900 and in character is basically similar to phase two. In fact, this was really a further extension of the previous phase but pushed outwards and into areas not used by the first.

Phase four refers to the period after the First World War when in the late 1920s and 1930s new housing estates sprang up. Some were built by the London County Council (LCC), others by private developers who bought areas of farmland and divided them into uniform plots. This filled in gaps in the existing built-up areas as well as spreading outwards to virgin lands. This era is characterised by the semi-detached house, often in the mock-Tudor style of the time. This phase is described in the important book *Semi-Detached London*, by Alan A. Jackson.

In addition, we can now add a phase five. This occurred after the Second World War, particularly boosted by the spread of railway electrification from the late 1950s onwards. Due to the intervention of the law pertaining to Green Belt land – a prohibition on further construction on land contiguous with the largely built-up area – developments now were taking place some 20 miles or more out of London, expanding the commuter area even further.

There were some pockets of development that don't fit into this pattern. A case in point is Woking, developed in the nineteenth century by the London Necropolis Company. After they dropped plans for a super cemetery on the Surrey heaths land on the south-eastern side of the railway was developed as an up-market commuter area, with land on the north side used for a low-class housing estate which is now largely torn down, but still evident in such places as the Chobham Road.

Then of course there were the new towns of the 1930s such as Welwyn Garden City and then those of the post-war era, all adding to the commuter area: places such as Bracknell, Hemel Hempstead, Crawley and Milton Keynes.

Edwin Course finds the connection between housing development and the railway as tenuous,[9] but one thing is certain: at some point in each case the railway emerged as an important factor in the lives of many of the inhabitants in terms of enabling them to get backwards and forwards between home and work. The inhabitants would not have been enabled to move to these places without some method of getting to and from their employment. Many of these new estates were clustered around existing, sometimes already electrified, railway lines but developers often contributed to the construction of new stations.[10]

Electrification was to expand the commuter belt right to the South Coast. There had always been some commuter traffic from places like Southampton and Bournemouth even in steam-hauled days, but in the 1960s the fast electric trains cut the journey time to two hours from Bournemouth. It could now realistically be viewed as a commuter town. Figures show big leaps in the number of season tickets sold on the line between the years 1965–70. In 1965, 10,000 season tickets were sold for journeys from Farnborough. In 1970, it had gone up to 22,900. Winchester season-ticket sales went up from 3,200 in 1965 to 7,100 in 1970. At Southampton they went up from 4,500 sales to 6,800 over the same years.[11] The Bournemouth line electrification proved such a success that in 1974 the fast service was up-rated from once every two hours to hourly and new rolling stock was provided.[12]

Railways such as the Southern were happy to expand their electrified systems, particularly in the thirties, when they had access to cheap government loans. By the time of nationalisation those railways with the largest commuter traffic were the same old suspects – the Southern, and the LNER focused on Liverpool Street.

The consequence of this expansion was that more people entered and left the centre of London on a daily basis, from more places than before, passing through transport systems that were not organised to cope with them. This inevitably led to congestion. The problems of London congestion – including those faced by its own customers once out of the railway station – were not the railway's concern. Yet there was no overall co-ordinating authority to deal with this. It was mentioned in Chapter 1 that the chance of creating a London railway group was dismissed at the end of the First World War, but that afterwards the London Passenger Transport Board was created in the 1930s. This had direct control only of the sub-surface and the Underground railways (as well as trams and buses), and was viewed as a competitor by railways such as the Southern. In the 1920s Sir Herbert Walker even went to parliament to fend off an attempt to expand the tube system further into – what was then – Surrey.[13]

The first emblem used by British Railways on the side of its motive power was the badge designed for the commission by Cecil Thomas. It had its critics, many pointing out that the lion looked rather anorexic. (Author, picture taken at the Mid Hants Railway. Permission granted from the National Railway Museum/Science & Society Picture Library to include images of BR material)

The original lozenge, or 'hot dog' as favoured by the Executive was tried out as a locomotive badge but didn't look right. Here a lozenge station sign is seen at Ropley, on the Mid Hants preserved railway, painted in the Southern Region green. (Author, picture taken at the Mid Hants Railway. Permission granted from the National Railway Museum/Science & Society Picture Library to include images of BR material)

The 1957 'achievement' was described by Modern Railways as a 'heraldic abortion'. This is the locomotive version, photographed on a preserved loco on the Mid Hants Railway, Ropley. (Author. Permission granted from the National Railway Museum/Science & Society Picture Library to include images of BR material)

The carriage roundel adapted from the crest of the 1956 heraldic device seen on the side of a preserved multiple-unit on the Mid-Hants Railway. (Paul Lund, picture taken at the Mid Hants 'Watercress' Line. Permission granted from the National Railway Museum/Science & Society Picture Library to include images of BR material)

Arrows were rather popular in symbology in the late 1950s and early 1960s. An example commissioned by BR was the Glasgow electric symbol designed by renowned graphic artist F.H.K. Henrion. Oddly, it was used only on stations and timetables, the heraldic symbol being borne by the power cars of the EMUs. (Author's collection/photograph Paul Lund. Permission granted from the National Railway Museum/Science & Society Picture Library to include images of BR material)

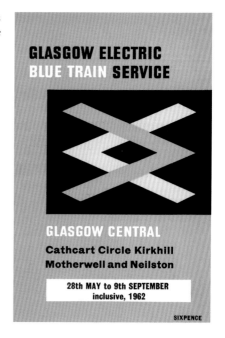

GLASGOW ELECTRIC BLUE TRAIN SERVICE

GLASGOW CENTRAL

Cathcart Circle Kirkhill Motherwell and Neilston

28th MAY to 9th SEPTEMBER inclusive, 1962

SIXPENCE

| sheet no. | 1/31 |
| issued | Jan 1965 |

colour B.R. Rail Blue
B.S.no
Munsell ref

| sheet no. | 1/32 |
| issued | Jan 1965 |

colour B.R. Flame Red
B.S.no
Munsell ref

| sheet no. | 1/33 |
| issued | Jan 1965 |

colour B.R. Rail Grey
B.S.no
Munsell ref

The 1960s Corporate Manual specified three bright cheerful colours for stock. In traffic they were often to weather badly, particularly as they were applied with a matt finish (due to production limitations the colours may not be reproduced accurately here). (Courtesy of Mike Bootman Collection. Permission granted from the National Railway Museum/Science & Society Picture Library to include images of BR material)

The cover of the 1985/86 BRB Reports and Accounts gives a good set of illustrations of the new motive power and liveries coming on stream in the 1980s; here are Pacers and Sprinters as well as the toothpaste InterCity livery, Network SouthEast and the grey freight livery before the advent of the Railfreight branding initiative. (Author's collection/photograph Paul Lund. Permission granted from the National Railway Museum/Science & Society Picture Library to include images of BR material)

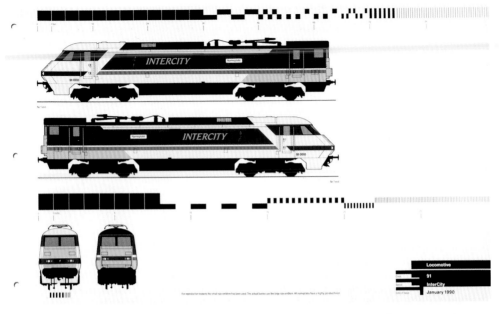

The Electra was the locomotive of the IC225 for the ECML electrification. This illustration is taken from volume 1 *Locomotives* of the livery handbook and shows it in the InterCity livery of the late 1980s and early 1990s, complete with the swallow logo and *sans* the British Rail identity symbol. (Author's collection/photograph Paul Lund. Permission granted from the National Railway Museum/Science & Society Picture Library to include images of BR material)

BR had high hopes of the APT, as is indicated on this souvenir bookmark and postcard. Sadly it was not to be. (Author's collection/ photograph Paul Lund. Permission granted from the National Railway Museum/Science & Society Picture Library to include images of BR material)

It's as Easy as 125.

The Journey Shrinker

-the network is spreading!

The Inter-City 125 was a truly iconic image and BR used it for all it was worth, both on literature promoting IC125 services and on anything else where a reason could be found. As with the corporate symbol, BR had commissioned an outstanding piece of design work. (Author's collection/photograph Paul Lund. Permission granted from the National Railway Museum/Science & Society Picture Library to include images of BR material)

For many years BR published its own holiday guides; each year there were five, covering different areas of the country. Like many other things, the holiday guides met their end in the 1960s. (Author's collection/photograph Paul Lund. Permission granted from the National Railway Museum/Science & Society Picture Library to include images of BR material)

The once numerous holiday 'specials' were in short supply after the cull of the 1960s. By the 1980s advance booking on certain trains to western seaside resorts was compulsory. The Runabout, or Rover, was a ticket that allowed you to travel where you pleased in a specific railway area for a limited period of time. (Author's collection/photograph Paul Lund. Permission granted from the National Railway Museum/Science & Society Picture Library to include images of BR material)

The cheap excursion, pioneered in the early days, was to come to an end in the British Rail era, but not before it was marketed under a number of different brands. As the 1975 Awayday leaflet shows, whilst much BR publicity literature had a slick, professional quality, some could still look amateurish. (Author's collection/photograph Paul Lund. Permission granted from the National Railway Museum/Science & Society Picture Library to include images of BR material)

British Rail decided to accommodate the car rather than fight it head on, and this proved to be a successful strategy. Car carriers, Parkway stations and railway-organised hire cars became part of the railway scene. (Author's collection/photograph Paul Lund. Permission granted from the National Railway Museum/Science & Society Picture Library to include images of BR material)

Railcards were to be one of BR's great marketing successes. As with the other BR leaflets the style changed through the years. Note the 'soft' drawings and captions such as 'Ready Teddy Go!' used in the late 1980s. The leaflets for disabled travellers have a more demure appearance. (Author's collection/photograph Paul Lund. Permission granted from the National Railway Museum/Science & Society Picture Library to include images of BR material)

Whilst BR competed fiercely with internal airline services, international air travel was an opportunity for rail. As the airliner replaced the ocean liner BR introduced new services and constructed new facilities for the jet age. Amongst these was Birmingham International, with five platforms to accommodate 13-coach Inter-City trains. (Author's collection/photograph Paul Lund. Permission granted from the National Railway Museum/Science & Society Picture Library to include images of BR material)

Another option offered to get people out and about, via train, was conducted rambles. Yet another healthy option was cycling. At one stage BR even fitted out some special vans with hooks to hang cycles for excursions organised by cycle clubs. (Author's collection/ photograph Paul Lund. Permission granted from the National Railway Museum/Science & Society Picture Library to include images of BR material)

In 1979 BR launched the Great Rail Club, later renamed Railriders, to encourage youngsters to travel by rail. The introductory magazine featured a chance to win Olivia Newton-John's latest album as well as railway and transport related items. (Author's collection/photograph Paul Lund. Permission granted from the National Railway Museum/Science & Society Picture Library to include images of BR material)

British railways had always had contacts abroad, enabling through bookings to the Continent and even further afield. BR continued to encourage foreign travel as part of its marketing. In the case of the *Night Ferry* (see first on the left) the train actually boarded a ship and was conveyed across the Channel. (Author's collection/ photograph Paul Lund. Permission granted from the National Railway Museum/ Science & Society Picture Library to include images of BR material)

British Railways had run a Staff Suggestions Scheme since 1948 – this is a page taken from a leaflet called *Ideas Pay* dating from 1955. In 1984 one chap won £1,000 for suggesting that the best way to improve the visibility of BR high-viz jackets was to wash them. Washing instructions, however, were already on the inside. (Author's collection/photograph Paul Lund. Permission granted from the National Railway Museum/Science & Society Picture Library to include images of BR material)

John Lewis' classic shot, taken from a DLR train, captures 86215, one of the production series of the first generation of 25,000V AC locos, in InterCity Executive livery heading a Norwich–Liverpool Street train. It is overtaking EMU 321-364 in NSE colours. Pudding Mill Lane, September 1995, when BR was still responsible, in parts, for running services. (John Lewis)

This competitive spirit had a negative consequence for the Southern commuter; as a result the Southern Region lacked sufficient distribution points from its own services into the inner city. All of its trains were concentrated into the termini and when the electric system expanded outward in the 1930s, and again after the war, the Southern found itself hobbled by running urban and inner-suburban services that obstructed its far more profitable outer-suburban business. North of the Thames such traffic was taken by railways such as the Metropolitan and the tube trains that had expanded vigorously northwards. Dr Beeching was well aware of this problem in the Reshaping Report, where he wrote under the heading 'London services':

> The rail system is capable of drawing passengers travelling daily to London from distances up to a hundred miles, and has ample spare capacity for doing so beyond a radius of about 20 miles. It is, therefore, in the railways' interest to foster growth of this longer distance traffic to achieve higher utilisation of the route system as a whole, but this development is itself restricted by the congestion of shorter distance traffic at the London end.[14]

Getting into London is one thing – getting out again is an entirely other proposition. At least during the rush hour you are going against the stream of traffic in one direction – you will probably have a seat on one leg of the journey. But it is still a huge problem. All of the main companies had viewed London as *the* destination, and journeys cross-London were very much catered for as an afterthought.

There were, and still are, cross-London routes such as the North London Line, the former West London Joint Railway and the East London Line – for a long time run as part of the Underground but now part of the main railway system once more. None of these offered services that particularly encouraged those wishing to travel across London. For most people, even today, it is a matter of going to one London terminus and taking the tube to another.

The trouble is that London's public transport is almost irredeemably unplanned, or at best half planned, with no oversight or great vision to direct it – or to mess it up even more.

During and after the Second World War there were attempts to bring about something better. The 1943 County of London Plan proposed a subterranean 'cross London link' stretching from Battersea through the centre of the city, connecting Victoria and Charing Cross, and out to Shadwell and Deptford. This was to be supplemented by a southern Underground loop taking in Charing Cross and London Bridge via Waterloo. It also proposed a north–south Underground connection to replace the Holborn–Blackfriars route.

The so-called 'Inglis plan', which emerged in 1946, proposed nearly 50 miles of deep-level, twin tunnels for full sized (i.e. Stephenson loading gauge) stock.

London Bridge was to be resited and was to be a hub from which five of the tunnels radiated. Another tunnel was to connect Stockwell, Victoria, Euston, King's Cross and Finsbury Park and thus extend out to the former Great Northern lines. This route eventually became the Victoria Line.

The various reports found themselves on Hurcomb's desk as from 1948. The BTC set up the London Plan Working Party and brought together London Transport and British Railways' staff. Out went the notions of placing the southern terminals underground and in came some more manageable proposals – one of which was to electrify the London Tilbury and Southend line, which was implemented. Another was to construct a new Underground line, designated 'Route C', which we now know as the Victoria Line. Despite the Commission's brief regarding integration, fulfilling such plans required additional expenditure which was not available at the time.[15] As I have mentioned, from 1953 integration was off the menu.

One new tube line and a smattering of electrification did not do much to improve London's transport situation. In the early 1970s the Minister for Transport Industries and the GLC commissioned another report from respected businessman David Barran, known as the 'London Rail Study', published in 1974. Of all the proposals put forward it was BR's plans for Crossrail that caught the eye of Barran and his colleagues. Barran thought it should be given a high priority. BR had started work developing the project as far back as 1967. In 1980 BR had another go at trying to foster some enthusiasm for cross-rail links with a booklet showing the possibilities. Yet again the east–west Crossrail proposal was mooted, together with north–south options.[16]

By 1980 there were enough reports on London's traffic problems to form a traffic jam all on their own, but no one in overall charge to ensure that plans were put into operation. The opportunity of the BTC as an authority embracing both BR and London Transport (LT) had been squandered for years and then finally discarded in 1962.

So the London transport system was under no direct unifying authority, but BR did have a monopoly of the surface lines into London – something that would be investigated twice by the Monopolies and Mergers Commission in the 1980s. One of the recommendations of the first investigation was that there should be unifying management for BR services into the capital. Perhaps it is a surprise that it took so long for this to come about, but of course it did involve four of the five regions and would have meant the setting aside of traditional rivalries. There were serious cultural differences between the Southern and the other regions. One in particular stands out: the Southern had long had an antipathy to 'real-time Control' such as was practised by the other regions, and by their predecessor companies.

Control was becoming established on British railways before the First World War. As I related in Chapter 1, Sir Herbert Walker had been put in charge of the

Railway Executive Committee during the First World War and had instituted the installation of 'Control telephones' so that the committee could talk to the different companies and important railway centres. Despite this, in peacetime Walker had an often stated aversion to Control, despite the fact that it was now common on the other companies' rail systems. Control removed individual initiative, he believed, and the best person to sort out problems was the staff member on the ground.[17] The case against Walker's viewpoint was put to me not so long ago by a controller in the present Waterloo Control Centre as we stood watching the trains moving in and out of the station; I was told that solving a problem in isolation often just moves that problem elsewhere, or has a knock-on effect on the rest of the system. Overall control is necessary to see that problems are solved with reference to or within the context of 'the big picture'.

There was real-time monitoring of operations by train supervision clerks, but unlike on the other companies or regions these people did not have the status of officers and certainly not of senior officers. They really did no more than use the control system to gather data and analyse it.[18] A telephonic system had been instituted during the Second World War to assist with the run-up to D-Day. It ran between selected stations and signal boxes and was of the 'omnibus' variety – in other words, it enabled every phone or a group of phones on the circuit to be connected at once.[19] Although this sounds like joined-up thinking, the reality was different. A message received at a station still had to be passed onto groups of people such as motive power and guards' foremen, not on the circuit, leading to a waste of time and effort.[20]

Nevertheless, for many years the Southern stubbornly maintained its stance that proactive control and joined-up communication was unnecessary. By the 1960s criticism of this attitude had grown. The Southern's response to this, initially, was propaganda rather than change. In the winter of 1962 it put out a brochure entitled *Want To Run A Railway?* with a cartoon on the front cover of a bowler-hatted chap leaning on his brolly and scratching his bowler hat in puzzlement. Inside, the same, now aggravated, commuter is saying 'I could run this lot a *!!?!** [sic] better than they do'. The brochure then goes on to point out how clever the Southern and its personnel are, and makes the point that Control is unnecessary by illustrating how individual initiative gets the job done. The final page shows the previously puzzled and vexed commuter now with blushes on his cheeks, embarrassed at being so silly for ever thinking he could have run such a complex operation. Such was the smugness of the Southern Region in the early 1960s.

The brochure earned a rocket from *Modern Railways* in an editorial under the heading 'Nobody runs this railway, mate', which commented: 'in this booklet management is introduced almost as an afterthought and described as maintaining no more than a "close personal interest" in operations.'[21]

The winters of 1962/63 and 1963/64 were particularly severe, with heavy snow disrupting Southern Electric services. In March 1964 G. Freeman Allen, editor of *Modern Railways* wrote analysing the Southern's troubles and describing its control methods and telecommunications system as 'sadly deficient'. This was to provoke quite a response from the former Superintendent of Operation on the Southern Region, S. W. Smart, CVO, OBE, who wrote an article published in the July 1964 edition of the magazine entitled 'The Southern Needs No Centralised Control'. This ran to four pages (including a summary of Allen's original points). Smart concluded by claiming that: 'Mr Freeman Allen's suggestion of a "centralised control" is unwarranted and impracticable.'[22]

However, it seems that S. W. Smart, CVO, OBE, former Superintendent of Operation on the Southern Region, was wrong.

A booklet[23] published by the General Manager's Office at Waterloo in January 1967 revealed that a new order was about to be implemented. It said: 'As from 6th February 1967 the function of the existing Train Supervision Offices will be completely revised. These offices will be replaced by Headquarters and Divisional Control rooms staffed by Controllers under the direction of a Deputy Chief Controller who will represent the General and Divisional Managers, respectively …'

Yes, the Controllers would now be 'representing the General and Divisional Managers' – very much a change in status.

On the front cover of the booklet the commencement date has in fact been stamped as '6 MAR 1967', but Control was coming. By 1969 modern control rooms had been installed at Victoria, London Bridge and Charing Cross, and one was in the process of being installed at Waterloo. The organisation and responsibilities of the control rooms differed between the divisions but all had the common theme of enabling direct communication between a controller authorised to make decisions and staff on the ground.[24] At long last, the Southern was under Control.

Having criticised the Southern so fulsomely over Control I do need to point out where the old company had done things right. Not only had it electrified substantial portions of its system by the time of the Second World War, but it had introduced a large number of flying and burrowing junctions – the inspiration for modern motorway junctions – that greatly eased the flow of traffic. By 1939 there were only two serious bottlenecks that had not been so reformed. These were Woking, where the Portsmouth line joins the South Western Main Line on the flat, and the bane of the South Eastern lines, Borough Market Junction. At Borough Market the initial planning of the line in the 1860s had envisioned Cannon Street as the main station and Charing Cross as a mere satellite. With the growth of the West End and the cessation of all but peak-time traffic flows at Cannon Street there was insufficient provision of tracks for the Charing Cross traffic. Neither of these two issues was resolved during BR's tenure. BR had laid plans in the 1980s for Borough Market to be substantially rebuilt but the problem has been that it lies within an area of very great historical interest, with many listed buildings. With the fulfilment of the much delayed Thameslink 2000 plans, the lines for the west passing through Borough Market will have been quadru-pled (four tracks in total) but that will not in fact increase the number of tracks to Charing Cross.

BR never had as much money to invest in the Southern Region as the Southern Railway, which was able to take advantage of cheap government loans during the 1930s. By the 1970s there was nowhere where the edge of quality was crumbling more than the Southern. Many of the units built in the late 1940s and 1950s had reached, or passed, their expected twenty-year life, whilst the replace-ments being built for the stock of the 1930s were based on the standard carriage of the early 1950s. This contrasted with other regions, where air-conditioned stock was being built as standard for long runs, as well as stock with air-sliding doors for suburban work. As has been referred to, such units were introduced by the LMS in the 1930s on Merseyside, and in the late 1950s in Strathclyde.

The Southern Region, by contrast, got the Mk1 in multiple-unit form on its newly electrified long-haul route from Waterloo to Bournemouth as late as 1967. Some new cars were built, while others were converted to multiple-unit formats from loco-hauled stock built in the 1950s. Complementing these, and available across the Southern Region, was the ubiquitous '4-VEP'. This was another remodelling of the Mk1 format, yet again taking advantage of the easily redesigned body by having hinged doors for every seating bay. The VEPs were high-density stock with an open format for second class, and compartments in first class, together with corridor connections and lavatories. They could be pressed into semi-fast or, if required, long-distance work. They were probably good value for the money. These, with the 4-REP tractor units, were the last Mk1 coaches to be built, with the last examples constructed as late as 1974 at York works. The Mk3 was already coming into production so the Southern really was getting third-rate carriages as-new.

Positive things about the 4-VEPs included their capacious guard's vans, built for moving post and packages at a time when the railways still handled that sort of thing. They could also accommodate a fair few bikes. They were the last gen-eration of multiple-units to show any generosity in this respect – the next ones would be focused keenly on getting as many seats into the space as possible.

The door to the brake compartment opened inwards on a VEP. To give the 'right-away' the guard would stand in the open doorway, usually with a beer belly threatening to infringe the loading gauge, watching to make sure that no one tried to board the train whilst it was starting. It's odd that it is possible to be nostalgic about something like that.

As well as using sub-standard stock as new the Southern had to put up with old stock re-dressed as new. There always seemed to be new stock for the newly electrified AC (Alternating Current) lines but not for the 'third-rail lines' south of the Thames. The money crunch of the 1970s inevitably meant that the units in service would have to continue in use for very much longer than was originally planned – now forty years instead of twenty was the accepted figure. As with the diesel multiple-units on the provincial and PTE services, refurbishment rather than replacement became the keyword. From 1979 British Rail Engineering at Swindon started to refurbish the units introduced for the Kent Coast electrification some twenty years before.[25] Some of these would outlast the century and British Rail itself. From 1981 large numbers of the EPB inner-suburban fleet were facelifted,[26] whilst work on the VEPs started in 1988. This included reducing the size of that large guard's van; it was a sign of the times.[27]

Capacity is of course a primary issue when it comes to suburban stock, or 'commutercans' as *Modern Railways* was wont to call them. BR did consider alternative solutions to the problem. There are basically two ways to go. You can pack as many people in as possible into the existing dimensions, or else expand the dimensions, either by increasing the length of trains or by building double-decker vehicles.

Bulleid had experimented with double-deckers after the war. He had already increased the width of his carriages by shaping the sides into a vertical curve, creating more room at waist level. These dimensions were followed by the BR Mk1 coach. Bulleid then embarked on another experiment: double-deckers. The standard British loading gauge was of course the primary inhibiting factor here. Bulleid solved the problem of the restricted headroom for the extra deck by interleaving the upper compartments with the lower ones, so that the feet of the upstairs passengers were at the head height of those in the lower compartments. Access to the upper compartments was via narrow stairways in the middle of the compartments (itself something of a waste of space, as there had to be one for each pair of components – upper and lower). The design was ingenious but when tested out in the field it was found to be unsatisfactory. Two prototypes were built for testing but no more after that. The loading and unloading times of these units were slower than conventional units as there were fewer doors per number of passengers – one to twenty four, rather than one to ten or twelve.[28] The two 4-DDs, as they were known, survived in service until the early 1970s as unique, freakish twins.

The idea did not go away though, and in the 1960s BR revisited it in the light of the Cartic 4 design of 1964. The Cartic 4 was an ingenious double-decker, car-carrying format that used the space below the normal floor level of railway vehicles as extra carrying space. On a railway there was no reason why this should not be done, as, within the confines of the loading gauge, there should be no obstructions above the level of the rail heads themselves. The Cartic 4s also used a shared bogie system (Cartic being an abbreviation of car-articulated) where adjacent carriages shared a mutual bogie.

The idea of the design was for carriages of no more than 46ft long, measured between the centres of the articulated bogies – this was determined by maximum permitted axle weight. Fourteen such carriages would approximate the length of a ten-coach train of Mk1 EMU stock. This was seen as an advantage, though, as the new design was to feature end doors only with two flights of stairs (up and down) per carriage reaching longitudinally from transverse end vestibules. It was said that the trains would allow for a 31 per cent extra seating capacity, giving 40 per cent in total, adding up to 500 extra passengers per train. (Presumably two decks increases the number of standing spaces.)[29]

The design was not even taken to prototype – doubtless the designers met the Southern's usual objection regarding loading and unloading. This was a good point, because trying to get 500 passengers through just two end doors would probably have been a nightmare and may even have presented some safety issues. In the 1970s the notion was revisited, but on this occasion the cost-per-seat construction was viewed as too high given that the carriages would have to be so short – on this occasion required to be so, it was said, by the Southern's restrictive loading gauge.[30]

In the 1980s the idea again came up – this time in the form of a proposal for four-wheel carriages on the same basic principle as the Class 141/2 railbuses. Again the loading and unloading issue was brought in as an objection. On top of that, Southern operators now wished such a format to bring about a significant reduction in frequency of the number of trains that needed to be provided, enough to substantially reduce track and signalling costs and to actually lead to the lifting of some track. As it could not bring that about, and would undoubtedly have led to a lowering in the standard of service, the idea was shelved once more.[31]

Not surprisingly, 'tinned commuters' have an irrepressible urge to spring from their containers at the end of their journeys; with the manually operated hinge doors this traditionally resulted in the doors being flung open before the train had stopped. This is actually quite dangerous and accidents did result. There can be little doubt that sliding doors that cannot be opened until the train has stopped are much safer than the manually operated, hinged doors. For a long time though the issue over which of the two designs was preferable hung on the question as to how quickly trains could load and unload from each of the two types. This was resolved, to the satisfaction of BR at least, with an experiment conducted at Doncaster works in 1967. Three hundred employees at the works spent a merry day testing the two types under closely monitored experimental conditions. The results came out in favour of the sliding door.[32]

Then, of course, there are the questions of who should operate the doors, and how should they work? This is a more involved question than most people would imagine. This issue was to be tested on three prototype units produced in the early 1970s. These comprised two four-car units and one two-car set of carriages, designated '4-PEP' and '2-PEP', as was appropriate. These units consisted of an entirely new design of carriage that was integral and built out of aluminium sheet. Three doorways were provided with air-powered sliding doors. New bogies were also trialled under these units. Under the 4-PEPs the suspension was relatively conventional, using the tried and tested swing bolster arrangement, but beneath the 2-PEP was a new design following the Continental practice of using rubber air bags for the secondary suspension. This design was to be chosen for future BR multiple-units.

The PEPs were very different to look at compared to previous SR stock. Gone was the curved side profile, replaced by a straight-sided, boxy look. The roofs were almost flat. The four-car units were painted all over rail blue with yellow ends and white lettering, but the two-car unit was finished in aluminium with red lettering, including a red corporate identity symbol.

Back to the matter of the doors. An instruction leaflet of the time informed passengers:

PEP

Our doors are different

The power-assisted sliding doors on the experimental PEP suburban train have been designed to provide quick and easy access, and at the same time to exclude unnecessary draughts.

THIS IS HOW THEY WORK

Boarding

To board the train, you must slide the doors open yourself when the train has stopped, unless someone opens them first from the inside. After you have moved them a short way they will slide open under their own power.

When you are on the train, you may pull the doors closed behind you if you wish. But any doors left open when the train is ready to start will be closed by the guard. The train will not move until all doors are fully closed and secured.

Alighting

Remember that the doors do not open automatically. When the train has come to a complete stop, slide the doors open yourself. This prevents doors being opened unnecessarily when no one wishes to get on or off, and helps to keep the temperature even throughout the train.

Don't forget – these sliding doors are different … YOU open them – WE close them.

Just a slight opening movement is all that's needed to start them opening. The power mechanism will do the rest …

As it turned out, not everyone did understand or read the instructions and a few people were rather more persuasive with the doors than they needed to be. Or perhaps it was actually due to the catch that was mentioned only at the bottom of the leaflet: 'As part of our passenger evaluation trials, the centre doors are not being used.'

There are tales of desperate passengers struggling to get the doors open and probably some missed their stops.[33] If commuters had ever thought that they were rats in an experimental maze, now they had confirmation.

For some reason BR persisted with these dodgy doors into the production phase and the Great Northern Electrics were fitted with them when they were built in 1976. It was not long before BR relented though, and in March 1977 leaflets duly appeared saying:

OPERATION OF TRAIN DOORS
Because of a few isolated incidents of passengers forcing the doors apart against the mechanism, the system of door operation on the electric trains between Welwyn Garden City/Hertford North and Moorgate is to be changed.
The alterations will begin Monday 21st March, when, for a temporary period, the sliding doors will be opened and closed only by the Guard of the train. The changeover may take a few days to complete.

It clearly shows the priority given to the comfort of Southern Region passengers that the first production batches of the new units were intended for other lines, even though the prototypes had been tested out on the Southern. As said above, the first lot went to the Great Northern electrification and the first third-rail units to the design were originally intended for the other prestige project, the Merseyrail reconstruction, but an 'urgent' need for new EMUs on Southern Region forced them to be diverted and built as four cars rather than three cars as originally planned. The Southern didn't hang on to them for long though, and they were off to Merseyside, *sans* one trailer, in the early 1980s. By that time the 'definitive' Southern Region multiple-unit, the 455, had arrived and the spare trailers were reused in those. The 508 units were noted for sliding on greasy rails, particularly on leaf mulch, and before it left for Liverpool one of the 508s provided some excitement by running through the buffers at Shepperton and very nearly destroying the Ian Allan offices – undoubtedly one for the conspiracy theorists.[34]

The Southern Region's third-rail system might have had to put up with antiquated stock for years but the new AC electrifications on other lines out of London brought brand new stock with them. From 1955 BR had undertaken a rolling programme of 25,000 volt electrification, much of it focused on the South East or on lines out of Euston, Liverpool Street and Fenchurch Street. South of the Thames 'third rail' had been extended to the Kent coast and then, in 1967, to Bournemouth. Sadly, with the Lea Valley scheme of 1969 electrification came to a temporary halt. In 1971 BR gained approval for the electrification of the King's Cross suburban lines out to Royston via Welwyn Garden City and Hertford North. The line also extended inwards using old tunnels to Moorgate. The latter involved some complications, as the use of 25,000 volts was not practical underground. BR's ingenious solution was dual voltage units, which switch over from 25kV AC to 750-volt DC and back again at Drayton Park. Overhead electrification was installed on 67.3 route miles of track, and 2.7 miles of underground track had 'third rail' laid.

The next electrification was the infamous so-called Bed-Pan line, which I have already referred to in relation to the introduction of Driver Only Operation (DOO). A DMU service had been instituted in 1960 and was claimed to be the most intensive of its kind in the world; it had been a success too, increasing traffic by a fifth over the old steamers and encouraging new housing development along the route.[35] As already stated, in the mid-1970s a primary argument for this electrification was the age of the existing DMUs but was also justified on the grounds of savings to be gained by DOO.[36] It was authorised in November 1976 at a cost of £80 million and involved the electrification from St Pancras out to Bedford and also the line from St Pancras through Barbican to Moorgate, making use of the tunnels of the so called 'Widened Lines' and forming a through, electrified route to the City. Because of the problems with the interchange between BR and LT at St Pancras a new interchange was built at King's Cross, known as King's Cross Midland Interchange station. The tunnels of the Widened Lines were built with enough clearance to enable the fitting of overhead lines so no dual voltage EMUs were required for the service through to Moorgate.

The entire fleet of EMUs for this service suffered significant failings which would have been discovered earlier but for the industrial dispute delaying their introduction. The problems were around the use of the BP20 bogie at 90mph (previously it had only been used at 75mph). It would have been discovered in the first one or two had they been introduced gradually and the others could have had their design altered as they were produced; sadly the whole class had to have the problem rectified – by the fitting of additional dampers – and this caused additional delays in the introduction of the service. By the mid-1980s this was all history and the line was flourishing with its customer base expanding once more.[37]

One of the cross-London link ideas that had been raised again in the BR *Cross London Rail Link* paper of 1980 was opening the old Snow Hill route. This ran from King's Cross and St Pancras to Holborn Junction and then on a bridge across the river at Blackfriars. It had not been used for regular passenger services since the First World War. A feasibility study was now funded by the Greater London Council and as a consequence the route was reopened to traffic and christened 'Thameslink'. Despite earlier scepticism of Southern Regional managers, business boomed.[38] Further expansions of Thameslink were planned by BR, but, as noted earlier in respect of Borough Market, the fulfilment of more extensive services in the form of Thameslink 2000 is only now coming to pass in the second decade of the twenty-first century.

A key turning point in the fortunes of the London and South East Sector (LSE) was the report of the Monopolies and Mergers Commission (MMC) ordered by the new Conservative government in April 1980.

Whilst making detailed constructive criticisms of the services provided, the report also made three key observations. The first was the connection between the price paid for a service and the standard it can attain; the second related to the financial constraints under which the commuter railway was being placed; and the third pertained to a lack of specific objectives.[39] The MMC did feel that the service could be run more efficiently and be better managed, but it also needed investment and a sense of purpose.

In terms of investment, though, LSE was to lose out in the 1980s with a paucity of new rolling stock introduced and the old Mk1s still in service. Meanwhile there was, in the words of Sir Peter Parker, 'heavy breathing' from the Treasury at everyone concerned to keep down fares, with some specific mention being made of London commuter fares.[40] In the light of the MMC considerations BR had launched the Commuters Charter – a very different sort of document from the Customers Charters of the 1990s. Parker used the document to try to open the debate as to who should pay for the London network, with the suggestion that a levy on businesses in London might be the way to go. This laudable idea didn't get anywhere.

As stated above, when it came to shabby stock, the Bournemouth route was a case in point. Here was a long-distance route that was still served by carriages based on the standards of the early 1950s. In 1988 new units were constructed for the line based on the Mk3 body shell and with air conditioning. Unlike their loco-hauled cousins these versions of the Mk3 had power doors – not of the sliding type and certainly not of the troublesome type tried on the PEPs, but of the 'plug' type. Plug doors are flush with the body side when closed and open by moving outwards and then to the side. The new units also boasted disabled toilets and a wheelchair space. Not everything about the 'new' units *was* new, however. In the best traditions of the Southern the motors were reused from the old units. BR, like its predecessors, was a master of 'make do and mend'.[41]

The new units quickly acquired the nickname of 'plastic pigs', amongst the staff. One theory is that it was due to them looking like pigs, although other theories abound. The spread of the nickname resulted in an infamous memo and briefings at which staff were instructed not to use this name on pain of dismissal. This, of course, was something of a tactical error as it simply spread it further and gave it the kudos of being forbidden. At some point a staff member also produced some plastic piggy badges to celebrate the new units – the perpetrator was sought but never identified.[42]

On 10 July 1986 the London and South East sector was relaunched as Network SouthEast. To the cynic it was simply a rebranding of the relatively new London and South East sector, but the man behind it had other ideas. After his success at launching ScotRail as a brand, Chris Green had moved south and been given what many would concede was the most difficult job on British Rail. At one level Network SouthEast was a makeover and Green made no bones about it. He launched Operation Pride at the same time as the new network name; this focused on image and cleanliness but also, and perhaps more importantly to the passenger, on punctuality, reliability and information. Since arriving in the south in January, Green had spent time staying in different places around the south-east and trying out the journey to work by train.[43] It's probably what many of his customers would have regarded as a 'good start'.

One of Green's immediate positive contributions was to oversee the introduction of the One Day Capitalcard. First introduced in June 1986 this enabled off-peak travel – after 9.30 a.m. – into London from a British Rail station as well as all-zones travel on LT rail and buses. In its first full year to June 1987 it sold 18 million tickets worth £33 million. Research found that 20 per cent of those passengers were new to rail yet the costs of handling the extra passengers was neglible after 9.30 a.m. Green states proudly that the extra income went straight into much needed train and station investment.[44]

One interesting event occurred in April 1988, when the services out of Liverpool Street were taken out of the massive Eastern Region and given their own, called the Anglia Region. The principal reason was that the Eastern Region had long been based at York, a very long way from the hustle and bustle of the London commuter services. The headquarters of the new Anglia Region was at Liverpool Street.

Although the second MMC report of 1987 found that since their first report in 1980 there had been no improvement in punctuality targets Green disputes this, stating that things were already beginning to get better – and continued to do so. The Monopolies and Mergers Commission were at least helpful in making the case that punctuality could not be improved without increasing expenditure.[45] One problem that Green was to face was the increasing difficulty in recruiting and keeping staff in the boom of the late 1980s. He comments that if staff were not available there was just no option but to cancel trains.

A lack of investment has been the thing that has dogged London's transport infrastructure. There have been plenty of ideas and plans. In 1989 the Central London Rail Study (a joint study by the Department of Transport, British Rail Network SouthEast, London Regional Transport and London Underground Ltd) came up with another set of analyses and recommendations. Yet again this included the idea of Crossrail. In 2012, as I write this book, they have just started excavations for this new line.

The amazing thing is that the London and South East network carried so many people, and carried them as safely, with so little money spent on it. It was so often the 'mend and make do' skills of the old companies, inherited and nurtured by BR, that enabled the government to get away with the relative lack of financial support for so long. It was those very skills in reinvigorating ancient equipment that led to the most criticism. Nowadays we expect everything to be new and bright and nice. Our forefathers could put up with a bit of recycling.

By the early 1990s the cracks were showing and the government was desperate to find some new way to get money into the system without having to pay for it out of public coffers. Or, alternatively, to find a way of putting money into it whilst at the same time concealing the amount being spent from the very many critics ready and willing to blow the whistle. If any one part of the system impelled the government into privatisation, it was Network SouthEast.

Speaking to me at the end of 2012 Chris Green voiced the opinion that London's rail system, with the number of interchanges between light and heavy rail, is the best of any city in the world. He may well be right.

11

A Golden Age?

The 1980s have come to be seen as a 'golden age' for BR, particularly the era of the first Robert Reid – 1983–90. This is a retrospective view that gained currency after privatisation, yet there are grounds to believe it to be so. It was an era in which BR was at last authorised to undertake long delayed electrification projects such as the East Coast Main Line, as well as to replace the archaic modernisation-era rolling stock that was becoming a serious maintenance cost burden. The fruit of previous expenditure was coming to maturity. By 1983 The IC125 fleet, although not consisting of as many units as BR might have wished, was operating at its full strength. Then of course there was the Channel Tunnel, something which BR was cut out of due to the Prime Minister's insistence that it should be a private project, but which still held out the hope of a bright future for UK rail since the system would now be linked directly to the rails of the European mainland.

On the downside, the 'crumbling edge of quality' was crumbling like nowhere else on the Southern Region, where archaic trains, some designed before the advent of BR, were still in service in the 1980s. Units dating from the 1950s were to outlive BR into privatisation. Meanwhile the payback that government required for allowing BR to invest in electrification and rolling stock was to be the achievement of the long cherished goal of Inter-City profitability. It was finally attained – with a little bit of fudging – in 1988–89.[1]

There had been a sense of gathering twilight over the nationalised railway at the beginning of the 1980s. It was badly hit by the recession and by strikes; passenger train miles were down from 19,100 million in 1981 to just 17,000 million in the strike year of 1982. Perhaps more ominously, sales of season tickets were down from 332.5 million to 268.2 million in that year.[2] The economic situation had changed since the launch of Inter-City back in 1966. The expansion of the motorway network and the deregulation of the long-distance road coach business meant that BR was now faced with tough competition. It was no longer just the airlines it had to worry about. Passengers who would have previously travelled by train in second class were now being wooed onto the road coaches. Market research showed that nine out of ten 'optional' passengers who had swapped to coaches had done so simply because of price.[3] The Western Region line to Bristol and South Wales was particularly badly hit, with off-peak leisure traffic dropping to the extent that by 1988 the original three-trains-per-hour service had been cut back to just two. By the mid-1980s the role of the IC125 on this route had changed fundamentally from that of high-speed, long-distance transport to a commuter vehicle, with people exploiting the fact that high speeds had now made towns as far afield as Swindon – halfway to Bristol – into London commuter towns.[4]

The recession of the early 1980s had also curtailed the business market, but this was across all transport modes. The main fear was that the traffic wouldn't come back once the recession was over. As a result BR was beginning to question the principles on which the success of InterCity had originally been based: high speed, comfort and regular interval services. The answer to the problem of competing with the road coaches was simple: compete on price or withdraw services. BR now had a bevy of promotional weapons, particularly the railcards, but inevitably with the high costs of running a railway there were times when the sums would not add up. When it came to business travel BR's answer was to go up-market and to attempt a reincarnation of the luxury, high-status railway of the past. This emphasis on quality and profit led to the demise of the traditional 'bucket and spades' excursion with a decision that if it was to pay then it had to go up-market. Selected coaches were refurbished to provide a high-quality environment for charter hire with an emphasis on VIP treatment and silver service catering.[5] Meanwhile InterCity pursued an aggressive policy of ridding itself of as many old carriages as possible. The emphasis of such marketing brands as Merrymaker passed decisively onto selling seats in scheduled services rather than guaranteed excursions. By 1993 there were just fifteen train sets run by InterCity's Special Trains Unit, which now also had a dedicated fleet of three electric locomotives and twelve diesels. The coaches were old Mk1s and Mk2s but four sets of Mk1s had been specially refurbished with open plan, first-class seating for dining.[6]

One reaction to long-distance bus deregulation was *The Nightrider*, a named train service from King's Cross to Edinburgh, Glasgow and Aberdeen. This was a de-luxe, entirely first-class train for 'night seated' passengers. Fares were as low as £12 for Edinburgh and £16 for Aberdeen – good even by 1982 standards.[7] In 1983 a Euston–Glasgow service was added. The service continued up until 1988 on the ECML, and until 1990 on the WCML.[8]

The 1980s were also to see a new phase of station reopening and even new stations being built. As referred to in Chapter 8, this was kicked off by the creation of the PTEs, but in 1981 the 'Speller' amendment to the 1962 Transport Act enabled BR to open or reopen stations on a short-term trial basis without having to go through the normal closure procedures if it didn't work out. The West Yorkshire Passenger Transport Executive, in conjunction with the University of Leeds, had done research on estimating potential demand for stations and the number of passengers needed to justify a new station on financial grounds. They had discovered that it was much smaller than was supposed.[9] All this led to something of a golden age of station openings/reopenings. Prior to Speller the greatest number of stations opened in a single year since 1960 was twelve, in 1978. In the 1980s the number of station openings took off with a high-water mark in 1987, when twenty-six were opened or reopened. From 1981 to 1994 a total of 212 stations had joined or rejoined the network.[10]

Nevertheless, 1982 saw what may well have been the first use of the infamous phrase 'closure by stealth'. This was an accusation levelled against BR by the Sheffield Passengers' Association in that year, and that was to be used as a charge against BR on many occasions until its demise. The Yorkshire Area Transport Users Committee noted that BR had withdrawn the summer Saturday service between Dore West Junction and Dore South Junction before consent had been given by the minister. It had been reinstated after representations by the TUCC. In its report the TUCC highlighted the suggestion of the Sheffield Passengers' Association that, due to Section 56 of the 1962 Transport Act, BR could minimise objections to closure by significantly winding down services before closure was announced. The TUCC thought seriously enough about the suggestion to send a paper on the issue to the Central Transport Consultative Council.[11]

One main line was to be closed in the 1980s. This was the Woodhead line, once held up as a shining example of electrification in the post-war era, and it was finally closed entirely as a through route. BR was to try, unsuccessfully, to close another main line – the old Midland route from Settle to Carlisle. After a five-year campaign this was reprieved by the Thatcher government in 1989 after attempts to sell it to a private buyer fell through.[12]

I explained in Chapter 2 how the big organisational change in the 1980s within BR was the development of Sectorisation, in fact a scheme that pre-dated the Tory election victory of 1979. Coupled with this there were changes in management practice and the general corporate view. The early glimmerings of this could be seen in the new regime on the Scottish Region. This was to see the image of the region transformed as it adopted the brand name 'ScotRail' and took on a new sense of pride and customer awareness. The beginning of the change can be dated to when Chris Green took on the role of Chief Operating Manager.[13] Later he was to rise to the post of Deputy General Manager and, in 1984, that of General Manager. A graduate of Oriel College Oxford, Green had entered BR as a management trainee in the 1960s and was just 41 years old when he was appointed to the prestigious role of General Manager of ScotRail.

Scotland is from the railway point of view – indeed from any point of view – an extremely diverse environment. It embraces a huge conurbation, Strathclyde, where more than 2.5 million people lived during the BR era. It also has some of the most remote areas of the British Isles with lines that have been almost continuously under threat of closure. And yet Scotland is at the end of the two most financially successful main lines in the UK – the two on which InterCity's profitability was to be based. As much as Scotland was a separate region that assumed its own identity, it was also essential to the system-wide InterCity operation.

Almost certainly the goad for the Scottish Region getting its act together was the Strathclyde PTE's (SPTE) ruminations about cancelling the Section 20 grants it paid out for some of the area's railway services. In 1981 the Strathclyde Regional Council announced that it couldn't afford to fund part of the £59 million Ayrshire electrification scheme. Meanwhile the PTE withdrew financial support from the Kilmacolm line and, in October 1981, the Minister for Transport gave BR permission to withdraw services.[14] In January 1983 BR and SPTE got together to plan a brighter future for rail with a joint review, the results of which were published on 13 December of that year. As peaceful relations with the PTE were slowly resumed a wave of expenditure was unleashed on the region.[15] In March 1983 the Paisley–Ayr and Ardrossan South Beach electrification was given the go-ahead.[16]

Chris Green was to oversee the spending of £37 million of investment into the Scottish rail system. This was spent on four major areas. These were opening and modernisation of stations, electrification, improved track and resignalling schemes, and upgrading facilities at maintenance depots.[17]

All 287 stations on the region were set for refurbishing, the small ones being given colours specific to the particular line they served, the large ones sporting a 'distinctive house style' using terrazzo tiles, TV information screens and bright fittings.[18] The trend of station closures was reversed with stations being opened and reopened. In 1984 there were four stations opened, in 1985 six, in 1986 another three and the same number again in 1987.[19]

As mentioned in Chapter 9, much new emphasis was put into staff training, particularly with respect to customer care; this was to be Green's great contribution to ScotRail and to the Sectors that he was subsequently to head – Network SouthEast and InterCity. There was also a new and robust attitude to industrial relations, and this resulted in ScotRail forging its own way in negotiating with the unions. The result was the Strathclyde Manning Agreement, allowing for DOO with 'flying' ticket inspectors and unmanned stations in the PTE area.[20]

The 'ScotRail revolution' was deemed to be enough of a success to warrant a book being published in 1987 entitled *Changing Trains – Messages for Management from the ScotRail Challenge*. It was written by Vivian Chadwick, at that time Deputy General Manager of ScotRail, and co-authored by industrial psychologist Valerie Stewart. The book highlighted such things as a need for a change in attitude – particularly underlining the need for a quality environment for customers and staff, ending the habit of doing things on the cheap and focusing on things such as presentation and cleanliness. Green was to freely confess that he took many of his ideas from other parts of BR, railways abroad and non railway organisations, but putting these concepts into practice was largely his initiative, backed up by others around him.[21]

In the early 1980s ScotRail was learning the lesson that 'putting the customer first' pays, but were other areas of BR?

In the document *InterCity Strategy* of June 1984[22] the following five elements are listed as the core strategy for InterCity. One: product. Two: sector definition. Three: price and volume. Four: resource management. Five, right at the bottom but at least not forgotten, was customer service.

The chapter on 'Customer Service Strategy' focuses mainly on physical things such as improved car parks, computer seat reservations and 'improved on train service' (presumably meaning reliability and punctuality catering). Finally, on page fifty it states (headed as 1), 'The customer comes first.'

At least they got there in the end. This was in spite of references earlier in the document to customer service being the key area where InterCity performed badly. Oh, and note that it is customer *service*, not care. As covered in Chapter 9, InterCity was to buck its ideas up and focus on staff training, but it is disappointing to find customer care listed so low at this point in BR's development – particularly as it is beneath Sector definition, which is at number two.

But what sort of customers were the staff supposed to be caring for? InterCity literature stressed that the service was for a range of customers. In 1989 John Prideaux was to tell the Royal Society of Arts that InterCity customers 'are typically affluent and predominantly young'. Few were travelling on their company's business and most journeys were to 'visit a friend'. He said: 'The typical intercity passenger [sic] was a girl [sic] in her twenties visiting a friend at the weekend.'[23]

Second class and discount travel accounted for £355 million of revenue for InterCity in 1984, but doubtless it was the premium traveller, in the first-class seat, who paid many of the bills. In 1984 first-class passengers contributed £56 million a year in revenue to BR. They also contributed further by taking up many fewer seats and thus fewer carriages than the standard-class passenger. Although accounting for only 12 per cent in total takings (the grand total also needs to include sleepers: £24 million and miscellaneous payments: £30 million) the profit levels were very high comparatively.[24]

Perhaps this needs no further explanation than a reference to the 1987 fares manual, where it says that the White and Blue Saver returns (with restrictions) were £53 and £42 respectively, whereas the cost of a first-class return was £121. The unrestricted standard return fare was still a bargain in comparison at £83. For even greater value, a person travelling on a railcard (not valid for first-class travel) was entitled to 34 per cent discount on White, Blue and Network Savers, so, allowing for a further discount of £14.30 from £42, there was only £27.70

to pay. At the weekend a '1980s Monica' (see p. 87) with a railcard could travel from London to Glasgow and back for £93.80 less than a first-class traveller. It is a simple case of cost-effectiveness: first-class passengers yield a profit over many fewer miles and occupy many fewer carriages.

BR needed not only to halt the erosion of first-class ticket sales but to increase sales generally. Yet by the mid-1980s it faced further competition on its main north–south routes. The M25 was scheduled to be completed in 1986 and it threatened easier car journeys from the north to the other side of London, as well as better travel connections by road with the London airports.

As mentioned in Chapter 4, BR had been worried by competition from the airlines for a long time; whilst speed had been seen as a priority, customer care – or the railways' lack of it – had also been seen as an important issue. Now that greater speed was no longer seen as the primary issue the railway sought to focus on customer care. Of course, air travel had changed since that time and the no-frills approach had lessened most people's expectations of air travel. The first-class traveller, however, still expected the best. As previously related, the modern railway carriage now used on most lines had come a long way since the 1960s. On many routes air conditioning was standard in all classes, seats were ergonomically designed and there was double glazing to keep out the enervating noise of high-speed travel. What more could the modern traveller desire?

In Chapter 8 I defined how the term 'Executive' had been used – and abused – for many years in various ways on BR services. In June 1983 the 'InterCity Executive Service' was launched, building on ideas from the existing Eastern Region Executive services. In January 1983 an eight-point action plan was introduced, featuring such things as parking spaces set aside for Executive passengers, tea and coffee served 'at seat' (in china cups) with a free local newspaper, improved public address announcements and window destination labels. Travellers Fare staff were also to be informed of passengers' names in advance, which should at least have discouraged any troublemakers! Further moves included negotiations with LT to see if Underground tickets could be purchased with an InterCity ticket, and catering trolleys in first class. In addition there were to be better menus and station information displays that highlighted Executive services. The preparatory work entailed more thorough cleaning programmes, although this wasn't announced as a plus point since it amounted to a tacit admission that trains weren't properly cleaned before. This decision yielded a bonus for second-class passengers as it meant the general upgrading of cleaning services throughout all trains.[25]

Despite the planning, the Executive initiative was not deemed a success; one aspect that drew criticism was the on-train catering, which was at that time in the hands of Travellers Fare. Quality was too dependent on which crew was on duty, and sometimes there was no catering at all.[26]

In 1985 BR decided to relaunch its most prestigious marque. In May of that year the last specifically designed Pullman coaches were withdrawn from main-line service as the *Manchester Pullman* – the last all-Pullman train – was withdrawn. In the same month the new Pullman concept was launched. This was really a revisiting of the Executive concept but under the Pullman brand, and it did offer what had always made Pullman special: the 'at seat' service. On certain designated trains, in carriages conveniently near the catering car, attendants would offer a free morning paper, tea or coffee as the customer liked it and meals, including the 'great British breakfast' for the early traveller. This was now to be provided on some services in first class without payment of a supplement.[27]

Shortly after the new Pullman concept was introduced all on-board catering was taken in-house by InterCity and more care was taken to choose the right personnel for Pullmans than with the Executive endeavour. There was talk of intensively briefing and grooming the Pullman attendants, who were chosen from the best and most suitable people.[28] All food was prepared fresh on the trains and the chefs were encouraged to create their own menus.[29]

Although not specially designed as Pullmans some of the new Mk3b First Open (FO) coaches that were built in 1984–85 were designated as Pullman and given names as well as being adorned with the Pullman crest. The names reflected the places the cars worked to – for example *John Lennon* worked on the Liverpool service. The new Pullman concept was, in the eyes of some, an ersatz Pullman but in just two years from their inception these trains had helped BR increase its first-class business by 20 per cent.[30] The number of Pullman service trains grew on the West Coast, East Coast and Western Region routes until, by 1991, there were fifty operating out of King's Cross, St Pancras, Euston and Paddington.[31]

The Mk3b FOs mentioned above were built instead of the last tranche of Mk3 sleeper coaches, which had come to be viewed as surplus to requirements by 1984. In the years 1978 to 1983 the sleeper business had dropped off from a peak of 811,000 bookings to just 475,000. This had initially been put down to the poor state of the Mk1 sleeper cars, once perceived as luxurious but now seen as shoddy and even dangerous in the wake of the Taunton sleeper fire. But the introduction of the Mk3 sleepers, with smoke alarms, did nothing to stem the loss of business. BR had to face up to the fact that it was a victim of its own success. Its high-speed daytime services were now attracting clientele away from the sleepers. The customers preferred a quick trip on an IC125 rather than a night's sleep on the slow train.[32]

The sale of the hotels in the 1980s meant that the railway catering organisation Travellers Fare became a directly controlled division of BR. It was still split between running station facilities and on-board catering, which were essentially competing enterprises. At stations, there were to be a lot of enterprising moves, such as the launch of the 'Casey Jones' burger brand in 1980. This was deliberately kept separate from the rest of Travellers Fare in terms of recruitment, organisation and image. It was such a success in all respects that people suggested that Travellers Fare start a similar operation to that of Casey Jones! Other successful initiatives were 'Trax', a sandwich outlet, and 'Trips', a brand which replaced the old railway cafeterias.[33] The last two were subsequently supplanted by Uppercrust and Quicksnack.[34] The first food court was opened at Euston on 27 June 1986.[35]

In June 1986 train catering was taken in-house by InterCity and became part of InterCity Catering Services.[36] Travellers Fare was retained to run the station catering facilities and subsequently became a limited company. It was now to have to compete with the private sector to run the units. By March/April 1988 eighty-nine competitive tendering processes were completed for station catering units, sixty-eight going to Travellers Fare and the other twenty-one to private competitors.[37] In December of that year Travellers Fare was the subject of a management buyout.[38]

The 1980s brought changes to on-board catering for the ordinary passenger. The wide aisles of the Mk3 carriages meant that trolleys could more easily pass up and down and in 1984 the NUR dropped its objection to them.[39] Although there was a small amount of unofficial action, the refreshment trolley quickly became a feature of many services. The Provincial services contracted private firms to operate these, the first being as early as 14 May 1984. By this time British Rail was divided up into sectors, and one result of this was rather amusing. Local managers in charge of Provincial services in North Wales hired a private firm to provide refreshment trolleys but overlooked the fact that one of the services turned into an InterCity service to London part way through its journey. Two trolleys, one private and the other Travellers Fare, started out at opposite ends of the train. The trolleys met somewhere near Llandudno, in a second-class saloon. Fortunately both sides took it well and the service was shared between them for the next few weeks.[40] Another conflict was the case of an enterprising steward on a Cannon Street–Hastings run who decided to take his trolley onto the platform at Cannon Street and ply intoxicating liquor to waiting travellers. The jealous manager of the station catering department knew his law, however; prior to 1988 (which this was) it was legal to sell alcohol on board a train, but a licence was required to sell it off-board on station premises. A phone call brought the British Transport Police and the enterprising individual was carted off to be questioned as to what he thought he was doing.[41]

An innovation tried from 1985 was with 'cook-chill meals'. This was piloted on the West Coast Main Line as 'Cuisine 2000', with Trust House Forte providing the prepared meals. The menus offered were very much of the upmarket variety, for example duckling in ginger and shallot sauce, but the project proved too ambitious.[42] The strains of providing a round-the-clock service over a 400-mile railway taxed THF management and logistics. Eventually the Cuisine 2000 food idea was taken back in-house and meals were once again prepared fresh on board.[43] This was not before more than fifty Mk3 catering vehicles were specifically and expensively converted to restaurant buffets for ready-made meals, including the West Coast Main Line's twenty-eight restaurant buffets with kitchens.[44]

InterCity was not the only sector to get new rolling stock in the 1980s. A start was made to phase out the elderly DMUs of the 1950s, mostly operated by the Provincial Sector, and replace them with new vehicles of modern design. BR's initial efforts to find a replacement for the 1950s DMU were hampered by the desire to meet conflicting demands, leading Roger Ford to make his famous comment that trying to pin down the ideal DMU replacement was like trying to 'nail jelly to a tree'.[45] One idea was to produce a diesel electric unit, based on the Southern's Diesel Electric Multiple-Units (DEMUs), which had always proved more reliable when compared to their diesel mechanical cousins. The advantage a DEMU offered was also the possibility that it could run together and in multiple with electric units, thus possibly forming the outer leg of a partially electrified route and a stopgap before full electrification. In 1982 BR unveiled two prototypes of a class, designated 210, one comprised of four cars, the other a three-car unit. These used a compact high-powered engine not only capable of matching the power of an EMU but also small enough to allow a side corridor beside the engine room – something that had not existed in the first generation of DEMUs. Reactions were mixed, with critics pointing to the fact that the seats didn't line up with the windows, thus allowing pillars to obstruct the view.[46]

The 210 was not to be the future of the BR diesel passenger unit. It was an expensive option and by the time it had been evaluated further, electrification projects were obviating the need for diesel units to be used in high-density operations in many areas. This left the services on which the old DMUs had always excelled – the cross-country and secondary services. Their replacements reflected two basic concepts: one was a return to the railbus and the other option was for a bogie-based vehicle.

The development of the high-speed freight vehicle (HSFV) in the 1960s (see Chapter 7) inevitably led to the notion that a modern four-wheeled passenger vehicle could be constructed that would be superior to the railbuses tried in the 1950s. BR was also now free from having to operate a sundries parcels service, meaning that the old operational problems outlined in Chapter 4 no longer applied. The new vehicles could be designed to focus purely on passengers.[47]

In 1977 BR commenced work on a new generation of railbuses in conjunction with British Leyland. This was to use the Leyland National body in conjunction with an underframe developed from the HSFV. The National bus was of integral construction and built out of modules, meaning that its length could be varied simply by changing the number of modules. The prototype railbus, designated LEV-1, was comprised of eight of these with a National Mk1 cab at each end. It had room for forty passengers.[48]

It was just the first in a number of prototypes. During the course of the development the bus body was considerably beefed up as it was felt that the road vehicle engineering wasn't sufficiently collision proof for railway use. The result of the rethink emerged in 1981 as what must surely be the ugliest vehicle ever built by BR, or perhaps any British railway company. The Class 140 was surely the railbus that Dr Frankenstein would have wanted to forget. Another important change at this point was that the 140 was not a single railcar but a two-car unit with a driving cab at each end. This would be the form that the production units would take.

The 140 was launched in June 1981 when it was demonstrated to the directors general of the seven PTEs before starting a nationwide tour. The director general of the West Yorkshire PTE was impressed enough to send a letter of intent to BR expressing interest in a fleet of 140s.[49]

As a consequence of the 140 prototype a further twenty units were built, this time with much improved aesthetics. After some teething troubles and some rebuilding these gave trouble-free service in Yorkshire, although they gave a bit of a rough ride at times. Several of the class were exported to Iran in 2000.[50]

In January 1984 British Rail ordered fifty new units of what were to become the 'Pacer' class (although the Cornish preferred the name 'Skipper'). Yet again built out of bus components it still looked more like a rail vehicle, although at £350,000 each the Pacer was much cheaper than a DMU. The aesthetics had been improved again. They had three-plus-two seating for 121 passengers, and the first units started operating in Manchester on 30 September 1985, under the auspices of what was at that time called the Greater Manchester PTE (GMPTE).

After initial teething troubles the Pacers proved themselves in service in terms of reducing the maintenance overheads of running the service, but they have never been a favourite with passengers. Despite all that work on perfecting the four-wheel ride they still have a reputation for being 'lively'. In Cornwall their use was short-lived as the length of the wheelbase conflicted with the tight curves on branch lines. Originally viewed as a single-vehicle solution to rural services, the design found its most extensive use as two-car units in metropolitan areas.[51]

The other sort of vehicle was more upmarket. The 'Sprinter' consisted of an integral body shell and rode on bogies. These were for short-haul work so were, in the first instance, only gangwayed within set, lacking corridor connectors for a through corridor for passengers to other units. That was to change with later versions. Initially two versions were commissioned in March 1983, one having been designed by BR (Class 150) and the other by Metro-Cammell (Class 151). The BR 150 was based on the excellent tried and tested Mk3 body shell, whereas the Metropolitan-Cammell design was new. In many ways the Metropolitan-Cammell units were regarded as superior, but because of some union objections to the original layout they were late coming into service and by that time the decision had been taken to order further examples of the BR type.[52]

The next range of Sprinters were dubbed 'Super Sprinters' and were to replace large numbers of cascaded loco-hauled coaches on longer routes. They were thus all designed with corridor connectors at both ends. Two versions were commissioned: the 155, built by Leyland Bus, and the 156, built by Metropolitan-Cammell.

Initially the 155s proved very unreliable but the 156s achieved very good availability and proved excellent value.

The Pacers had been developed from the idea for a single-vehicle railbus but had ended up as two-car – sometimes three-car – multiple-units. For the Sprinters the reverse happened as Provincial decided that two-car units were surplus to requirements on many routes. Thus 155 Sprinters were sent to Hunslet and converted to single-car units with a cab at each end. Known to enthusiasts as Skateboards, they became the natural successors to the single-car 'bubble cars' – the single-car versions of the modernisation-era DMUs. Skateboards can work in single or be teamed with any other member of the 141–150 and 153–158 family to strengthen a service.

Given the general success of the Sprinter class a further development was planned. In 1989 the class 158 'Express Sprinter' was introduced. Sadly this proved to be too ambitious as the new body shell was initially troublesome.[53] Twenty-two of the 158 Sprinters were modified to become Class 159, taking over from loco-hauled trains on the Waterloo–Exeter route from 1993.

Whatever the technical difficulties, the new rolling stock – particularly the Sprinters – heralded a new look and an entirely new level of comfort for the Regional/Provincial passenger. Whether it was down to this or the business boom of the late 1980s, or a mixture of both, the sector's fortunes were to be transformed. Passenger miles increased by 15 per cent from 1987 to 1991, and between 1981 and 1990, 106 miles of railway and 122 stations were reopened to passengers under the sector.[54] The Pacers and Sprinters were a further step in the relentless march of the multiple-units and the demise of the loco-hauled passenger train.

A spin-off from the development of the Leyland Experimental Vehicle (LEV) and the association with British Leyland was the Leyland coach. This was a development of the LEV railbus project which BR undertook with British Leyland. The coach was basically a Leyland bus body mounted upon a recycled Mk1 underframe, thus yet again proving that railways are masters of 'make do and mend'. Despite being experimental and not officially in BR stock the Leyland coach did see some use. Passengers were not generally impressed. It seems that our grandfathers would have accepted – or put up with – things that are no longer acceptable to us; perhaps we are spoiled; we are certainly more demanding. The Leyland coach was a pretty desperate, cheap option that basically presupposed that the edge of quality had already crumbled back a couple of stages. It was also a retrograde step in prolonging the separate underframe/body mode. Goodness knows what the Health and Safety Executive would have made of it post the Clapham rail disaster. With the push upmarket that we have described above it was unlikely that InterCity would be interested in it and the scheme was abandoned in the mid-1980s.[55]

As well as new rolling stock there was also substantial electrification in the 1980s. Some schemes were extensions of, or the connecting up of, suburban electrification schemes, but there were also some medium-distance routes such as those in East and West Anglia and the third-rail electrification of the Hastings route. Then, of course, there was the big one: the East Coast Main Line. It had now been delayed for more than thirty years since it was first considered in the 1950s – indeed delayed for more than sixty years if you date it from when the NER first proposed electrification from north of York.

Since the electrification of the WCML costs had come down substantially with the view that the overhead equipment of the 1960s era had been over-engineered.[56] Money was also saved in the West and East Anglia electrifications by cascading stock from elsewhere – the locos came from the WCML which was to be getting the new Class 90s. Many of the EMUs were refurbished examples. After all, the routes out to Cambridge, Harwich and Norwich did not have to compete with motorways and airlines and were thus a low priority for new stock.[57]

The ECML was a different matter. With major motorways and those dratted internal airlines something prestigious had to be cooked up. It needed to look good in the press photos and do the business. By this time the Advanced Passenger Train (APT) and tilting technology had finally been abandoned so BR cooked up the 225 – in fact a 140mph train (225km/h is equivalent to 140mph). The traction method chosen was based on the tractor-trailer concept first developed for the Bournemouth electrification on the South Western Main Line and then further developed by the Scottish Region for the Edinburgh–Glasgow services.

By the mid-1980s the advantages of a nose cone in terms of lessening atmospheric resistance were well proven. Such designs were also a success in terms of public image, but the power unit of the 225 was to be a single locomotive, not a power car each end, as was the case with the IC125. As a locomotive it was to be detached and reattached to rakes of coaches and maybe used for other duties. It would thus need to have a cab at each end. The problem was that the turbulence created by a streamlined locomotive cab facing inwards against the end of a carriage is much greater than a normal 'blunt' end. Thus the new Class 91s were designed with a streamlined end and a blunt end, both containing driving cabs. This prompted *Modern Railways* to enquire whether turntables might not be required.[58] In fact turntables were not to be needed. The Class 91 locomotives were all to be northwards facing, hauling the trains in that direction. For southbound running the driving would be done from specially built, non-powered Driving Van Trailers, or DVTs, with streamlined fronts at the London end.[59]

The carriages to be used were the new Mk4s, developed by Metropolitan-Cammell from their successful Class 156 Super-Sprinter design.[60] The big difference was that, unlike the Sprinter, the sides of the Mk4 sloped upwards towards the roof, like the APT. This was in the hope that tilting might be added later. The Mk4s were mounted on Swiss SIG bogies because the BR version was not up to the job in time for the production run.[61] They were originally available in two flavours: Pullman (first) and Standard. Some of the standard vehicles were fitted with disabled spaces and had suitable lavatories. There were also catering vehicles that included a kitchen and buffet and seating for twenty first-class passengers.[62]

The electrification was completed to Leeds by 1988 and to Edinburgh via York in 1991. At last the other important main line to Scotland was electrified.

The largest investment of all in terms of railway infrastructure in the last 100 years must surely be the Channel Tunnel. Although ultimately to be cut out of the process of constructing it, British Rail made a significant contribution to its initial planning.

The idea of a Channel Tunnel was a long-held dream stretching back to the very early nineteenth century, and probably even earlier. Inevitably, with the growth of the railways the idea of a railway tunnel emerged. In 1887 a Channel Tunnel company was formed with the South Eastern Railway (SER) as a shareholder.[63] Things got as far as digging test borings (during which the SER discovered the Kent coal seam, much to its benefit) but the tunnel, needless to say, was not built at this point. There was much discussion in the inter-war years but again nothing happened. In 1948 the BTC inherited the SER's block of shares in the Channel Tunnel Company via the Southern Railway, and when the idea – and the company – was revived once again in 1957 the BTC necessarily became a partner.

Brian Robertson was keen on the idea and plans were very advanced by 1961, as the BTF film *Modelling for the Future* shows. This illustrates the tunnel – or tunnels – using proprietary models, including the Minic slot car system. The tunnel shown is basically as we know it today – two tunnels, one for each direction with a service tunnel in between and car carriers ferrying passengers and cars through the tunnel to and from terminals at each end. This vision, simple to construct using Tri-ang toy trains, was not to be completed in 12in to 1ft scale (full size) for another thirty years.

Dr Beeching was rather less enthusiastic about the tunnel but work continued. On 8 July 1966 the French and British Prime Ministers, Georges Pompidou and Harold Wilson, announced a decision to actually build it.[64] The year 1975 was set as a target date, but the Labour administration that took over from the Conservatives in 1974 was much less keen on the tunnel than the governments that preceded it, and the scheme was once more aborted.

The tunnel dream was kept alive in the form of the mousehole. This was a proposal that it should consist of only a single tunnel with a single track that would facilitate trains travelling in both directions organised into flights (first in one direction, then in the other). This was refined into a plan, initially circulated by BR in a private document in 1981, that proposed a tunnel of Continental (UIC) loading gauge with a service tunnel running alongside.[65]

But already the political landscape had once more changed in the tunnel's favour. The election of the Conservative Party in 1979 resulted in Margaret Thatcher becoming prime minster. Thatcher was pro-tunnel, provided that the British government didn't have to pay for it. In September 1981 agreement was forged with President Mitterrand of France for the commissioning of a joint Anglo-French study of the options for the tunnel. This reported seven months later but then the two governments decided to await the outcomes of legal, financial and organisational reports into the tunnel. Essentially, the work that had already been done was being redone.[66]

In France the construction was to be financed by the government, but on the British side money was to be raised from private companies. Tenders were accepted from companies wishing to build the tunnel (and to finance the British contribution) and the winners were an Anglo-French consortium called Channel Tunnel Group/France Manche, that consisted of a conglomeration of banks and construction firms.

The tunnel they built was the one that had been planned with the help of British Railways in the late 1950s and early 1960s.

With the tunnel construction in private hands all that was left for BR to do was to link it to the main rail infrastructure and provide an international terminal. The first international terminal was built at Waterloo and required extensive modifications to the infrastructure as well as new works to enable trains from the tunnel to reach it.

The High Speed Rail Link was to be constructed by a British Rail subsidiary called Union Railways.

British Rail's preferred option was a line to King's Cross under central London but various proposals were shot down by government. The choice of the Stratford route was announced on 9 October 1991. From the political viewpoint it had the key advantages of not rampaging through the gardens of as many suburban Tory voters as the direct route, whilst at the same time promising regeneration for an area in the East End of London. Bob Reid II was furious, though, and clearly felt that BR was being mucked about for political reasons. He described the whole matter as a 'pantomime' and pointed out that it would add twenty minutes to the journey and take commuters far out of their way.[67] The bizarre Stratford route is what we are stuck with, though, albeit with St Pancras now substituted for King's Cross.

So by the late 1980s it seemed that BR had dispelled the doldrums. Like the rest of Britain, it seemed to have new energy and purpose, a new spring in its step – or its wheel. But there are doubters of the 'golden age' thesis, and Terry

Gourvish is amongst them. In his book *British Rail: From Integration to Privatisation* he points out that in the 1980s fares were high. There was also the matter of the decline of the rail freight business. He also points to a lack of investment in infrastructure compared with countries like France, who spent five times as much in the period 1987–91. There is of course also the issue that much of the BR investment was paid for in one-off sales from its property portfolio.[68]

A parliamentary select committee report of 1989 found that while there had been a 2 per cent increase in spending on roads between 1 April 1986 and 1 April 1988, there had been a massive 45 per cent reduction in spending on rail and a 19 per cent reduction on London Transport buses and Underground. BR's external financing limits had fallen by 43 per cent. The committee recommended a halt to cuts in BR's PSO grant and an increase in support for Network SouthEast to relieve congestion. There was also much criticism of BR's performance figures, with strong suggestions that they had been massaged to look better than they were.[69]

In 2003 Tony Blair was presented with a paper entitled *Where Has All The Money Gone*, which detailed a projected £21 billion rise in rail infrastructure costs until 2010/11. The simple disorganisation of the privatised rail system, requiring that unchallenged and uncoordinated decisions be brought together and made to work, was a substantial part of this, together with increased safety expenditure. But another part was the backlog of track re-laying that Network Rail traced back to 1985.[70]

To the passenger a main issue was the lack of staff as personnel continued to disappear in the 1980s. In 1991 a code of practice was agreed between BR and the Central Transport Consultative Committee (CTCC) to ensure that better facilities were provided at de-staffed stations – these were to include better communication, full access to ticket options, including through booking, adequate lighting, proper cleaning and sheltered seating. The CTCC considered that too many stations were already unstaffed and stated that there should be no more relegated to this state.[71] As if to rub salt into the wound of those who used unstaffed stations, in 1993 InterCity brought back luggage-carrying porters (for a fee of £2) at main stations in addition to the Customer Welcome Teams, introduced at forty main stations from 1992.[72] There could be no doubt whose business was the most valued.

12

The Safety Case

nthony Hidden's report into the Clapham Junction accident stated of
BR's safety culture that 'The best of intentions regarding safe working
practices was permitted to go hand in hand with the worst of inaction
in ensuring that such practices were put into effect.'[1] His words were damning,
but were they really fair? The truth is that British Rail had a rather good safety
record, and there were many years when it lost precisely zero – *nought* – passengers to accidents. That is something that could never be said of our homicidal
road system. In his book *Danger on the Line*[2] former British Rail safety officer
Stanley Hall makes the point that no coherent pattern emerges from an analysis
of those accidents where ten or more people died in the years from 1967 to
1989. The accidents at West Ealing on 19 December 1973, the fire at Taunton
on 6 July 1978 and the accident at Polmont on 30 July 1984, all had totally different causes and, whilst carelessness was a factor in two of them, no universal
pattern could be discerned.

The Hidden Inquiry was an unusual affair conducted under a rarely used piece
of legislation, Section 7 of the Regulation of Railways Act 1871,[3] which gave the
minister the power to hold an investigation into a railway accident in open court.
This power had only ever been used twice before for the main railway system –
in the case of the Tay Bridge disaster of 1879 and the Hixon level crossing disaster
in 1968. Normally in BR's time inquiries into accidents, whether major or minor,
had continued to be carried out by the Railway Inspectorate that had been established in accordance with the Railway Regulation Act 1840. When the railways
were nationalised in 1948 the decision was taken to retain the long-established
Inspectorate as a separate body. Throughout its existence BR benefited, as the
private companies had, from its criticism and experience. As before, its role was
advisory and it was not a prosecuting authority – until 1990, when it was placed
under the Health and Safety Inspectorate with, it would seem, little regard for the
previous nature of its role.

The first major incident to take place on British Railways after nationalisation was the Harrow and Wealdstone disaster, and a disaster it was, killing 112 people and injuring more than 300, eighty-eight seriously enough for them to be detained in hospital.[4] It all started to go wrong at Harrow and Wealdstone when the driver of the Perth–Euston sleeper ignored stop signals and consequently his train ploughed into the back of a suburban passenger train which was standing at the station platform. This was densely packed with 800 passengers in nine carriages. The three rear carriages were compressed into the space of one. Sadly that was not the end of it; the engine at the head of the Perth–Euston sleeper was obstructing the down fast line and the 8 a.m. Euston–Liverpool–Manchester train collided with it at significant speed. The destruction was 'altogether exceptional' in the words of the investigating officer.[5]

The Harrow and Wealdstone disaster brought forward once more the call for ATC – Automatic Train Control. This title is in fact something of a misnomer, as it is in fact more of a warning system. British Railways decided to call it the Automatic Warning System, or AWS. This was a system that warned the driver when approaching a signal at caution. If the driver didn't acknowledge it by pressing a plunger, it made an automatic brake application. He has the power to override this – an issue we shall come to. ATC/AWS systems had been around for a long time and the Great Western Railway, uniquely amongst the four group companies, had fitted all its main lines with its version of ATC by 1939.[6] It was alone though, despite the fact that a committee chaired by Colonel Pringle of the Inspectorate had reported on such systems in 1922 and pressed for the universal installation of ATC. Apart from on the GWR no notice was taken of this recommendation; the reorganisation of the grouping was undoubtedly amongst the causes (the GWR was, uniquely, almost immune from such turmoil). In the late 1920s Colonel Pringle chaired another committee which, yet again, pressed for installation of ATC; nothing came of this either.

When the Railway Executive (RE) was formed in 1948 the need for ATC was appreciated but matters got bogged down in questions and experiments over what form ATC should take. The GWR system had some issues and in general the RE preferred the Hudd system that had been deployed by the LMS on the LT&SR. Finally minds settled on a modified version of the Hudd system and plans for this were in preparation when the Harrow and Wealdstone accident took place. In his report on the accident Lieutenant Colonel Wilson reported the Railway Inspectorate's long insistence of the need for ATC, and commented:

In the 41 years 1912-1952, Formal Inquiries were held into 640 Train Accidents in which 1,416 persons were killed. Of these accidents, 66, or rather more than 10 per cent, might have been prevented or mitigated by Automatic Train Control of Warning type, but it will be noted that the fatalities which might have been saved were 28 per cent of the 41-year total, or 399 lives in all, including 112 at Harrow.[7]

The fitting of AWS to British Railways lines was to be a long and protracted process. The Executive had planned for it to be fitted on 6,700 route miles. Despite a further commitment in the modernisation plan the installation was only nearing completion in 1985, when 6,313 route miles had been fitted (and this included replacement of the old GWR system).[8] AWS had to compete with other priorities in a financially constrained organisation being pressured to cut costs. Meanwhile people died.

There was also an objection to its installation from the Southern Region. To see why it is necessary to explain the Southern's four-aspect signalling system, used to organise its intensively trafficked routes into London. Signals in a four-aspect system have four lights: red, green and two yellows.

They display the following aspects:

Red – Danger – stop at this signal
Green – Proceed – line is clear
Double yellow – Preliminary caution – next signal is single yellow
Single yellow – Caution – next signal is red

The issue over AWS arises because the system was devised only for warning signals in a simple two-indication system. In a four-aspect system it would have to apply to all signals and would trigger the same warning at the double yellow as at the single yellow (and also at the red). The concern of the Southern Region was that, with so many signals triggering the warnings, cancellation would become automatic for drivers – particularly those of EMUs capable of slowing down in the distance between the single yellow and the red due to their electro-pneumatic brakes. It was feared that one day someone would cancel the warning at a single yellow without thinking about it, with fatal consequences.[9] Eventually the system was installed on the SR, but the concerns of the Southern were to be proven as valid by subsequent events.

Meanwhile, other matters concerned the railway engineers. Apart from trains crashing into each other the railways are also confronted with the problem of ensuring that the trains stay on the track, particularly at high speeds. This means that the track must be in a fit state to bear trains. Proper construction is one prerequisite, regular maintenance the other.

No one can dispute that the switch to continuous welded rail (CWR) that was started in the mid-1960s was a significant contribution to safety. The joints in traditional track resulted in stresses and fatigue due to the impact of the wheels against the rail ends. The old system comprised of short lengths was in need of regular inspection and occasional remedial action if disaster was to be averted. On occasions that action was not taken in time; sometimes bureaucracy got in the way of urgent action.

On Sunday 5 November 1967 the 19.43 Hastings–Charing Cross service was approaching Hither Green on the up fast line.[10] It consisted of twelve coaches, formed of the special diesel electric multiple-units built for the Hastings line. The third coach of the train derailed but the train continued on for a quarter of a mile with the passengers becoming more and more alarmed. The wheels of the coach then encountered a set of points which caused the derailed coach, together with the one in front of it and the two behind it, to fall over and slide for 250yd. During this time the coach sides were ripped off and the passengers inside were crushed and mangled between the moving debris and the track. Forty-nine people died and twenty-seven were seriously injured.

The cause of this disaster was found to be a broken rail; a piece had sheared away from the end as a result of the stresses that the track had been placed under. Colonel McMullen, reporting for the Inspectorate on the disaster, was scathing as regards the standard of maintenance on the section and of management, right the way up to the Chief Civil Engineer. The primary cause had been a bolt hole that had been weakened by the stresses that the track was placed under – a fracture had spread outwards from this, eventually weakening the whole rail and causing it to break. Such a fracture is known as a 'star' crack, due to the shape of the fractures radiating out from the bolt hole, suggesting the rays of a star.

It was not the first such accident of this kind. Just a few months earlier the *North Britain* express travelling from Edinburgh to Leeds became derailed whilst travelling at 75mph between Acklington and Chevington. On this occasion, mercifully, the carriages had remained upright, there were no fatalities, and only nine passengers out of the 160 total needed hospital treatment.[11]

The whole issue of broken rails had been causing some alarm in railway circles for a while and in his report for 1966[12] Colonel McMullen had already pinpointed it as a cause of concern and highlighted the fact that such incidents were increasing year on year: 238 in 1964, 279 in 1965 and 383 in 1966. Particularly high in number were star cracks of the type that had caused the Hither Green disaster, and 179 had occurred over a three-year period, comprising 47 per cent of all rail breakages. The trend was particularly high on the Southern and the Eastern Region.

Why might this have been? Colonel McMullen had an answer, stating that: 'It will be noted that this category of fracture in particular is appreciably greater on lines where electric multiple-unit trains operate more than on other lines, due possibly to the heavy battering which the rail ends receive from this type of traction.'

And one with which BR's own engineers concurred:

They are firmly of the opinion that the smaller diameter of the wheels of electric and diesel locomotives and, particularly, the relatively high un-sprung weight on the wheels of diesel-electric and most electric locomotives and on electric and diesel-electric multiple-unit sets resulting from axle-hung traction motors, have a more punishing effect on the track generally than steam locomotives, particularly if the condition of the track is not very good, and produce increased stresses at rail joints that contribute to fatigue failures. The increase in the speed of passenger trains, in the axle loads of high capacity freight vehicles, and in the higher average speed of freight trains must also contribute, as must the increase in the number of stress cycles on rail joints arising from the relatively large number of axles with axle-hung motors and the running of long trains of high capacity freight wagons.[13]

Colonel McMullen was to criticise strongly the maintenance regime of the line with a focus on the chief officers responsible: 'all of whom were, I think, prepared to accept too low a standard of maintenance.'[14] Colonel McMullen's sensible solution to the problem of fatigue cracks at rail joints was an obvious one – reduce the number of joints by continuing to replace short rail sections with CWR. On the LMR this had not been an entire solution, as the practice of electric arc welding had also led to cracks developing in the joints.[15] The truth was that British Railways was on a learning curve when it came to the new technology of modern traction and how it affected the track. The organisation was now learning the downside of decisions that had been hailed as positives a decade before. As related in Chapter 7, the axle-hung, nose-suspended traction motors had been recognised as a mistake and had not been continued in the IC125s or the Class 87 electric locomotives.

Star cracks are not the only issue that short-length rails suffer from. To some extent all rails suffer rail creep – this is where the rail moves longitudinally through the chairs or clips holding it – although modern technology such as the Pandrol clip has led to a significant reduction in this phenomenon. In the days of short-length rail it was particularly serious as gaps were left between sections of rail to allow for expansion due to heat. If creep causes these gaps to close up along a sequence of rails, then in hot weather they reach the point where they just instantly buckle. This is most likely to happen when they come under further stress – the passing of a train over them produces precisely this effect.

Tattenhall Junction had formerly been the point at which the Whitchurch line departed from the Crewe–Chester main line, but the branch had been closed since 1964 and the track simplified. The point still bore the name of the junction, though. The main line was inspected by the traditional method of walking. This was done three times a week, on Mondays, Wednesdays and Fridays, come rain or shine, fair weather or foul, by leading trackman A. Pinnington. Mr Pinnington had been a railwayman since 1946 and a leading trackman since 1967.

In February 1971 Pinnington had become concerned about a section on the up line approaching the junction where he had noticed rail creep.[16] Shortly after noticing it Pinnington brought the matter to the attention of his superiors and made entries in his Report Book. On 20 March and 23 March Pinnington recorded 'very bad rail creep – needs attention' twice in the official book.

In mid-May things were decidedly worse and on 23 May Pinnington made a record of the extent of the creep in his Report Book and filled out a patrol-man's action slip. By this time he was concerned about the prospects of the rail buckling in hot weather. When he handed these in his superior made a point of going to look at the site in person and returned with the remark: 'I will get it put in to be done.'

By his own testimony the permanent way supervisor responsible, Mr M. Garratt, had walked the line himself early in 1970, had noticed the rail creep and had scheduled work to be done on 9 May and 16 May. This had not been carried out however, as it had proved impossible to get possession of the line since it had conflicted with maintenance work on the Manchester line. He had inspected the track again on 11 May but did not consider the creep significant enough for urgent action, and when he received the reports from his subordinates he there-fore rejected them. His focus was taken instead by another section of the line which he believed needed more urgent attention.

In mid-June Pinnington used waterproof chalk to mark three sleepers at the site 'very bad creep'. He mentioned this to the track chargeman in charge of the permanent way gang working on the line, who made no comment.

The day of 2 July 1971 was gloriously sunny. It was a great day for a school outing to the seaside and 380 children set out on a school excursion special from Smethwick to the North Wales seaside resort of Rhyl. If their parents had known of the state of the track they were to pass over they probably would never have been allowed to go. Salty, sandy and sunburned the children returned along the stretch of line that had so concerned Mr Pinnington. The signalman accepted the train into the section at 18.01 and expected it to arrive five minutes later. At 18.08 he was looking down the line when he observed it coming towards him with a trail of rubble and dust following. The signalman rushed out onto the platform and raised his hands above his head to indicate danger. The driver slowed the train and came to a stop. Soon after, the guard arrived on the platform; he had been sitting in the rearmost, tenth coach when suddenly it had jumped into the air and begun to sway violently. He had grabbed hold of the handbrake and had seen sparks flying from beneath the coach. Then the coach had struck the bridge and turned over. Luckily he was able to climb out. The rest of the train had continued, although a part of the side of the ninth coach was lying on the track. In the tenth coach two children had died.

In his inquiry Major Rose came to the inevitable conclusion that the cause of the disaster was that the rails had finally given way and buckled under the tenth coach, causing it to leave the track and collide with the bridge. The blame lay squarely with Garratt, and the report exonerated Pinnington who, the Major felt, had done as much as he could to alert his superiors to the danger. The report revealed that Garratt had been involved in a dispute with his superiors over the manning needed to maintain the line, and despite being given an extra ten-man crew had still considered he was understaffed, although Major Rose found that he couldn't agree with this and instead considered that Garratt had been a man out of his depth and unable to cope with modern methods of track maintenance.

Major Rose also commented about the lack of communication between the men on the ground and those in the Divisional Engineers' Office. He made criticisms of the organisational structure in which authority was centralised at divisional level and not delegated to individuals lower down.

For the rail passenger, level crossings do not present the danger that they represent for the road user, for whom a misstep at these locations can be fatal. Normally the effect of an incident at a level crossing is one of inconvenience to rail users, however awful may be the consequences for those who get in the way of a moving train. Passengers do occasionally suffer minor injuries when a train brakes or collides with a car or truck, but as a railway vehicle is very much more robust than a road vehicle it is usually the occupants of the latter that suffer the consequences. It is not always so, though. There have been incidents at level crossings which have resulted in rail passenger deaths.

The issues of road and rail have occupied the minds of the authorities from the very earliest days in Britain. The 1839 Highway (Railway Crossings) Act had required:

> Wherever a railroad crosses or shall hereafter cross any turnpike road or any highway or statute labour road for carts or carriages in Great Britain the proprietors or directors of the company or proprietors of the said railroad shall make and maintain good and sufficient gates across each end of such turnpike or other road as aforesaid at each of the said crossings, and shall employ good and proper persons to open and shut such gates, so that the persons, carts, or carriages passing along such turnpike or highway shall not be exposed to any danger or damage by the passing of any carriages or engines along the said railroad.

Further stipulations were made in the Railway Clauses Consolidation Act of 1845, particularly requiring that gates should be closed across the railway when no train was passing. By the 1950s the traditional style of gated level crossing so mandated was proving irksome to both the railways and the road user. Road traffic could be held for a considerable time due to the manual nature of the operation. It also became quite difficult to recruit people to the role in the 1950s due to high employment, further lending weight to the case for automation.[17]

The 1954 Transport Act allowed lifting barriers to be installed upon permission being received, for each separate case, from the Minister of Transport, but the crossings still had to be manned. With the need for a modern solution pressing, in 1956 Colonel McMullen, on behalf of the Railway Inspectorate (RI), went on a fact-finding mission to France, Holland and Belgium to see how things were done there. The Colonel found plenty of automatic crossings functioning safely and wrote a positive report, culminating in the Minister for Transport being given the power to relieve British Railways from its previous responsibilities at a particular crossing (each case being taken individually) and to order that automatic barriers could be installed. The restrictions laid down led to only two such crossings being installed by 1961 but in that year Colonel McMullen went to see the situation in the US and Canada and on his return wrote a report leading to a lifting of some of these restrictions. It still was not enough and by 1963 there were only six automatic crossings, but further lifting of the restrictions meant that the number had risen to 205 by 1967 – most of these in rural areas.

The type chosen was the 'automatic half barrier' (AHB) type.[18] These permitting vehicles to escape if the barriers came down when they were on the crossing, since they only blocked the carriageway leading on to it, not the egress. It was decided not to link the automatic crossings with the signalling system as it would make it more costly.

To warn road users of the new crossings a standard leaflet was devised entitled 'Automatic Level Crossing Half Barriers'. This differed from one crossing to another only in the name and location printed on the front. Its main focus was on getting people to obey the red lights and the barriers but it did mention, on page three, the need for herders of animals and drivers of exceptional or heavy loads to phone before crossing. Signs to this effect were also placed on the road before the crossings. Sadly these warnings proved to be insufficient.

On 8 November 1966 a small low-loader arrived at a level crossing at Leominster and proceeded to cross, only to become grounded as it passed over the crossing. The driver got out to see what the trouble was and was told by some railway workers nearby that an express was due at the crossing in just a few minutes. At that moment the lights on the crossing started to flash and the signalman who was present told the lorry driver that he had no way to halt the train. The lorry driver returned to his cab and began to move the lorry slowly by over-revving the engine and working the clutch. He got it out of the way just as the express passed through. The train came to a halt half a mile from the crossing.

This near-miss led the owners of the low-loader, Robert Wynn and Sons Limited, to send a letter to the Department of Transport describing the incident and criticising the short warning time given by such crossings, as well as the fact that there was no way of stopping trains in an emergency. The reply the firm got was bureaucratic in style; it justified the design of the crossings on the basis that they had ministerial approval and stated the rather obvious fact that vehicles weren't supposed to become stationary on the crossings. It pointed out that trains take a long distance to stop and that was why there was no way to stop them at such places. This letter was later to be condemned as 'remarkable for its arrogance and lack of insight'.[19] Nowhere did the letter point out that drivers of vehicles with exceptional or heavy loads were supposed to telephone the signalman and check whether it was safe to cross.

On Saturday 6 January 1968 another Robert Wynn and Sons Limited transporter was conveying a transformer from the English Electric plant at Stafford to their plant at Hixon. It was a colossal vehicle with sixteen axles, eight at each end and with two six-wheeled tractors, front and rear. The transporter was such that it had its own steering cabin. In total this 'juggernaut', together with tractors, was 148ft long, weighed 162 tons and could only travel at just over 3mph. It required a police escort and followed a route agreed in advance with the Department of Transport. Towards the end of its journey it had to cross the West Coast Main Line at a crossing at Hixon. This had recently been converted to a crossing of the automatic half barrier type. When a train 'struck in' the lights automatically started to flash and the barriers lowered. There was only 24 seconds between this warning and an express train reaching the crossing. It was not enough time for a 148ft-long vehicle, travelling at just over 3mph, to clear the crossing.

The police escort went over the crossing first, the policemen not even considering the risks of the transporter crossing the line. There were warning notices together with instructions for drivers of heavy loads to stop and phone the signalmen but neither the police escort nor the transporter's drivers heeded them. The transporter had just begun to cross when the lights activated and the barriers started to lower. This was, in the words of the report, to the 'consternation' of its crew.[20] From that point things happened very fast. Both of the drivers of the tractors accelerated as hard as they could, struggling to get the juggernaut clear of the railway line. They were unable to do so and an express train hit the transporter, killing three men in the cab of the locomotive, including the driver, as well as eight passengers in the train. Forty-four passengers and a restaurant car attendant were injured, six seriously. The actions of the transporter drivers prevented a far worse disaster as they had moved the bulk of the transformer out of the way and the train had struck a part of the vehicle instead, meaning that less damage had occurred. The Report of the Public Inquiry was to commend them both, particularly the driver of the rear tractor who actually worked very hard to put himself in the way of the train. The Inquiry was to find that the main blame fell on Robert Wynn and Sons for failing to acquaint their drivers properly with the rules regarding the use of automatic half barrier crossings. The police and the Department of Transport also came in for a share of the blame. British Rail was entirely innocent of any fault; it was one of those cases where the railways were the victims of other people's negligence.

The Hixon Report also recommended the continued installation of AHBs, but others got cold feet and there was a pause of some ten years in which very few automatic crossings were installed.[21] It was only after a new appraisal was published in 1978[22] that confidence in automatic crossings was slowly restored in Britain.[23]

All untimely deaths are tragic but some are definitely more ghastly than others. That is especially true of the Taunton sleeper fire tragedy of 6 July 1978.[24]

The cause of the accident was, to put it bluntly, negligence of the kind that so often occurs in large organisations when people are under pressure, and where changes and alterations are made to equipment and procedures and no one has time to think through the consequences.

In those days the 21.30 Penzance–Paddington sleeper train changed locomotives at Plymouth and as it did so additional carriages were added to the front of the train. On the night of 5 July 1978 there were three carriages from Plymouth: a full brake and two sleepers. These had been standing at the platform in Plymouth station since approximately 22.30 so that the occupants could board and make themselves comfortable for the night. Fifteen minutes before departure they had been backed on to the front of the train from Penzance and the electric train heating was switched on. The vehicles now formed coaches A, B and C of a nine-coach train lettered A to J.

At this time electric train heating on the sleeper coaches was something relatively new; sleeping car W2437 – the middle of the three vehicles from Plymouth – had been fitted with electric train heating in 1976. The train left at 00.30. It stopped at Newton Abbot and Exeter, where the driver and guard were relieved. It departed Exeter at 01.54.

As the train passed through Whiteball tunnel the sleeping car attendant in the coaches D and E noticed a smell of burning and went to investigate. Going forwards into coach C he found thick smoke and immediately returned to his pantry and pulled the communication cord, then went forward again shouting 'Fire!' and banging on doors in order to raise the alarm. He attempted to get into coach B, but the smoke was too thick. He had pulled the communication cord at exactly the same time as the driver had operated the brake, leading to some confusion, as initially the driver couldn't understand why he was unable to take off the brake again. He then saw fire coming from the train and notified the nearest signal box by using a lineside telephone before joining the other train staff in attempting to fight the fire and evacuate passengers. Thankfully the train had come to a stand near to a road and the emergency services were able to access the scene comparatively quickly.

In total twelve people died, including one who was amongst the sixteen taken to hospital as critically injured. All of those who died inside coach A died as a result of carbon monoxide poisoning; however, one man from the coach escaped but collapsed and died from a heart attack. Another from coach C died of a heart attack and another lady expired later in hospital as a result of pneumonia.

How had the fire started, and why had so many passengers been overcome by poisonous gas before they could escape?

The two carriages had previously formed a down train from Paddington and this had produced soiled bedding which needed to be returned to the laundry at Old Oak Common (London) for cleaning. It was a long-established practice for this to be stripped off and collected into bags which were then piled, together

with bags of fresh bedding, into the vestibules at the London ends of the coaches.
The habit of stacking these bags in this position dated from the time when the
carriages were steam heated. Now they were electrically heated. The heater had
proved hot enough to cause the bags and their contents to smoulder and to give
off toxic fumes. Right above the heater was the vent that allowed air from the
vestibule to pass into the sleeping compartments.

On at least one previous occasion bags of linen were set on fire by the electric
heaters at the ends of the coaches. This should have been a wake-up call but the
danger associated with this practice was not made known.[25]

British Rail often came in for unfair criticism but it was also capable of an
unbelievably crass ability to display its own failings in public. In the August 1979
edition of *Modern Railways* Alan Williams delivered a too well deserved rocket to
BR for:

> the increasingly common habit of leaving the smashed remains of locomotives
> and rolling stock in full public view long after the contretemps that brought
> about their demise has passed. In bygone days, if the wreckage could not be
> moved immediately, decency demanded that at least it be securely sheeted
> over …

He continued:

> for sheer bad taste it would be hard to rival Wolverton's latest effort in parking
> the charred remains of last year's Taunton sleeper fire – complete with smoke-
> blackened windows – in full view of the West Coast Main Line.[26]

On Monday 12 December 1988 the 07.18 Basingstoke to Waterloo train was
proceeding along the stretch of line between Earlsfield and Clapham Junction.
It was a crowded commuter train with between fifteen and twenty people
standing in the cage of the guard's van. The rest of the train was so packed
that the guard could not get up and down it to clip tickets. Its speed was
about 60mph when it approached signal WF138 in the cutting to the south-
west of Clapham Junction station, beside Spencer Park. The driver, Alexander
McClymont, observed that WF138 was green, indicating that he could proceed
at his current speed. The AWS confirmed this via the correct sound and by
showing a completely black disc on the indicator. As the train was about 30yd
away, however, the indication changed from green to red. The very fact that
it changed in that way suggested a fault in the signalling installation, or an
obstruction on the line.

At first Driver McClymont made an emergency brake application but then
realised that it would bring the train up short of signal WF47, where he would
have to alight and telephone the signalman to report the incident. He stopped at

signal WF47 and, all things being right, should have been able to be confident that signal WF138 was still at red and properly protecting the rear of his train.

Driver McClymont's call to Clapham A signal box was answered by Signalman Cotter. McClymont told Cotter what he had observed but Cotter said that according to the indications in the box there was nothing wrong with the signal. McClymont was, in the words of Mr Hidden 'a little aggrieved' by this response but he didn't have long to dwell on it. As he put down the receiver there was a loud crash and his train was pushed forward several feet in front of him. He picked up the phone again and this time was able to tell Cotter that something definitely was wrong and that casualties were involved. Cotter acted immediately by putting all signals to danger and sent the emergency code – six bells – to the neighbouring signal boxes.

The collision that had occurred had involved two additional trains. These were the 06.14 from Poole (which had actually started that morning from Branksome, due to reasons not connected with the accident) and the 08.03 empty stock working to Haslemere from Waterloo. The Poole train had passed through signal WF138, which had reverted to green since the time that driver McClymont had observed it change from green to red. As a consequence of the signal's indication the driver of the Poole train, Driver Rolls, had continued on at around 50mph. At some point before the impact Driver Rolls must have seen the Basingstoke train; there was a very sharp emergency brake application. The train collided with the back of the Basingstoke train at around 35mph. What Driver Rolls thought and experienced in those seconds before the crash will never be known, since he died as a result of the collision. However, his action in applying the emergency brake certainly saved many lives.

As the Poole train hit the rear of the Basingstoke train the 8.03 empty stock train to Haslemere was alongside the Basingstoke train on the adjacent line. The front driving carriage, of the Poole train veered right off its own tracks to collide with the second coach of the Haslemere train. As a result the front driving carriage of the Haslemere empty stock train ran on for several yards down the track.

The accident triggered the selectors on the diagram board at Raynes Park Electrical Control Room where Mr Roland Reeves was working. The alarm bell rang and lights on his board began to flash. He worked quickly to isolate the current to the relevant sections.

The current was now off, but despite this there was a fourth electric train that was still in motion. Driver Pike, on board the 06.53 Waterloo to Waterloo roundabout service, thought that the power failure might be on board his own train and decided to allow it to coast into Clapham Junction, where at least it could be easily moved out of the way of other traffic. It passed through one signal at green and another at double yellow and was then approaching WF138. The two yellows should have meant that there was at least one, normally two, block section(s) and a further signal – at red – between him and any obstruction.

Thus he was travelling at about 60mph when he came upon WF138. Some 250yd from the signal he was able to see the trains beyond it and employed the emergency brake; the train stopped just 187ft from the rear of the Poole train. Further disaster had been averted. Driver Pike himself went back to signal WF138 and from there phoned Mr Cotter at Clapham Junction box, telling him that WF138 was now showing a yellow aspect. Cotter replied that it should be showing a red aspect. Pike's response was blunt: 'Red aspect be damned. There are three trains standing in front of it, and it is still showing one yellow.'

Yet again the signalmen were being told what their instruments should have been indicating, but were not. The cause of the malfunction was not at all far from Mr Cotter – it was in the relay room adjacent to the Clapham Junction A signal box. There a surplus live wire, left over from a deactivated signal, had been dangling down unattached so that as it moved it interfered with the contacts of WF138. It had caused the deaths of thirty-three people and serious injury to sixty-nine others. The engineer responsible had never been trained properly for the role of wiring the signals, nor had his work been supervised or checked.

British Rail crash investigators were quickly on the scene and established the direct cause of the disaster. Bob Reid I also arrived and immediately admitted that British Rail was to blame.[27] The Transport Minister of the time, however, ordered a public inquiry as per Section 7 of the 1879 legislation rather than simply allowing a normal investigation by the Railway Inspectorate (RI). The inquiry was conducted by Anthony Hidden QC.

There are many who question why a public inquiry was instigated by the minister rather than the Railway Inspectorate simply being allowed to continue with its work. The reason why it was done for the Tay Bridge disaster was that the Inspectorate had been involved in the approval of the structure and thus their role needed to be examined. They had also been involved in the approval of the type of level crossing at Hixon. Beyond that, Hixon involved matters to do with road traffic and police which were beyond the remit of the railway inspectors. Many attribute political motives for the calling of a 'Section 7' inquiry – that the government was out to do down BR – but some justification can be found in the report on page 115. In fact the RI had been overseeing the Waterloo Area Resignalling Scheme (WARS) – but only partially – and the role it had, or should have had, was confused by 'unworkable' legislation. The RI itself had not helped matters through ambiguous guidance as to what sort of schemes needed approval. Even so, it actually had no power to force the railway to submit its plans in timely fashion. Hidden considered that the RI had been 'placed in an extremely difficult position'. Thus it seems that there was a good reason to hold such a judicial inquiry, if only to find out that the will of parliament, however badly expressed, was not being carried out, and why.

As mentioned in Chapter 9, Hidden was to fiercely criticise BR's recruitment procedures as not being able to equip the railway with properly trained people. He was also to find fault in the organisation of the Waterloo Area Resignalling Scheme that was at the centre of the accident. First conceived in 1978 WARS had had a chequered history in both its planning and enactment stages. The signal and telegraph (S&T) department of the Southern Region had been subjected to four reorganisations in eight years between 1982 and 1988.[28] Hidden considered that on top of poor planning and management practice the reorganisations had played their part in the accident, in that people had been given positions of responsibility for which they were unsuited.[29] There had also been a serious effect on staff morale.[30]

Hidden was thorough and had much else to say, but was he just in his criticism of BR as an organisation where safety was 'the appearance' and not 'the reality'? Stanley Hall considers that Hidden had extended his criticisms too far, to the whole of BR when he had only looked at the signal department of one region. When investigations were undertaken on the other regions no such similar problems were uncovered. Moreover, such an accident involving poor wiring was unheard of before.[31] British Railways carried millions of passengers safely every year and in many of those years it had not a single fatality amongst its customers. Viewed from that perspective, Hidden's remarks seem to be quite unjustified.

Hidden was not to direct any of his criticisms in the way of the government, yet it was they who had put pressure on the board to cut investment and costs, and so had inspired the many reorganisations to serve this purpose.[32] The board's lack of money was the primary and root cause of the accident.[33]

One interesting point that Hidden was to make was in respect to the different ways that BR treated driver error and the so-called 'wrong side failures', or WSFs – the railways' term for equipment failures that lead to a dangerous situation. In the case of driver errors leading to so called 'Signals Passed At Danger' (SPAD) incidents there had been a great deal of monitoring and investigation, yet in the case of WSFs there was no proper monitoring or attention given. The Court of Inquiry asked for details of WSFs on the Southern Region from 1985–87 and BR had difficulty finding out how many there had been, despite the help of a computer system called FRAME (Fault Reporting and Maintenance Evaluation).[34]

Hidden's remit did not permit him to consider that the root of this was a long-standing culture, stretching back into the nineteenth century, where railway managers had sought to blame individuals for failures and to deflect criticism from equipment – for which the company could of course be blamed. This issue was to emerge again when the Health and Safety Executive (HSE) investigated a set of 'small incidents' of the type often characterised by the railways as 'movement accidents'; these don't involve trains colliding but nevertheless bring death and injury to railway premises. For a while there had been concerns that people were falling out of trains at speed, something which BR was quick to put down to passengers' own misconduct. Yet the HSE found that there were indeed issues with the type of door mechanism used on Mk2 and Mk3 stock. It was to find that BR had investigated the issue with a blinkered approach that had focused on the internal mechanism of the lock and not on how deficiencies of both the lock and the frame interacted to bring about a dangerous situation. BR had also been too quick to dismiss the incidents as being down to 'aberrant passenger behaviour'.[35]

In 1991, when the eight Asian guards from Paddington complained that they had been discriminated against when applying to be drivers, the Commission for Racial Equality was to find that BR had imported a psychometric test from the Dutch Railways and used it to as a tool to ascertain the proneness to SPADs amongst applicants. This was in spite of the conclusion by the Dutch Railways' own psychologists, who also served as consultants to BR, that the solution to such incidents had to be found in technical systems and not in the assessment of personnel.[36]

But it wasn't just BR who chose to blame individuals rather than look at the technical and organisational issues. The law did so too. There is a history that is too long of prosecutions against railwaymen for causing disasters when really efforts should have been expended on improving mechanisms and systems. Perhaps few cases are as grotesque as that of Bob Morgan, the unfortunate driver of the 12.17 Littlehampton–Victoria train on Saturday 4 March 1989. This was a terrible example of the long-feared and predicted accident where a driver automatically cancelled the AWS warning at double then single yellows resulting in insufficient distance to stop the train for the red. Still travelling at 55mph, it struck the rear of a train heading to Victoria from Horsham at Purley. Five passengers died and thirty-two were injured seriously enough to be kept in hospital.

After Clapham the popular mood was in favour of punishing someone. Up to that point no train driver who had pleaded not guilty to causing an accident had been convicted, and the circumstances under which Bob Morgan had made his tragic error were well understood and had long been predicted.[37] Nevertheless, his lawyers advised him to plead guilty to the charges of manslaughter and he was sentenced to eighteen months' imprisonment, with twelve suspended. Later Morgan appealed against his sentence and it was reduced to four months; he was released almost immediately.[38] Some seventeen years after the event Bob Morgan appealed against his conviction, basing it on new evidence that showed that the signal he had passed had a history of being passed at danger and the perils of this should have been known. It was a difficult appeal because Morgan had pleaded guilty at his original trial and normally there is no legal way back from that situation. On this occasion, however, it became clear that Morgan had been deprived of a rightful defence as details of the signal's history had not been known at the time. As a consequence his conviction was quashed and he was, after seventeen years, exonerated.[39] Sadly, Bob Morgan did not live for long afterwards as he died in a sailing accident in 2009.[40, 41]

A fatal accident at Purley occurred in the wake of the Clapham disaster and Hidden was asked to draw conclusions relating to that incident as well. This led him to recommend the fitting of the Automatic Train Protection System, this being a system that not only warns the driver when approaching a yellow signal but then gives him a further nudge before automatically applying the brakes to prevent him going through a red. The minister of the time rode the wave of public concern and stated categorically that the money would be found for such a system, however much it cost. However, subsequent trials on the Great Western main line involving IC125s threw up serious technical problems and the price tag rose from the initial £250 million to £750 million. The cost came to be questioned but by this time, in mid-1994, BR was well on the way to being privatised so there were serious distractions. There was a second possibility which BR had not considered: the Train Protection and Warning System (TPWS), a system built as an improvement to the existing AWS. By the time this came up for consideration Railtrack was in charge of the infrastructure, so whatever happened is out of the time frame of this book.[42]

In the light of the Clapham disaster major changes were undertaken in BR's safety culture. Bob Reid II made a personal commitment to change. A Safety Panel was established in May 1990 and the board took direct responsibility for safety. Whereas in the past safety matters had rarely reached board level, from July 1990 the Chairman's Group devoted a whole monthly meeting to safety. The Safety Committee, which had met only four times a year, was disbanded at the end of 1990 and its responsibilities assumed by the Chairman's Group. The Production Management Group became the Safety Management Group. The new organisational change known as Organising for Quality (OfQ) involved the creation of clear lines of responsibility for safety.[43]

Also in 1990 the Railway Inspectorate was removed from the Department of Transport and placed within the Health and Safety Executive.[44] This involved the London staff moving from Westminster to Bayswater but elsewhere regional RI inspectors were already based in HSE offices, so from that point of view it made little difference. The move to the HSE had been contemplated for some time but even before it took place there were siren voices warning that the tradi-tional role of the RI could be compromised by transferring it into a prosecuting authority. In 1990 Stanley Hall voiced concern that the role of the Inspectorate could change from one of co-operation and advice to one of interference with threats of prosecution, with negative results.[45]

For the time being Hall's concerns were not heeded, but events outside the scope of this book were to prove his concerns justified and the Cullen report into the Ladbroke Grove disaster was to recommended the re-establishment of a separate body with the sole responsibility of advising on railway safety.[46]

Meanwhile, when the Railway Inspectorate arrived in the offices of the HSE, on 3 December 1990 it was proudly re-titled 'Her Majesty's Railway Inspectorate'.[47]

With the introduction of modern signalling and the safety installations that often accompanied it the railway looked to ways to simplify track installations.

The most contentious example of this is the transformation of so called 'double-lead junctions' into 'single-lead formation'. Traditionally where a two-track subsidiary line met a two-track main line, each track joined its respective counterpart by its own set of points. This meant that one of the tracks needed to reach its counterpart on the far side. Inevitably it had to cross the other, nearest, main line track by a diamond crossing. That was okay, since when a train crossed the diamond from the subsidiary line both sets of points, on both tracks of the main line, were switched over to the subsidiary line. This meant that if a main-line train on the other track went through a red signal it would be sent down the subsidiary line rather than into the side of the train crossing the direct path. This is known as 'flank protection'.

In a 'single-lead junction' the situation is rather different. The subsidiary line becomes a single track prior to the junction – both tracks merge into one. They then join the main line by the nearest of the main-line tracks. A train destined for the track on the far side must cross onto those by another set of points. This sounds more complicated but it has the advantage of eliminating crossovers, which, because of their need to have gaps in the rails, are expensive to maintain due to the stresses that arise from wheels striking the ends of the rails. The downside is that protections are removed. A situation is set up whereby head-on collisions are possible if drivers ignore signals at danger. The proponents of single-lead junctions tended to argue that they are no more dangerous than any single line, but as safety experts such as Stanley Hall point out, that misses the point that specific protections – such as token systems – exist on single lines. They do not just rely on drivers observing signals.[48] The history of relying on drivers always observing danger signals is not a happy one. In the late 1980s and early 1990s there were three accidents involving single leads and the issue had already become one of concern with the Inspectorate.[49]

These incidents led up to the Newton accident. At Newton two double-track routes, one from Glasgow to Carlisle, the other from Kirkhill to Hamilton, occupy different platforms, but a junction exists at the end of the station to allow trains to move from one route to another. For the sake of simplifying this junction the Kirkhill to Hamilton route was single-tracked for a short stretch so that the connecting track from the other line could join it at a single set of points. It sounds wonderfully simple when you say it like that but the effect was to create a needless situation where trains were headed towards each other in potential head-on conflict, with only the driver's unwavering attention to signals to keep everyone safe.

On the evening of Sunday 21 July 1991 it seems that the attention of Driver Reginald McEwan did indeed falter. The train he was driving was the 21.55 Newton–Glasgow. It departed the station at 21.56 only to collide head on with the 20.55 Balloch–Motherwell train. It occurred on the singled stretch at a combined speed of 60mph. Both drivers and two passengers were killed. Twenty-two other passengers were injured.

By this time the responsibility for the track had been apportioned and divided between the sectors and this led to an unseemly row, reported by both British Transport Police and the Strathclyde Police, in which InterCity and ScotRail managers squabbled amidst the wreckage over which one 'owned' the disaster.[50] In the days after the accident ASLEF were to be fiercely critical of the existing safety regime, including the use of single-lead junctions and the lack of ATP.

As well as the ongoing RI investigation the board sent a troubleshooter northwards in order to deal with the fall-out from the accident and to establish some facts about what had happened from a managerial perspective. Peter Rayner was to write two reports about the implementation of the single-lead junction at Newton: one was titled *How the Decision Came About* and the other was *Why the Decision Came About*. These reports were to tell the tale of how the three rail businesses who used the junction – InterCity, ScotRail and Railfreight – had argued amongst themselves in the years between 1986 and 1990 over the costs of re-laying the junction. Rayner was to find that the confrontational way in which the investment rules had been applied by the three organisations had resulted in the absolute minimum requirements being met at the junction. In his report *Why the Decision Came About* Rayner was to castigate the junction design as an example of how not to organise a railway junction.[51]

The Railway Inspectorate's official report was to be more measured, but it dismissed claims previously proffered by British Rail[52] that single-lead junctions offered no greater risk than single lines, stating: 'The perception of increased risk at single-lead junctions is ... supported by analysis and experience.'[53]

Perhaps most significantly, the Operations Manager of ScotRail told the inquiry on day two that the double lines would be reinstated at the junction.[54] This was indeed done and was in operation from 30 January 1994.[55]

Peter Rayner, the troubleshooter of the Newton incident, was not to serve BR for much longer. He was an outspoken critic of the 'Organising for Quality' regime, arguing that the logical and provably safe regional system was being abandoned to make privatisation easier, and that safety was being compromised in the process.[56] Having made his views known he was made redundant on All Fools' Day 1992, only to receive an offer from the board to return as an adviser for £150 for every day that he worked, and an extra £12,000 per annum on his pension. The proviso was that he should refrain from criticism of the rail industry. He refused the offer and went on to become a champion for rail safety during the run-up to privatisation.[57]

As Peter Rayner recognised, the single-lead saga was further proof that cost cutting is the major threat to rail safety, and it was to serve as a prelude to the disasters that were to plague the privatised railway.

Hidden's remarks were unfair to British Rail; BR was a much safer railway than Hidden's conclusions stated. But he had hit on the underlying issue behind the Clapham accident and many other safety failures, namely money. This undoubtedly put the government on alert regarding the problems in the railway industry and spurred on the quest to find ways of financing the railways other than through the public purse. With many of the BR subsidiary businesses and surplus land sold off by the early 1990s, the only way to go was privatisation. Privatisation also had the additional bonus that it might shift the responsibility for failure – or even catastrophe – onto other desks.

13

Disintegration

When we reorganise, we bleed.

Gerry Fiennes

Undoing the nationalisation of 1948 was not on the agenda of any of the post-war governments from the 1950s through to the 1970s. The state ownership of utilities and certain services – mail, telephones, gas, electricity, and the railways – was accepted as part of what came to be viewed as the post-war consensus in British politics. The 1953 Act forced the BTC to sell off its lucrative road freight business but that was really a one-off. The sale of Thomas Cook was really nothing but the righting of an anomaly. The company had been owned by Wagons-Lits at the time when the Nazis overtook Paris. For the sake of not having it controlled directly from Berlin the firm's British assets were transferred into a company jointly owned by the four British Railway companies – from there it went into the British Transport Commission and, from 1963, into the holdings of the British Railway Board. In 1972 it was at last liberated.[1]

Jon Shaw traces the beginnings of policy change within the Conservative Party to the late 1960s. The Conservative research department's committee on nationalised industries had come to believe that there was a need for a programme of denationalisation, but took the view that they would not be able to get enough money for the railways to make it worthwhile.[2] After Margaret Thatcher was elected as leader of the Conservative Party, as long ago as 1975, the Young Conservatives had called for the rail industry to be privatised by means of allowing private operators onto the network – essentially fulfilling parliament's original intention that the railways should be public roads to which all had access.

Privatisation was to develop slowly after the Conservatives were elected. The large 'showpiece' privatisations did not start until after the 1983 election. However, steps were taken quickly to move certain assets and holdings of the BRB into a state from which they could be privately capitalised – in fact, privatised.

Peter Parker had been urging that such a step be taken since 1977,[3] but he probably didn't bargain on the consequences. He had taken the view that the need to limit the Public Sector Borrowing Requirement (PSBR) was constraining investment in the rail industry. The government saw another possibility: that selling off assets owned by the board could help reduce the PSBR. Thus in December 1980 British Rail Investments Ltd was set up as a wholly owned subsidiary to the board, holding the assets and shares of several organisations. These were Sealink UK (a ferry operator inherited from the private companies that had passed to BR via the BTC), British Transport Hotels Limited, British Rail Hovercraft Limited (an unlikely extension of the maritime interest that was started in the mid-1960s) and BR's non-operational and office properties.[4]

It was not long before the government's real motives were made plain in the 1981 Transport Act which authorised the sale of the subsidiary businesses.[5] Privatisation started quickly, hovercraft going as early as October 1981, the hotels sold off in dribs and drabs from 1982–84 and Sealink in 1984. Also privatised at this time were two other BR assets: the Superbreak mini holidays (February 1983) and the Slatford Laundry (September 1983).

That was just the start; from 1987 privatisation began in earnest. Here is a summary of the sections that were sold:

British Transport Advertising (responsible for placing adverts in stations and lineside hoardings) – August 1987
Doncaster Wagon Works – October 1987
Horwich Foundry – August 1988
Travellers Fare – December 1988
British Rail Engineering Limited – April 1989
Golden Rail – May 1989[6]

At the same time British Rail Property Investments Ltd was set up to sell off 'surplus' land and otherwise exploit British Rail's lucrative property assets.[7] It was this that was to raise much of the money that paid for the rolling stock investment of the 1980s.[8]

But all this time the government resisted calls to privatise the railway system itself, despite plundering it for its other assets. The calls never went away, though. After the deregulation of the buses in 1985 proved to be a fiasco it was perhaps little wonder that Thatcher got cold feet. Anyway, as a Conservative MP who had survived the defeats of 1964 and 1966 in the wake of the Beeching report, and who had subsequently served as a shadow transport minister during six long years of opposition, she must have had some inkling of how dangerous it was to mess with the railways. According to Christian Wolmar,[9] Nicholas Ridley, Secretary of State for Transport, approached Thatcher after the bus fiasco to press for the privatisation of BR; he was given short-shrift by the PM and forbidden from mentioning the railways to her again.

In 1987 Paul Channon was appointed to the Transport role. Despite Thatcher's caution regarding rail privatisation, Channon was permitted to tell the 1988 Conservative Party conference that privatisation options for BR were to be investigated by the Department of Transport.[10] This investigation yielded five possible options; these can be summarised as BR plc, regional, sectorisation, track authority and 'hybrid' – a mixture of the previous options.

The 'BR plc' option was essentially the sale intact of the existing railway as a whole. This was not favoured, since previous sales of that kind – such as British Telecom and British Gas – were deemed not to have brought benefits to the consumer. With hindsight, it was felt that competition should have been introduced by breaking up the monopolies. It was also felt that BR was uneconomic due to its complexity, although the fact that it was continually deprived of the cash needed to make it more efficient would be a better explanation for this.[11]

The regional option would be something like a return to the old groups – the details to be worked out. This obviously evoked some nostalgia but it is not clear that any of those involved in the decision-making process had any real historical knowledge of the group era. They perceived a problem over through trains between regions, also that each region would have to have a mix of different traffic, diluting management focus. There would also be a loss of economies of scale – but wasn't that inevitable in breaking up BR anyway? Come to that, BR had never been able to take advantage of this due to the drip feed it had been on; it had only been able to order small amounts of items such as sleepers at any one time.[12]

Sectorisation would mean the preservation of the existing BR businesses, but a difficulty was perceived over the problem of track ownership. There was also the issue of competition – there would be none as each sector would in itself be a monopoly. Sectorisation was also deemed to avoid a problem of 'operational transparency' – presumably this was meant to mean that costs could be allocated clearly and management responsibility for an area defined.

Then there was the track authority model. Basically, the track would be run by a single company and slots (paths) let out to whoever wanted to, and could, run a service. This was identified as problematic because of the simple practicalities of organisation. It would involve high transaction costs, the track company would be remote from users and the investment situation would be complicated. It was also viewed as unsatisfactory due to this proposed company remaining a monopoly.

Then there was the hybrid solution: a mix of the above to bring about the best possible combination. Or it might bring about the worst. With the cynicism of perfect hindsight, many will have an opinion on that one.

By the 1989 party conference Channon had been replaced by Cecil Parkinson, also a keen privatiser who intended to say something about privatising BR. When Thatcher saw a draft of his speech he was asked to 'cool it', however.[13] He did manage to persuade Mrs Thatcher that a failure to mention the issue would seem like backing down, so he got permission to state that a review was being undertaken.

By February 1990 the British Rail Board were confident that privatisation had been shelved once more, only to have the matter reopened just eight months later by the leaking of details from a DTP seminar and a statement by Parkinson at the party conference that privatisation was not a matter of 'whether' but 'how and when'.[14] Shortly afterwards he made an announcement to parliament[15] and established another working party to look at the matter.

Soon after the 1990 Tory Party conference came the matter of the annual election of the Conservative Party leader – in fact the election of the Prime Minister by the ruling party. Thatcher had been politically wounded by the Poll Tax issue and she was supplanted by John Major. Major was much more enthusiastic than Thatcher about privatisation.

Looking back at the Major years it is hard not to do so with some disbelief. John Major came from a circus family and this was rather appropriate as his administration was very much like a circus clown's car, regularly backfiring and falling apart whilst its occupants haplessly tumbled out and proceeded to make fools of themselves. Indeed, it seemed as if every Conservative politician was involved in a grotesque competition to find ever more extraordinary and bizarre ways to humiliate themselves in public. Major himself had fired the starting gun on all this with his call for the party to get 'back to basics': a call to remoralise society with supposed Victorian values. The press took it as a declaration for an open season on revealing politicians' antics – of which there were all too many. Major himself turned out to have had an extra-marital affair himself.[16] To cap all of this Major was faced with a dwindling majority. In late 1996, Labour and the Liberal Democrats capitalised on this by dropping the 'pairing' arrangements. This was a system whereby if an MP had an unavoidable reason, such as illness or important meetings, for not being able to vote on a crucial issue, his 'pair' in the opposing party agreed in a spirit of honour not to vote either, thus cancelling out the missed vote. Cancellation of this arrangement meant that every Conservative MP had to be mobilised for crucial parliamentary votes. This included the Prime Minister, who had to fly back from summits and meetings abroad to vote in parliament. Against this background of incompetence and hypocrisy, the railways of Britain were privatised.

By 1991 the working group established by Parkinson had reported; its recommendation was for a hybrid solution but with the London commuter network vertically integrated. By that time the tea party had once more shuffled around the table to leave Malcolm Rifkind at the Transport plate. Rifkind was not at all keen on the hybrid structure and much preferred the sector solution that would leave InterCity intact. Yet more analysis followed.

It was during this time that the track authority model was examined and certain problems identified. The Treasury had pushed the track authority model in the belief that *individual* train paths could be auctioned to the highest bidder, but when this idea was analysed it was seen to be impractical. It was recognised that for commercial purposes a railway timetable is planned in such a way that services interlock and serve each other. Putting such a timetable together by auctioning paths would be excessively complicated and it would also mean financial uncertainty for the bidders. The supposed solution was franchising – a whole group of services in a particular area would be taken over by a single company. It was a compromise that inevitably reduced the fundamental aim of the privatisation – increasing competition. The reality of a railway as a co-ordinated, organised system essentially thwarted this aim.

By the end of 1991 no clear decision had been taken and rather than show any clear leadership Major allowed his Policy Unit to advance its own solutions based around the regional concept, which had little but sentimentality to recommend it.

John Major famously demonstrated that his grasp of history could be obstructed by misplaced nostalgia and sentimentality when he suggested that the fiftieth anniversary of the D-Day landings in 1994 should be a day of national celebration. The Royal British Legion objected on the grounds that D-Day had been a day of carnage, and insisted that the fiftieth anniversary of VE Day the following year was the right time for celebration.

By 1992 things had been thrashed out well enough for the Conservative manifesto to spell out the structure that privatisation would eventually take. The existing passenger services would be franchised out to different operators while a part of BR would remain in charge of the track. Individual stations might be sold to private companies, though. There would be a regulator (one, at this stage) who would be responsible for handing out franchises, ensuring fair access to the track and ensuring that contractual commitments were followed. It was hoped that the franchisees would recapture the spirit of the old regional companies and foster the local pride and commitment that nationalisation had destroyed – although some might think that modernisation and the service cuts insisted on by the Conservatives in the late 1950s and early 1960s had rather more to do with this. It did seem very odd that the party that had done so much to bring the railways into the modern age and to a hardnosed, economic reality were now trying to turn the clock back to a sentimental vision of the past.

In something of a shock result the Conservatives won the election of April 1992, and the new Transport Secretary, John MacGregor, started work trying to put some flesh on the bones of the proposals.

In July 1992 the government unleashed a white paper called *New Opportunities for the Railways*. It made clear that the government believed that the profit motive needed to be at the centre to encourage improvements in rail services by making them more responsive to customer needs. It was thus necessary to end the monopoly and increase competition, allowing management the freedom to develop ideas independently of government intervention.

As had been said in the manifesto, companies would be locally based and reflect local identities and, it was thought, would increase the pride of employees in providing high-quality services to the public within their area. It was also argued that smaller companies would increase efficiency because their management would be closer to the public and yield up greater opportunities to cut out waste and reduce costs in general. Despite the emphasis on freedom some standards such as punctuality, reliability and overcrowding were to be written into contracts and rigorously enforced by the franchising authority. Those in breach of these would face penalties up to and including loss of their franchises.

At some time between the issuance of the 1992 manifesto and the publication of *New Opportunities for the Railways* someone had twigged that a single regulator would be in a contradictory position. On the one hand he would be handing out government subsidies with a duty to protect the public purse; on the other he would have to function as an independent authority ensuring fair play and guarding the interests of the passengers. If a service was failing and the company asked for more money, yet a case could also be made that it could be managed better, did the regulator argue it out with himself?[17]

Thus was born the schism of regulation between the Office of the Rail Regulator (ORR) and OPRAF – the Office of Passenger Rail Franchising. The ORR was to be the independent operator responsible for seeing fair play and guaranteeing passenger interests, whilst OPRAF was to represent the public interest in respect of government apportioned money; it would award the franchises and subsidies.

The opposition parties, Labour and the Liberal Democrats, were fiercely opposed to the break-up of BR, the Labour Party even going so far as to promise that the railways would be renationalised when they came to power. Privatisation also had an opponent in the Tory ranks in the form of Robert Adley, the MP for Christchurch and a keen railway enthusiast. Adley was a peculiar sort of person; born Jewish but converting to Anglicanism he became a somewhat passionate anti-Zionist. He also took a keen interest in the politics of China, simply and only because it was the last country on earth to operate steam locomotives on its main-line railways.[18] His attitude towards the railways was as much driven by emotion as other people's, it was just that Adley also knew rather more about railways and what was practical. He was chairman of the Transport Select Committee at the time when the white paper was released and was fiercely critical of it, arguing that it was vague and should have been preceded by a green paper (discussion document). He further remarked that those ministers and officials who had appeared before the committee didn't have a clue about how it would all work.[19] Unfortunately for the railways Adley's influence on the proceedings was to be cut short when he collapsed due to a heart attack and died in the Brompton Hospital on 13 May 1993. In the opinion of commentator Christian Wolmar, the privatisation act would have been a much better one had Adley lived.[20]

Bob Reid II also weighed in with his opposition to the way the privatisation was taking place. He took the analogy of the oil industry by arguing that anyone could produce oil, but that the core business for a company like Shell lay in the filling station. Reid was in favour of privatising the behind-the-scenes businesses but keeping the public face of the railways as BR. This was exactly not what the government envisaged though; they had formed the belief that BR *was* the problem and that its brand was poison in the public mind.[21]

It was in the House of Lords that the government got the roughest ride. Many Tory peers were against the bill, including former Transport Minister Lord Peyton. Amongst the concessions the Lords insisted on was that BR itself should be allowed to bid for franchises. The government viewed this as somewhat counterproductive but the point was conceded, subject to the discretion of the franchising director. The franchising director then denied BR the right to bid for the first round of franchises, and it then gave up.[22]

Although BR itself had been ruled out of the bidding process, the government did give management buyout teams a leg-up in terms of a grant of £100,000 to cover legal and other costs incurred whilst bidding for franchises. It was said that this was in recognition of the fact that existing managers were already busy running a railway. Also, if an MBO (Management Buy Out) bid offered up to 5 per cent lower it would be regarded as equivalent. Directors of the existing BR businesses were expected to give overall financial details of their businesses to the franchising director, who chose what would be shared with outside bidders.[23]

In order to sell the privatisation to critics, and to sell the railway itself, the government had to water down the proposals in order to accommodate so-called network benefits. As mentioned in Chapter 1, ever since the days of the Clearing House and Edmondson, passengers had been able to book through to their final destination by buying a single ticket, however many companies they travelled with. There was also the 'turn up and go' ability – you buy a ticket and hop on the first train, regardless of who operates it. It was felt that this ability had to be retained. But this cut across one of the fundamental aims of the privatisation, which was to enable railway companies to issue their own tickets and undercut each other in order to keep prices down. In the end a kind of fudge was arrived at where companies are forced to sell a range of universal tickets but can also sell tickets exclusive to their own services. This complicates matters for passengers and explains why the chap or chapess seated next to you may have paid a lot less for their ticket. Another issue was railcards – something else which it was felt needed to be preserved, but which obviously restricted the companies' abilities to organise their own prices and discounts.[24]

Yet another set of concessions were made regarding closures and service reductions. It was recognised by critics that subsidies would have to rise greatly if services were to remain in their current form whilst being run by independent companies. It was also feared that the privatisation would lead to a new round of closures. These points were conceded by the government, who accepted a rise in the Public Service Obligation Grant (PSO) and agreed to strict closure procedures.[25] It was another blow to the intentions behind privatising the railway, probably one for the better.

What emerged was essentially a poor attempt to salvage the best of a joined-up system whilst trying to make it work better through inward competition. Whatever sense it all made, or was supposed to make, got lost in the political dogma and spin.

Meanwhile, BR had to get on with the job of running the railway. In the hopes of whipping up some enthusiasm, in 1991 British Rail had published a document called *Future Rail – The Next Decade*. It was a rather nebulous document deploying words like 'opportunity' and 'challenge', together with the usual stuff about strategies and visions for the future, all printed in double space type with lots of white areas, pictures and a few graphs. At least 'meeting the needs of the customer' was top of the list of priorities now, with the statement: 'the cornerstone of our strategy is to satisfy our customers by identifying what we can do well and concentrating on doing it better.'[26]

As well as the privatisation British Rail was subject to another notion emanating from the startling mind of John Major: The Passengers Charter. This was a spin-off idea from the Citizens Charter, which basically gave the public an outline of what they ought to be able to expect from government – no rights were given by these charters, and in fact the government made the point of ensuring that they were 'judge proof'.

In the case of the Commuters Charter a similar condition was spelt out on page three, under 'Conditions of carriage':

> This charter sets out our commitment to you and to raising our standards. It does not create any new legal relationship with you as a result of what we say we will do …

The 'conditions of carriage' were of course the traditional get out for the railways which have enabled them to vary terms and conditions and basically tell you where to get off – literally – if you don't like them.

The only real teeth of any kind that the new charter had was an ability to offer discounted season tickets (season ticket holders only, of course) in the case of repeated delays. But there was a catch. Writing in *Rail* magazine Steven Knight revealed that BR was adding in so-called 'charter minutes' into the timetables to ensure that even late-running trains arrived 'on time'.[27] Was this cheating? It was certainly moving the goalposts.

Throughout the period in which privatisation took place the railways' financial position grew steadily worse due to the recession of the early 1990s and the government's slashing of the Public Sector Obligation Grant (PSO). In 1992/93 the PSO was £1.14 billion, but for 1993/94 it was slashed to just £950 million.

There was a severe lack of investment in the system; while the government was keen to point to record levels of investment this included all money spent on the system, including new projects such as the upgrading for the Channel Tunnel. The reality, when abnormal spending on major upgrades and new projects was stripped out, was that the system was under-resourced to maintain standards.[28] This was something that the private railway would inherit – and take the blame for.

With the exception of the Channel Tunnel major plans were on hold. Even rolling stock orders dried up, with the last being authorised in 1992 for the 465/6 EMU Networkers.[29] It was to be 1,064 days before another order for new stock was placed.[30] Railway development was effectively on hold for a number of precious years while the privatisation took place. The old equipment got even older.

Even before the legislation was passed steps were afoot to allow private companies to operate passenger services. The day after the Queen's Speech of 6 May 1992, which announced the privatisation of the railways, Stagecoach, the Scottish bus group, unveiled plans to run night seated coaches on the Aberdeen–Euston sleepers.[31] InterCity had announced the withdrawal of this service and Stagecoach had approached with an offer to run them instead. Six Mk2d coaches were specially refurbished at Derby works to Stagecoach's specifications and painted in a smart new Stagecoach Rail livery. It contrasted rather gratingly with the InterCity livery, but it was no worse than what could happen when stock of different BR sectors were mixed.

Despite the optimistic start Stagecoach was unable to make the plans work and on 1 November the service was withdrawn. A source inside Stagecoach indicated that only half of the 116 seats had been sold. InterCity took over the operation of the coaches, once more with Stagecoach taking a block booking of seats and selling them through their own outlets.[32] Meanwhile Richard Branson had met with InterCity Director Chris Green to persuade him to allow Virgin Trains to operate over the prime long-distance routes from London to York, Newcastle, Edinburgh and Manchester. Branson believed that the railways could offer real competition against short-haul, internal airlines.[33] Doubtless there were those in BR who felt that Branson had come to tell his granny all about sucking eggs the traditional way, but this wasn't the time to boast about the entrepreneurial successes of the nationalised railway.

The first and most significant date of the privatisation was undoubtedly 1 April 1994.

To all intents and purposes BR, as the operator of a unified, integrated railway system, ceased to exist on that day. The infrastructure, track, stations and light maintenance depots ceased to be owned by British Rail and were handed over to Railtrack, a separate government-owned company.[34] All of the passenger rolling stock was transferred to the three new rolling stock companies – or ROSCOs[35] – which were finally transferred to separate government ownership in August 1995 and sold to private ownership early in 1996. By February 1996 all twenty-five of the 'passenger operating units' became Train Operating Companies vested in British Rail as subsidiaries.[36] The fledgling Railtrack still needed BR's skills, personnel and experience to run it. For this reason BRIS – British Rail Infrastructure Services – was created. BRIS had a contractual relationship with Railtrack to maintain and operate the infrastructure.[37]

BR had been broken up into a large number of different companies inclusive of the three bulk haul freight companies, infrastructure services companies, maintenance companies, group services and a few others to boot. Some estimate there were over a hundred but I counted ninety-three, adding up those listed on pages seventy-four to seventy-five of the 1995–96 BRB Reports and Accounts. All these were to be sold individually from 1995 to 1997.[38] The British Railways Board report contained an interesting insight into the effects of the break-up, saying: 'Each business unit charges prices calculated to enable it to be a self-sustaining commercial company … This has led to much higher charges for many items than had to be attributed to them while BR was a single corporate entity.'[39]

The Organising for Quality structure, so painstakingly built by the two Bob Reids, was peremptorily dismantled.

The very first passenger service to be privatised was, in theory, the charter operation – those excursion services that had gone upmarket in the 1980s. This was sold (not franchised) on 1 April 1995. The purchaser was pop music millionaire Pete Waterman through his Waterman Railways Company. As Waterman was to admit to *Rail* magazine just a few months later, he hadn't bought what he thought he had. One of the problems was that operators now needed to be authorised to run services through the possession of a licence. Waterman Railways did not have one of its own and the only organisation that did possess a system-wide, national passenger licence was Rail Express (RE) Systems, which ran the Royal Mail traffic. This was still in British Rail's hands. Waterman Railways was to discover that running a charter train service under Rail Express's auspices was much more expensive than they had believed it would be. RE was now passing on every penny of charges that had previously been absorbed into the whole BR organisation.[40] In truth, all Waterman had purchased were some leftover carriages and locos. It wasn't a going concern and had utterly no chance of receiving a government subsidy.

The franchising of the passenger operations proceeded slowly. The first three Invitations To Tender (ITTs) were issued by the franchising director in May 1995. These were for South West Trains, Great Western and London Tilbury and Southend (LTS). The results were announced in December. Things were not entirely straightforward, though. The winner of the LTS franchise was a management buyout team and it later emerged that a scam run by lower levels of management had bolstered the financial results of the line. The award for the franchise was annulled, the management buyout team was ruled out and the other bidders invited to re-tender. It was hardly an auspicious beginning. Things got worse when the first privatised train was substituted with a bus because of engineering work. The first true privatised train had extra coaches laid on in the expectation that enthusiasts would want to be a part of the new era. None of them did.[41]

To help the first tranche of franchises through, the government had set aside yet another notion that underlay the privatisation – the 'open access' idea. This would allow other operators to run competing services in a franchise area where the existing franchise holder did not operate services. With the privatisation in its early stages this was considered to pose too much of a financial risk that might frighten off franchise bidders and so the open access idea, although revived later, was initially blocked. Yet another key principle of competition had had to be sacrificed to get the job done.[42]

Then there was the scandal of the rolling stock operating companies. These were transferred over to the government in 1995, British Rail receiving nothing for them despite the fact that there were millions of pounds' worth of rolling stock, representing a massive public investment. The government was free to do as it pleased with them and it did, selling them off for a mere £1,743 million. In just a few months one of the companies, Porterbrook, initially sold for £298 million, was sold on for £528 million.

Alan Williams was to denounce this as 'Shocking disgraceful and scandalous'.[43] When it came to look at the matter, the National Audit Office was a lot less than impressed too; as with so many of the privatisations, public assets had been sold beneath their true market value.[44] In 1996 Railtrack itself was floated on the stock exchange, again at a lower price than the public had a right to expect for an asset they had owned.[45]

Nevertheless, further sales and franchising took place through the years 1995–97. The last passenger franchise handed over was ScotRail on 31 March 1997. Interestingly, seventeen of the twenty-five were awarded to management buyout teams – in combination with outside investors, of course. BR had spent £2.2 million in support of those teams. In terms of legacy, the management skills it had nurtured were still present in the system after privatisation. They had to be. I have found no hard statistics but doubtless many of the other winners hired ex-BR managers as well. Chris Green was one of those, being taken on by Virgin as Chief Executive from 1999.[46]

The sale of the infrastructure service companies and other auxiliary operations was achieved by 7 June 1997. With the sale of Railfreight Distribution on 22 November 1997 British Rail had ceased to have any operational interest in the railway system of Great Britain.[47] All that remained was the BRB residuary that managed pensions, the rump of property no one else wanted, and the archive of material that the BRB had accumulated, stretching back to the days of yore, much of it stored in an old Great Western Railway building near to Royal Oak station.

This archive was sifted through on a three-stage process by the National Archives, the National Railway Museum and the Historical Model Railway Society. It was a huge job, in which this author played a part. The building on Porchester Road was subsequently converted into luxury flats, doubtless a more lucrative enterprise than its previous role of storing a treasure trove of national historical importance.

14

What did BR do for us?

S o, to coin a famous phrase: what did BR do for us?
 Much of this book has sought to answer that very question.
 BR unified a once disparate and chaotic system. In organisational terms this was rather belated, due to the political interference of the 1953 Act, which set in stone the partial independence of the too-long enduring regions, but unification finally started coming together in the 1980s.

BR modernised the system and brought about a technological revolution from the very foundations of the rail bed (new techniques in constructing high-speed railways – see Chapter 7) upwards to the rolling stock that ran on them. Many of the advances BR introduced were the result of in-house, world-beating research work. Other advances included electrification at 25,000 volts, and the Pandrol rail clip that was spotted and improved by the gifted engineers BR trained. At its best BR was a treasure house of technological expertise.

BR redefined what the railways of Britain were for – it was something that needed to be done, if any railway system at all was to survive for the future. There are still those who resent Beeching, but he merely carried out what cowardly politicians had been putting off ever since 1948. The fact was that the services he cut were very expensive to run and if they had charged the customers what it actually cost to run them, road travel would have been a much more attractive option. Many of them had already chosen road travel anyway.

An essential part of the redefinition was the discovery of the importance of speed and time-intervals services – what BR branded Inter-City, InterCity or *InterCity*. BR also embraced the modern arts of design and marketing to sell the redefined service. It became a world leader in these matters, just as it did in technology. Its corporate design manual remains a benchmark of corporate image making worldwide.

BR also provided a range of 'social' railway services, finally paid for by the government (when the politicians finally awoke to the fact that it was politically necessary). These were of varying quality, perhaps hardly surprising considering the way that the money was squeezed.

BR finally managed to get movement on the long-held personnel issues, particularly recruitment and training. The downside was that many jobs were lost, and many of those were in 'non essential' customer-relations roles. The train can depart on time without a ticket clerk at the station, but not without a driver. In fact it can be on time without passengers.

One black mark on BR is undoubtedly that it took a long time to get a grip on its costs – where the money was going. This was pointed out by many commentators and it was a failure that BR inherited from its forerunners, but which it should have done more, more quickly, to rectify. Again, the entrenched regional structure that was reinforced by the 1953 Act can be seen as one cause of this, but it is undoubtedly more complex than that.

So, British Railways oversaw the most enormous change in the railway system of Great Britain. In this book I have tried to explain that in terms of passenger services, and have also referred to the enormous change in freight services. There is a question as to whether this could have been achieved by anything other than a state owned and run railway. Also, we could question whether private companies would have put up with the situation that British Railways was faced with for so long. My personal view is that the private companies would simply not have survived the 1950s with the same demands placed upon them – certainly not in the form in which they had existed pre-war. Consequently, they would not have had the organisation or the will to bring about the fundamental changes needed – to take a holistic view that only a national carrier could take. A *national* plan was required to speed up city-to-city passenger services and to dispense with the wagon load and sundries freight. Even if we accept the logic of the argument for eventual privatisation, it is hard to argue other than that nationalisation was a necessary stage that the railways had to pass through to transform them into a service fit for the modern world. Whatever, it needed government to bankroll the changes and government is still paying for much of the railways' operation today, and will have to provide funds or guarantees for construction in the future.

What did it all mean for the passenger?

We have seen the kind of services that were run before the changes of the late 1950s and 1960s. It was an old world of inefficiency against which market forces proved the greater efficiency of the car, of the lorry, of the road bus. Those who couldn't afford a motor vehicle, or who didn't have a bus service available, got left at home, unless they could cadge a lift from someone. The railway trunk routes have now returned to their originally intended market: the long-distance passenger. There are now fewer places you can travel to and from by train, many fewer places, but if you wish to catch a train from one major centre to another it will now be a darn sight quicker to get there, and very much more comfortable than it was fifty years ago.

Above I mentioned BR's ground-breaking research. There is the question, though, as to whether it was the role of a national rail carrier to get involved in research. Of course it had inherited such facilities from the LMS – a private company, but should it have been using public funds to develop new technologies, even if it was for the wider benefit of mankind?

Clearly the politicians from the 1960s to the 1970s thought so and they bankrolled it. It does raise the question as to an appropriate use of public funds, though, particularly when it goes wrong – such as the APT did. Are politicians and even railway managers really the right people to spot a good idea and spend public money to develop it? Judging by some of their choices and ideas (theories about helicopters, and also the aborted Maglev idea) it is possible that the answer is no. On the other hand, there is no doubt that the Derby Technical Development Centre was a true national asset, like Farnborough is to the aeronautical industry. The loss of Derby was a loss to the nation. Today it is merely a business park and research is no longer done there. Doubtless it now makes a lot more money for its current owners than it ever did for BR.[1]

What else did BR do?

It certainly gave us a good laugh, regularly and often; from 'leaves on the line' to 'the wrong type of snow' it was the butt of many jokes. Some of the people who made them probably regret they ever did, now. Privatisation certainly spoiled the fun and privatised railways have caused more anger than laughter. Nevertheless we can look back on *The Goons'* parody of the British Railway Ham Sandwich and innumerable other sketches down the years that reflected on BR's real or supposed frailties. It was an old friend you felt comfortable laughing at and it didn't hit back. Parodying any of the current crop of private companies would probably land you in some legal trouble.

There is of course the fraught matter of how BR behaved as a custodian of our railway heritage. Some of the most important archaeological sites in railway history are in Britain and were, or still are, functioning railway sites.

BR got no special grant to look after the buildings in its charge. Indeed, *Modern Railways* commented that Bob Reid II kept a 'commendably straight face' when he said, 'The Treasury should ask us "are you spending enough to maintain those national assets which have been entrusted to you?"'[2]

These assets included over a thousand listed buildings (of course, they were already *sans* one heritage propylaeum). In 1979 SAVE Britain's Heritage published a book entitled *Railway Architecture*, the introduction of which was pretty damning in its assessment of BR's care of the railway heritage. BR was the worst vandal since the Reformation, according to SAVE, and it listed a number of demolitions of significant structures, starting with the Euston Arch and including the destruction of the St Enoch train sheds at Glasgow, the demolition of Birmingham New Street and the Great Viaduct at Crumlin.[3]

It was a great shame, but then you can't keep everything, in the manner of obsessive hoarders, and some of these buildings stood in the way of great improvements in the railway infrastructure, as well as allowing sales of land to fund new rolling stock.

What is a nationalised railway to do?

Well, in 1983 it curried favour with John Betjeman – a fierce critic of the destruction of the arch and campaigner for the saving of St Pancras – by naming an electric locomotive after him, the naming ceremony tactfully taking place at St Pancras and not at Euston. Afterwards Betjeman was presented with a model of the Euston Propylaeum.[4] Since that time – long after the demise of BR – a statue of Betjeman has been erected at St Pancras.[5] Meanwhile, a campaign has been started to restore the Doric Arch, whose pieces were reportedly saved by the demolition contractor.[6] The Euston Arch Trust (http://www.eustonarch.org/trust.html) lists its patrons as Sir William McAlpine and Michael Palin. For the time being, however, it is an ex-propylaeum. It has ceased to be.

As well as the structures still being used, British Rail retained responsibility for many that were no longer used by the system; the tracks may have been lifted and the signals taken away, but station buildings, tunnels, bridges and viaducts often remained. Once beautifully maintained station gardens ran riot now that the ordered way of life that created them had departed. I have been told tales of railwaymen breaking off their duties early to go scrumping in such places, where long-untamed orchards of apples, plums, pears and quinces spread and fruited amidst riotously overgrown flower beds and vegetable patches. Of course, buildings such as station masters' houses could fairly easily be disposed of as dwellings and this often happened. Other uses included restaurants, such as the former station at Polegate, now used as a restaurant and pub.

But there were some structures that defied easy re-employment. In 1991 the British Rail Property Board published a brochure entitled *Disused Railway Viaducts: Their Future In Your Hands* (hint, hint!) listing no fewer than seventy-four disused viaducts – twenty-four of these had already been sold, fifty more awaited a buyer. The brochure considered that: 'the optimum solution is for the Government to take over responsibility for them' (nudge, nudge!) but was ready to sell them to anyone prepared to take them off the board's hands.

There was the Charlton Viaduct of the former S&DJR, with its 'intriguing feature' of a gradient change midway across it. It towered over the neighbouring property of the drinks company Showerings (of Babycham fame) who purchased it for £5 and landscaped the area around it. 'Could your Company benefit from such a fine backcloth?' asked the brochure.

There was the Lower Largo Viaduct which 'forms an attractive centre piece to the village'. The local council bought it for £1 (and received £70,000 toward maintenance from the British Rail Property Board).

There were the two listed viaducts purchased by Sustrans, described as 'an imaginative organisation that creates and maintains safe and attractive routes for cyclists and pedestrians, usually using redundant railway lines'. These viaducts had been converted to pedestrian and cycle paths together with a third one, which they leased.

If the Railway Reformation has anything to compare with the great, ruined monasteries of the religious Reformation it is surely these: huge edifices that remain beached long after the tide of exuberance that led to their construction has retreated.

Would the railways have fared any better in private hands? Would there have been fewer closures, perhaps? Reading some books you get the impression that closures were the direct result of nationalisation; the notion being, presumably, that once the railway system had been handed over to bureaucrats and politicians it had automatically been sentenced to neglect and decline. The corollary of that idea is, presumably, that had the private companies been allowed to continue they would have maintained the traditions of service regardless of profit in the dedicated, selfless way that we are so used to seeing from big business.

It is all highly unlikely; certainly Hurcomb's vision of an integrated transport system contained the notion that railways would be closed where road transport could do the job more efficiently; in the end the profit ethos cut much the same cloth that central integration should have cut.

Had the private companies continued as they were, with the same legislative constraints, they would have faced all the same problems that BR had faced; they had already been complaining vociferously about the 'unfairness' of legislation in the run-up to the Second World War with their Square Deal campaign, although it has to be said that not all transport analysts and economists saw the system as being loaded against the railways.[7]

It is quite possible that more closures and not less would have taken place if private ownership had been retained. Or perhaps some alternative to nationalisation would have been found to help out the railways. The LNER's 'landlord and tenant' proposal may well have become a reality and today's system, with many operators, may have evolved rather than being imposed as a revolution as different companies tried to run different lines, the Big Four withdrawing and new companies bidding for the option to run them.

In terms of improving the system, after the war the companies did not lack any ambition or ideas for reconstructing the network. In 1946 the LNER published a pamphlet entitled *Forward: the LNER Development Programme*. According to the pamphlet this programme was a five-year plan in two parts. Firstly there was to be the restoration of pre-war standards of service. Secondly progressive improvements, based on modern designs and scientific research, were to be introduced.

The booklet informed its reader that: 'Nothing can be done as quickly or as cheaply as in 1938, but progress must be resumed.' It then went on to list the litany of shortages and needs that faced the railway system – rolling stock for passenger and freight locomotives overdue for repairs, many miles of track in need of renewal, stations, depots and other buildings in need of rebuilding, repair and repainting.

The LNER had squirreled away a trust fund, worth £40 million, during the war which was intended for arrears of maintenance – and that is all it would cover. A New Works programme would require an additional £50 million, excluding electrification and additional rolling stock.

The Great Western Railway put its best foot forward in an even more substantial volume, by an illustrious author. This was *Next Station*, running to 113 pages, written by Christian Barman and published in 1947 on behalf of the Great Western Railway by George Allen and Unwin.

Of course it needs to be pointed out here that these plans may have been part of the companies' propaganda in the face of – by that time inevitable – nationalisation. Nationalisation may have been acting as a goad to do better. Perhaps the ongoing threat of it, rather than its implementation, would have brought good results.

There is no reason to think that the group companies wouldn't have got on with the job of reconstructing the railway post-war. What they would not have been able to do was to bring the resources of a unified system to bear on the great problems the system faced, or to bring about the system-wide changes needed.

The group companies owe their treasured status to the fact that they were never faced with the tough decisions and challenges of the 1950s and 1960s.

As to the question of whether the railways should have been re-privatised, the jury seems to have been in on that one for a while. It was never a popular privatisation and must have contributed to the Conservatives' destruction at the polls in 1997. More than that, it may have been a 'poll-tax-on-wheels' at the time but it has turned out to be a 'millstone-with-legs' that keeps on running for the Conservatives; the latest debacle over the West Coast Main Line franchising has yet again led to their competence in running the railways being called into question. If there is one conclusion to be drawn from the contents of this book it must be that the railways are likely to be much better off without politicians meddling. Ironically, when they tried to withdraw from being the railways' masters they couldn't even get that right. Now there is more political interference in the railways than ever.

The biggest criticism of the privatisation, heard from many quarters, is that it split the railway up into so many components; there are those who argue that a railway is properly an integrated system where all the parts are supposed to work together, not be set at loggerheads. The other criticism that follows from that is the sheer cost of administering the current railway, in which lawyers must now play a significant role. It was designed so as to make it difficult to put it back together again – it was a Humpty-Dumpty privatisation designed to ensure that it could never be re-nationalised. It was in so many ways a spiteful act of the scorched earth variety, from a party that knew its time in power was nearly over, more than a cohesive transport policy.

Setting aside for a moment the practicalities, one question that should be asked is: should BR be brought back? Ellie Harrison, spokesperson for 'Bring Back British Rail', whose Facebook page (http://www.facebook.com/bringbackbritishrail) boasts over 25,000 'likers', certainly thinks so. She argues for a railway run for people rather than profit, and with public money going directly into improving services rather than bolstering the profit margins of private companies. Chris Green, the ex-BR manager referred to in this book and rightly described as 'the best chairman BR never had' takes a different view. He argues for the private railway on the grounds of the swiftness with which investment decisions can be taken – an example he gives is that it took ten minutes to get agreement to spend £50 million on extra coaches for the Pendelinos. He states, and quite rightly, that it would have taken a year or more to get agreement for that money from the Treasury (what he doesn't say is, if that money had been made available at all). He points to air-conditioned commuter trains, manned stations and mobile security guards as examples of things BR could never have achieved. He believes that with each decade the railway gets better, steps another rung up the ladder. The only downside in Chris Green's view is the administrative costs of the current system.

As so often, it seems to be the organisation that is the problem – if only we can change that!

Probably what the railways need right now is a rest from organisational change. They have bled enough. If Gerry Fiennes was right then they have bled oceans full. For outsiders to come in with another set of theories and upset it all again would only cause more havoc. In 2011, I was privileged to see – with a group from the RCTS – the modern railway working at its best; the wonderful integrated control room at Waterloo where staff from South West Trains and Network Rail work side by side to keep the trains moving in and out of the largest, and the greatest, of London's great termini. The overall impression I got was that train operators and the track operator were working together better than they have ever done. Traditionally there was always a spirit of rivalry and non-co-operation between such departments, even when they were receiving their pay cheques from the same company. As Chris Green points out, there would never have been track engineers in the control rooms in BR days. In some ways it could be said that privatisation has brought a structured set of remedies to traditional issues within the railway system. Issues that needed to be sorted out.

Does it really matter who owns the railways, as long as they are run well? Privatisation wasn't really that big a deal anyway – British Rail had already made all the important changes needed to bring the railway into the modern age. This is why the name of the man associated in the public mind with those changes – Beeching – is still so potent. The reason why people feel so strongly about him is because those changes took from us more than just a way to get from Blandford Forum to Midsomer Norton. They attacked an idealised, idyllic view of Britain as somewhere timeless and unchangeable. It is the vision captured by Edward Thomas in 'Adlestrop':

Yes, I remember Adlestrop –
The name, because one afternoon
Of heat the express-train drew up there
Unwontedly. It was late June.

The steam hissed. Someone cleared his throat.
No one left and no one came
On the bare platform. What I saw
Was Adlestrop – only the name

And willows, willow-herb, and grass,
And meadowsweet, and haycocks dry,
No whit less still and lonely fair
Than the high cloudlets in the sky.

And for that minute a blackbird sang
Close by, and round him, mistier,
Farther and farther, all the birds
Of Oxfordshire and Gloucestershire.

The poem captures perfectly the atmosphere of a country station in the middle of nowhere on a summer's afternoon – in fact the desolation of a station that saw little traffic and most likely no profit. Even on a lovely midsummer day there is no one waiting for a stopping train, ready to take the opportunity of the express' unscheduled stop. What we love about this vision of the country station is the peace and isolation; which is exactly what made Adlestrop unprofitable. The station was closed on 3 January 1966.

Thomas's 'Adlestrop' is a vision of Britain that belongs to a sunny day before the First World War, over a hundred years ago. It does not belong to today.

Glossary

4DDs	Two experimental, double-deck 4-car multiple-units designed for the Southern Railway by O.V.S. Bulleid. They were not deemed a success.
4-VEP	British Rail Class 423 EMUs, having hinged doors for every seating bay.
AHB	Automatic half barrier.
AH-NS	Axle Hung-Nose Suspended traction motor.
APT	Advanced Passenger Train, an experimental tilting high-speed train, also referred to as the 'tilting train'.
APT-E	An experimental APT that would provide a test bed for the new technology.
ASLEF	Associated Society of Locomotive Engineers and Firemen.
ATC	Automatic Train Control.
AWS	Automatic Warning System.
BoT	Board of Trade.
BR	British Rail.
BRB	British Railways Board.
BRCW	Birmingham Railway Carriage and Wagon Works.
BRIS	British Rail Infrastructure Services.
BTC	British Transport Commission.
BTF	British Transport Films.
Cartic	meaning 'car articulated' this was a double-decker, car-carrying format that used the space below the normal floor level of railway vehicles as extra carrying space.
CIS	Corporate Identity Symbol.
CME	Chief Mechanical Engineer.
CM&EE	Chief Mechanical and Electrical Engineer's Department.

CTCC	Central Transport Consultative Committee.
CWR	Continuous Welded Rail.
Deltic	Diesel locomotives built by English Electric, named after their Deltic power units.
DEMU	Diesel Electric Multiple-Unit.
DMU	Diesel Multiple-Unit.
DOO	Driver Only Operation.
DVT	Driving Van Trailers.
ECML	East Coast Main Line.
EMU	Electric Multiple-Unit.
EOC	Equal Opportunities Commission.
EPB	Electro-Pneumatic Brake train, an EMU train incorporating electro-pneumatic brakes.
FB	Flat bottom (rail).
FO	First Open (coaches).
GER	Great Eastern Railway.
GGPTE	Greater Glasgow Passenger Transport Executive.
GGTS	Greater Glasgow Transportation Study.
GLC	Great London Council.
GMPTE	Greater Manchester PTE.
GNR	Great Northern Railway.
GWR	Great Western Railway.
HMRS	Historical Model Railway Society.
HSDT	High Speed Diesel Train (also HST).
HSE	Health and Safety Executive.
HSFV	High-speed Freight Vehicle.
HST	High Speed Train.
IC125	Inter-City 125, the brand name of British Rail's High Speed train fleet.
ICT	Independent Commission for Transport.
Integral	A method of construction where strength is built into the body of a vehicle and there is no underframe that can serve as a vehicle by itself.
ITT	Invitations To Tender.
L&Y	Lancashire and Yorkshire Railway.
LB&SCR	London, Brighton and South Coast Railway.
LCC	London County Council.
LCDR	London Chatham and Dover Railway.
LEV	Leyland Experimental Vehicle.
LMR	London Midland Region.
LMS	London, Midland and Scottish Railway.
LNER	London and North Eastern Railway.

LNWR	London and North Western Railway.
LPTB	London Passenger Transport Board.
LSE	London and South East Sector.
LSWR	London and South Western Railway.
LT	London Transport.
LTE	London Transport Executive.
LT&SR	London, Tilbury and Southend Railway.
LTS	London, Tilbury and Southend Line.
Mk1	The designation given to the original standard carriage upon the advent of the Mk2.
Mk2	The first monocoque carriage built as a standard type by BR. Also, in later versions, the first to offer air conditioning to second/standard-class passengers.
Mk3	A further development of monocoque body construction with bogies and suspension derived from BR research. Capable of 125mph and used in the IC125.
Mk4	Carriages constructed for the East Coast electrification in the 1980s as part of the IC225 trains.
MBO	Management Buyout.
MMC	Monopolies and Mergers Commission.
MU	Multiple-Unit.
NER	North Eastern Railway.
NSE	Network SouthEast.
NSR	Norwegian State Railways.
NUR	National Union of Railwaymen.
OfQ	Organising for Quality.
OPRAF	Office of Passenger Rail Franchising.
ORR	Office of the Rail Regulator.
OWW	Oxford, Worcester and Wolverhampton.
PEP	Experimental EMU trialled on the Southern Region, prefixed by 4 or 2, depending to the number of cars within the unit.
PSBR	Public Sector Borrowing Requirement.
PSO	Public Service Obligation (grant).
PTA	Passenger Transport Authority (or Area).
PTE	Passenger Transport Executive.
RCH	Railway Clearing House.
RCTS	Railway Correspondence and Travel Society.
RE	Railway Executive.
RI	Railway Inspectorate.
ROSCO	Rolling stock company.
S&DJR	Somerset and Dorset Joint Railway.

S&T	Signal and Telegraph – later Telecommunication – Department.
SELNEC	South East Lancashire North East Cheshire passenger transport area.
SER	South Eastern Railway.
SPAD	Signal Passed At Danger – a classification of types of railway accident.
SPTE	Strathclyde Passenger Transport Executive.
SYPTE	South Yorkshire Passenger Transport Executive.
THF	Trust House Forte.
Time-Interval Service	Also known as a clockface service. This is where trains run from a specific place to a specific destination at specific intervals, such as every half past the hour.
TPWS	Train Protection and Warning System.
TSSA	Transport Salaried Staffs' Association.
TUCC	Transport Users Consultative Committee.
WARS	Waterloo Area Resignalling Scheme.
WCML	West Coast Main Line.
WSF	Wrong Side Failure.
WYPTE	West Yorkshire Passenger Transport Executive.
XP64	Experimental train designed to demonstrate improved fixtures and fittings conceived by the British Rail Design Panel for express trains. It was unveiled in 1964, hence XP64.

Notes

Chapter 1

1 Philip Bagwell, *The Railway Clearing House in the British Economy, 1842-1922*, George Allen & Unwin (1968), pp. 56–7, Jack Simmons and Gordon Biddle (eds), *The Oxford Companion to British Railway History*, Oxford University Press (1997 edn), 'Excursions', p. 150.

2 Jack Simmons and Gordon Biddle (eds), ibid., 'Parliament And Legislation', p. 364.

3 Philip Bagwell, quoted in *The Transport Revolution From 1770*, Batsford (1974), p. 171.

4 Mark Casson, *The World's First Railway System*, OUP (2009), pp. 16–29.

5 Philip Bagwell, *The Railway Clearing House in the British Economy, 1842–1922*, George Allen & Unwin (1968), p. 15.

6 Ibid., p. 34.

7 Henry Parris, *Government and Railways in Nineteenth Century Britain*, Routledge & Kegan Paul (1965), p. 24.

8 Mark Casson, op. cit., p. 26.

9 E. Eldon Barry, *Nationalisation in British Politics: The Historical Background*, Jonathan Cape (1965), p. 80.

10 G.A. Bonner, *British Transport Law by Road and Rail*, David & Charles (1974), p. 23ff.

11 Railway and Canal Traffic Act, clause 2.

12 Philip Bagwell, op. cit., for a full account of the RCH.

13 Frederick S. Williams, *Our Iron Roads*, Bemrose and Sons (1883). For an early account of this process p. 311.

14 Philip Bagwell, op. cit., p. 50.

15 Ibid., pp. 56–7.

16 Susan Major, *The Million Go Forth: Early Railway Excursions 1840–1860* (http://www.academia.edu/529584/The_Million_go_forth_early_railway_excursions_1840-1860_The_excursion_agent_as_social_entrepreneur). *The excursion agent as social entrepreneur*, Institute of Railway Studies & Transport History, University of York.

17 Philip Bagwell, op. cit., p. 55 and Jack Simmons and Gordon Biddle (eds), op. cit., 'Time', pp. 512–3.

18 G.P. Neele, *Railway Reminiscences, London 1904*, quoted in Philip Bagwell, ibid., p. 225.

19 Philip Bagwell, ibid., p. 263.

20 Emil Davies, *The Case for Railway Nationalisation*, Collins Clear Type Press, 1913, quoted p. 222, 'Report to The Board of Trade 1907'.

21 Charles E. Lee, *Passenger Class Distinctions*, The Railway Gazette (1946), p. 65.

22 Frederick S. Williams, op. cit.

23 E. Eldon Barry, *Nationalisation in British Politics: The Historical Background*, Jonathan Cape (1965), pp. 83–4.

24 Jack Simmons and Gordon Biddle (eds), op. cit., 'Nationalization; The Concept of', p. 339.

25 E. Eldon Barry, op. cit., p. 96.

26 Geoffrey Alderman, *The Railway Interest*, Leicester University Press (1973), p. 195.

27 Ibid., p. 195.

28 CAB/23/21, p. 186.

29 CAB/23/21, pp. 186–7.

30 CAB/24/121, p. 3.

31 CAB/24/121, p. 3.

32 Michael R. Bonavia, *The Nationalisation of British Transport*, St Martin's Press (1987), pp. 5–6.

33 See *The Oxford Dictionary of National Biography*: Reith, John Charles Walsham.

34 Michael R. Bonavia, op. cit., p. 6ff.

35 CAB/65/19/6.

36 http://www.labour-party.org.uk/manifestos/1945/1945-labour-manifesto.shtml.

37 The Board of the London and North Eastern Railway, *The State and the Railways: An Alternative to Nationalisation*, 'Memorandum'. See also Michael R. Bonavia, *A History of the LNER 3: The Last Years 1939–48*, George Allen & Unwin (1983), p. 86ff.

38 Terry Gourvish, *British Railways 1948–73*, Cambridge University Press (1986), p. 35.

39 HC Deb, 5 May 1947, vol. 437, c. 143.

Chapter 2

1 Quoted in Terry Gourvish, op. cit., p. 138.

2 *Railway Magazine*, September 1953: 'Rehabilitating British Main Lines / A Useful High Speed Service', p. 577 and 'Restoring British Permanent Way', p. 584.

3 Transport Act 1947, Part 1, Section 3(1).

4 British Transport Commission, *The Organization Of British Transport* (1948), pp. 18–9.

5 John Elliot, *On and Off the Rails*, George Allen & Unwin (1982), p. 89.

6 Terry Gourvish, op. cit., p. 138.

7 HC Deb, 28 January 1960, vol. 616, cc. 371–3.

8 Terry Gourvish, op. cit., p. 322.

9 Michael Bonavia, *British Rail: The First 25 Years*, David & Charles (1981), p. 124.

10 Sidney Weighell, *On the Rails*, Orbis (1983), p. 49.

11 Terry Gourvish, op. cit., pp. 360–1.

12 *Modern Railways*, May 1977, p. 165.

13 *First Report from the Select Committee on Nationalised Industries, Session 1976–7*, 'The Role of British Rail in Public Transport', p. 177.

14 *Modern Railways*, November 1983, p. 601.

15 Terry Gourvish, *British Rail 1974–97*, OUP (2004), p. 101.

16 Ibid, p. 138.

17 *Modern Railways*, June 1974, p. 248.

Chapter 3

1 C.J. Allen, *Titled Trains of Great Britain*, Ian Allan, 5th edn (1967), pp. 180–1.

2 David R. Lamb, *Modern Railway Operation*, Pitman's Transport Library (1926), pp. 122ff.

3   Ibid, p. 126.

4   Richard Woodley, *The Day of the Holiday Express*, Ian Allan (1996), p. 21.

5   David St John Thomas and Simon Rocksborough Smith, *Summer Saturdays in the West*, David & Charles (1973), p. 77.

6   Quoted in Alan A. Jackson, *The Railway Dictionary*, Sutton Publishing, 4th edn (2006), p. 67, 'clockface service'.

7   Quoted from *The Way To Enjoy Party Outings*, British Railways Western Region (1951).

8   Quoted from *Party Outings From London and the Suburbs, c. 1957*.

9   Quoted from *Party Outings By Rail*, North Eastern Region, 1961.

10   Jack Simmons and Gordon Biddle (eds), op. cit., 'Hop-pickers trains', p. 209.

11   D.W. Winkworth, *Southern Special Traffic*, The Irwell Press (2000), p. 53.

12   D.W. Winkworth, *Southern Titled Trains*, David & Charles (1988), p. 46.

13   *Trains Illustrated*, No. 31, *Express Trains*, p. 6.

14   Transport Act 1947, Section 6, p. 12.

15   Philip Bagwell and Peter Lyth, *Transport in Britain: From Canal Lock to Gridlock*, Hambledon & London (2002), p. 135.

16   Charles E. Lee, *Passenger Class Distinctions*, The Railway Gazette (1946), p. 70.

17   Keith Parkin, *British Railways Mk1 Coaches*, HMRS & Pendragon, 2nd edn (1990), p. 79.

18   Ibid., p. 79.

19   Michael Bonavia, *British Rail: The First 25 Years*, p. 180.

20   Michael Harris, *LNER Carriages*, Atlantic Transport Publishers (1995), p. 44.

21   Neil Wooler, *Dinner in the Diner: The History of Railway Catering*, David & Charles (1987), p. 109.

22   Neil Wooler, op. cit., pp. 108–9.

23   British Railways, *1958 Facts and Figures*, p. 12.

24   C. Hamilton Ellis, *Railway Carriages in the British Isles from 1830 to 1914*, George Allen & Unwin (1965), p. 217.

25   Ibid., p. 64.

26   Ibid., p. 211.

27   Ian Carter, *Railways and Culture in Britain*, Manchester University Press (2001), pp. 173 & 219.

28   Ivor Smullen, *Taken for a Ride: A Distressing Account of the Misfortunes and Misbehaviour of the Early British Railway Traveller*, Herbert Jenkins Ltd (1968), p. 72.

29   Mike and Trevor Phillips, *Windrush: The Irresistible Rise of Multiracial Britain*, HarperCollins (1999), pp. 86–7.

30   Correspondence from Malcolm Peakman.

31   Alan A. Jackson, *London's Termini*, David & Charles/Pan (1969), p. 177.

32   Jack Simmons and Gordon Biddle (eds), op. cit., 'Malicious Damage', p. 306.

33   Charles E. Lee, *Passenger Class Distinctions*, The Railway Gazette (1946), p. 27.

34   http://www.britishpathe.com/record.php?id=41470.

35   Regulation of the Railways Act 1868, clause 20.

36   Repealed by Statute Law Revision Act 1959.

37   Document headed 'British Railways Revised Rule Book –1972', BR.87109/2, p. 11.

38   Leslie James, BA, LLB, FCIT, *The Law of the Railway*, p. 251. Bye-law 9 actually read: 'No person of the male sex above the age of 12 years shall travel or attempt to travel or remain in any vehicle or place on the railway marked or notified as being reserved or appropriated for the exclusive use of persons of the female sex.'

39   David Jenkinson, *The History of British Railway Carriages 1900–1953*, Pendragon (1996), see the illustration on p. 190.

40   Ibid., p. 191.

41   H.A.V. Bulleid, *Bulleid of the Southern*, Ian Allan (1977), p. 93.

42   Ibid., p. 97.

43   Ibid., p. 98.

44   Terry Gourvish, *British Railways 1948–73*, p. 34; Riddles is quoted there as saying: 'fortu-
      nately for me those other boys were so engaged on their own jobs that I could simply say
      to the Executive, "I'm going to do this" and I did it … I think we were left a lot to our
      own devices.'

45   David Jenkinson, op. cit., p. 290.

46   Ibid., p. 295.

47   C. Hamilton Ellis, op. cit., pp. 92 & 97.

48   Keith Parkin, op. cit., p. 8.

49   G. T. Moody, *Southern Electric 1909–79*, Ian Allan (1979), pp. 86 & 247.

50   Keith Parkin, op. cit., p. 8.

51   Ibid., p. 8.

52   Ibid., p. 9.

53   Story told to me by historian Adrian Vaughan, the signalman involved being a friend of
      his.

54   C. Hamilton Ellis, op. cit., pp. 216 & 236.

55   Keith Parkin, op. cit., p. 82.

56   John Johnson and Robert A. Long, *British Railways Engineering*, Mechanical Engineering
      Publications (1981), p. 66.

57   Jack Simmons and Gordon Biddle (eds), op. cit., 'Hop-pickers trains', p. 209.

58   *Trains Illustrated*, Vol. X, No. 103, April 1957, p. 175.

59   *British Railways Yearbook*, 1963 edn, p. 6.

60   Mallaband and Bowles, *Coaching Stock of British Railways*, RCTS 1976/78/80.

61   *Camping Coaches for Delightful and Inexpensive Holidays* (1955), British Railways.

62   Ibid.

63   Ibid.

Chapter 4

1   Report on Revision of Passenger Train Services to Combat Air Competition on the East
      Coast Route, Liverpool Street, 5 December 1956, p. 1.

2   Robert Tufnell, *Prototype Locomotives*, David & Charles (1985), p. 58.

3   R. C. Bond, *A Lifetime with Locomotives*, Goose & Son (1975), p. 234.

4   Colonel H.C.B. Rogers OBE, *Transition from Steam*, Ian Allan (1980), pp. 6–7.

5   'Bad railways? Blame it on the 1950s', BBC News website, Thursday 16 May 2002,
      http://news.bbc.co.uk/1/hi/uk/1989357.stm.

6   Colin Buchanan, *Traffic in Towns: A Study of the Long Term Problems of Traffic in Urban Areas*,
      HMSO (1963), p. 24 and Penguin Books (1963), pp. 31–2.

7   British Transport Commission, *Modernisation and Re-equipment of British Railways*, 1955, VI,
      'Economics of the Plan', pp. 30–2.

8   British Transport Commission, *Modernisation and Re-equipment of British Railways*, 1955, II,
      'Outline of the Plan', p. 6.

9   Ibid., pp. 6–7.

10   Ibid., p. 7.

11   Ibid., p. 7.

12   *Railway Magazine*, September 1953: 'Rehabilitating British Main Lines / A Useful High
      Speed Service', p. 577 and 'Restoring British Permanent Way', p. 584.

13   Two such films, from 1952, *Day to Day Track Maintenance parts 1 &2* can be seen on the
      BFI's BTF collection 'Points and Aspects'.

14   *Railway Magazine*, September 1953, 'Restoring British Permanent Way', p. 584.

15   Alan Williams, *Not the Age of the Train*, Ian Allan (1983), pp. 53–7 (see his acerbic comments).

16   Valerie Stewart and Vivian Chadwick, *Changing Trains: Messages for Management from the ScotRail Challenge*, David & Charles (1987), p. 23.

17   David N. Clough, *Hydraulic Versus Electric: the Battle for the BR Diesel Fleet*, Ian Allan (2011), pp. 59–71.

18   See Brian Reed, *Diesel Hydraulic Locomotives of the Western Region*, David & Charles (1975) for dates of withdrawals.

19   John Glover, *BR Diary 1958–1967*, Ian Allan (1987), pp. 26–7.

20   John Johnson and Robert A. Long, op. cit., p. 183.

21   British Rail Fleet Survey 8, *Diesel Multiple-Units – The First Generation*, p. 27.

22   Evan Green-Hughes, *BR First Generation Railbuses*, Ian Allan (2011), particularly pp. 3–10.

23   Ibid., pp. 9–10.

24   Ibid., p. 6.

25   E.S. Cox, *Diesel and Electric Traction on British Railways*, United Kingdom Railway Advisory Service (1961), p. 32.

26   Reshaping Report, p. 18.

27   Evan Green-Hughes, op. cit., p. 74.

28   Report of the Railway Electrification Committee, 1927 and Report of the Committee on Main Line Railway Electrification, 1931.

29   John Johnson and Robert A. Long, op. cit., p. 223.

30   Brian Webb and Alan A. Duncan, *The AC Electric Locomotives of British Rail*, David & Charles (1979), pp. 20ff.

31   Brian Haresnape, *British Rail 1948–78: A Journey by Design* (Ian Allan), 1979, p. 111.

32   Ibid., p. 92.

33   Ibid., p. 92.

34   Ibid., pp. 92–3.

35   Ibid., p. 93.

36   Ibid., p. 101.

37   Jonathan M. Woodham, *Oxford Dictionary of Modern Design*, OUP (2006), pp. 123–4.

38   Keith Parkin, op. cit., p. 102.

39   Colonel H.C.B. Rogers OBE, op. cit., p. 77, col. 1.

40   G. Freeman Allen, *British Railways Today and Tomorrow*, Ian Allan, 3rd edn (1962), p. 69.

41   G. Freeman Allen, *The World's Fastest Trains*, Patrick Stephens Ltd, 2nd edn (1992) p. 84.

42   Brian Webb, *The Deltic Locomotives of British Rail*, David & Charles (1982), pp. 76 & 81.

43   Ibid., pp. 32, 36, 61, 67 & 81.

44   *Modernisation and Re-equipment of British Railways*, para. 58, p. 19.

45   *British Railways Magazine: North Eastern Region*, February 1957, p. 45.

46   Recommended Code of Practice for Minor Stations Improvements, British Transport Commission Design Panel, Architects Study Group (1961).

47   Cecil J. Allen, *Titled Trains of Great Britain*, Ian Allan, 5th edn, p. 6.

Chapter 5

1   Based on figures in D.L. Munby, *Inland Transport Statistics Great Britain 1900–1970*, Vol. 1 (A.H. Watson (ed.)), OUP (1978), pp. 117–9.

2   BRB, 1963 Reports and Accounts, p. 19.

3   Reshaping Report, p. 21.

4   British Transport Commission, *Modernisation and Re-equipment of the Railways* (1956), p. 32.

5   http://en.wikipedia.org/wiki/List_of_closed_railway_lines_in_Bavaria#1950s.

6   Richard Marsh, *Off the Rails*, Weidenfeld & Nicolson (1978), pp. 166–7.

7   G.F. Fiennes, *I Tried to Run a Railway*, Ian Allan (1967), p. 114 ff.

8   Reshaping Report, p. 20.

9   Independent Commission on Transport, *Changing Directions*, p. 325.

10 Ibid., p. 324.

11 Policy Studies Institute, *Social Consequences of Rail Closures*, p. 104.

12 *Modern Railways*, June 1980, pp. 244–5.

13 R.E. Burroughs, *Great Isle of Wight Train Robbery: Story of the Isle of Wight Railway Closures*, Railway Invigoration Society (1969), p. 37.

14 C.J. Wignall, *British Railway Maps and Gazetteer, 1825–1985*, Oxford Publishing Company (1985).

15 John Thomas, *Forgotten Railways Scotland*, David & Charles, 2nd edn (1981), p. 66.

16 http://www.bbc.co.uk/news/uk-scotland-south-scotland-20206538.

17 Reshaping Report, p. 15.

18 Reshaping Report, p. 14.

19 *Report on Dieselisation of Passenger and Freight Services in the West of England*, British Railways Western Region (1955), p. 45.

20 Ibid., p. 45.

21 David St John Thomas and Simon Rocksborough-Smith, *Summer Saturdays in the West*, David & Charles (1973), p. 48.

22 G.F. Fiennes, op. cit., pp. 114–6.

23 *Modern Railways*, May 1967, p. 262.

24 Ibid.

25 Ibid., November 1967, p. 605.

26 Reshaping Report, p. 13.

27 Trunk Route Report, Map 21.

28 John Gough, *British Rail at Work: InterCity*, Ian Allan (1988), p. 70.

29 Roger Ford and Brian Perren, *HSTs at Work*, Ian Allan (1988), p. 47.

30 Terry Gourvish, *British Railways 1948–73*, p. 629.

31 Ibid., p. 630.

32 G. Freeman Allen, *British Rail after Beeching*, Ian Allan (1966), p. 146.

33 O.S. Nock, *Britain's New Railway*, Ian Allan (1966), p. 209.

34 Ibid., p. 210.

35 'Inter-city and main-line trains will be accelerated and made more punctual': British Transport Commission, *Modernisation and Re-equipment of British Railways* (1955), para. 8(i), p. 7.

36 O.S. Nock, op. cit., p. 209.

37 G. Freeman Allen, *British Railways Today and Tomorrow*, Ian Allan (1955), p. 83.

38 *Modern Railways*, March 1966, p. 131 and March 1967, p. 120.

39 *1967 Southern Travellers Handbook*, British Railways Southern Region, p. 186.

40 *Modern Railways*, September 1966, p. 486.

41 *Modern Railways*, April 1967, p. 177.

42 *Modern Railways*, April 1964, p. 249.

43 *Trains Illustrated*, December 1962, p. 405.

44 *The New Tradition*, Eighth Rail Report, BTF, 1968. The British Transport Films Collection, Volume Four, *Reshaping British Railways*.

45 Keith Parkin, op. cit., pp. 121–2.

46 Cecil J. Allen and B.K. Cooper, *Titled Trains of Great Britain*, Ian Allan, 6th edn (1983), p. 90.

47 'Let British Railways do the long drive', leaflet for 1961.

48 British Railways Board, *Britain's Growing Railway, An A-Z Guide*, Railfuture (2010), p. 55.

49 *Modern Railways*, November 1988, p. 590.

50 BRB Reports and Accounts, 1965, p. 32.

51 BRB Reports and Accounts, 1965, p. 4, para 16.

52   Harold Pollins, *Britain's Railways: An Industrial History*, David & Charles (1971), p. 178.

53   Terry Gourvish, *British Rail 1974–97*, p. 481.

54   Ibid., pp. 480–1.

Chapter 6

1   Raymond Report, p. 7.

2   Ibid.

3   Keith Parkin, op. cit., p. 64.

4   *Modern Railways*, January 1965, p. 3.

5   George Dow, *Railway Heraldry*, David & Charles (1973) pp. 246–8.

6   Brian Haresnape, op. cit., p. 107.

7   Ibid., p. 107.

8   Jonathan M. Woodham, op. cit., p. 182.

9   http://www.doublearrow.co.uk/manual.htm.

10   British Railways Board, *British Rail Architecture, Design and Environment* (1989), p. 4.

11   George Dow, op. cit., p. 250.

12   British Rail Architecture, op. cit., p. 4.

13   Alan A. Jackson, *The Railway Dictionary*, p. 11.

14   *Modern Railways*, January 1965, p. 27.

15   http://www.telegraph.co.uk/culture/art/art-features/9214460/Margaret-Calvert-inter-view-Caution-woman-at-work.html.

16   Simon Garfield, *Just My Type*, Profile Books (2010), pp. 148–59.

17   *Modern Railways*, January 1965, p. 28.

18   *Railway Magazine*, August 1978, p. 414.

19   *Railway Magazine*, January 1979, pp. 47–8, and *British Rail Locoshed Book*, Ian Allan (1979), cover and p. 2.

20   Brain Haresnape, op. cit., p. 122.

21   Colin J. Marsden and Darren Ford, *Encyclopaedia of Modern Traction Names*, Channel AV Publishing (1998), p. 5.

22   Ibid., pp. 3–5.

23   Ibid., p. 214.

24   D. W. Winkworth, 'Named British Express Trains' in *Railway Magazine*, October 1978, pp. 477–9.

25   G. Freeman Allen, 'Passenger Marketing In The West Midlands' in *Modern Railways*, July 1970, pp. 294–6.

26   'Personalising Crack Trains' in *Modern Railways*, November 1972, p. 403.

27   Ibid.

28   Dave Peel, *Locomotive Headboards: The Complete Story*, The History Press (2006).

29   Colin Boocock, *Railway Liveries: BR Traction 1948–1995*, Ian Allan (2000), pp. 49–50.

30   British Rail Architecture, op. cit., p. 9.

31   *Railway Magazine*, November 1978, p. 568.

32   Colin Boocock, op. cit., p. 66.

33   'Designing the Network' in *Modern Railways*, January 1987, pp. 25–9.

34   *Modern Railways*, January 1965, pp. 26–34.

35   *Modern Railways*, May 1987, p. 268.

36   British Rail Architecture, op. cit., p. 10.

37   Keith Lovegrove, *Railway Identity, Design and Culture*, Laurence King Publishing Ltd (2004), p. 141.

38   Mike Vincent and Chris Green (eds), *The InterCity Story*, OUP (1994), p. 68.

39   *Modern Railways*, April 1989, p. 175.

40 *Identity Management: Regional Railways*, brochure sent to staff on 11 June 1992.
41 Edgar Anstey, *The Work of the B.T.C. Film Unit*, British Railways (Western Region) London Lecture and Debating Society, Session 1960–1, No. 466.
42 Ibid., p. 6.
43 *Travelling with British Rail: A Guide for Disabled People*, The Royal Association for Disability and Rehabilitation (1985), pp. 169 & 173. *British Rail 1979: A Guide for Disabled People*, The Royal Association for Disability and Rehabilitation (1979), pp. 153 & 157.

Chapter 7

1   *Modern Railways*, July 1963, p. 29.
2   Keith Parkin, op. cit., pp. 30–7.
3   Ibid., p. 37.
4   Ibid., pp. 30–7.
5   Michael Harris, *BR Mark 2 Coaches: The Design That Launched Intercity*, Venture Publications (1999), p. 19ff.
6   Ibid., pp. 26 & 37.
7   Ibid., p. 27.
8   Ibid., p. 28.
9   Ibid., p. 28.
10 John Johnson and Robert A. Long, op. cit., p. 288.
11 *Modern Railways*, July 1964, pp. 2–9.
12 Michael Harris, op. cit., p. 92.
13 Ibid., p. 90.
14 Ibid., pp. 55–66.
15 Ibid., p. 68.
16 Ibid., p. 58.
17 Ibid., p. 68.
18 John Johnson and Robert A. Long, op. cit., p. 291.
19 *Modern Railways*, December 1962, p. 461.
20 *Modern Railways*, December 1966, p. 648.
21 *The Listener*, 16 March 1939, p. 566, quoted in K.G. Fenelon, *British Railways Today*, Nelson (1939), pp. 58–9.
22 John Johnson and Robert A. Long, op. cit., p. 453.
23 O.S. Nock, *Two Miles a Minute*, Patrick Stephens Ltd, 2nd edn (1983), p. 84.
24 *Modern Railways*, August 1965, p. 450.
25 John Johnson and Robert A. Long, op. cit., p. 456 and Stephen Potter, *On the Right Lines*, Frances Pinter (1987), p. 50.
26 Stephen Potter, ibid., pp. 69–72.
27 Hugh Williams, *APT: A Promise Unfulfilled*, Ian Allan (1985), p. 10.
28 John Johnson and Robert A. Long, op. cit., p. 191 and Colin J. Marsden and Brian B. Fenn, *British Rail Main Line Diesel Locomotives*, OPC, 2nd edn (2000), p. 27.
29 Roger Ford and Brian Perren, op. cit., p. 10.
30 http://www.paxmanhistory.org.uk/paxeng34.htm#y3j.
31 'Co-Co' and 'Bo-Bo' are the Continental Notation for the axles under a locomotive. 1 signifies a single unpowered axle, 2, two adjacent unpowered axles, etc. Letters signify powered axles: A is a single axle, B, two adjacent powered axles, and so on. The small 'o' suffix indicates that each axle is powered by its own traction motor. Hence a Bo-Bo machine has two bogies, each with two axles, each powered by its own traction motor.
32 *Modern Railways*, May 1971, p. 206.

33   Gemma Curtin and Kenneth Grange, *Making Britain Modern*, Black Dog Publishing (2011), p. 160.

34   Ibid., p. 166.

35   Ibid.

36   *Kenneth Grange at the Boilerhouse*, Conran Foundation (1983), p. 47.

37   Stephen Potter, op. cit., p. 124.

38   Ibid., p. 130.

39   Ibid., p. 134.

40   Ibid., pp. 135–6.

41   British Railway Board Reports and Accounts, 1965, p. 51.

42   John Johnson and Robert A. Long, op. cit., pp. 427ff.

Chapter 8

1   Terry Gourvish, *British Railways 1948–73*, p. 451.

2   Commuters Charter, p. 1.

3   Terry Gourvish, *British Railways 1948–73*, p. 451.

4   http://www.pteg.net/NR/rdonlyres/54A4F498-0487-46BF-AD8F-65276A4F5860/0/25YearsofPTEs.pdf.

5   *Transport Policy: An Opportunity for Change*, BRB, p. 44.

6   P. Semmens, *Electrifying the East Coast Route*, Patrick Stephens Ltd (1991), p. 30.

7   *Modern Railways*, April 1976, p. 127.

8   John Glover and Colin J. Marsden, *London Transport Railways and PTE Systems*, Ian Allan (1985), p. 104.

9   John Glover, op. cit., p. 114.

10   Iain Frew, *Britain's Electric Railways Today*, Electric Railway Society/Southern Electric Group (1983), p. 36.

11   *Modern Railways*, October 1990, p. 521.

12   http://www.metrolink.co.uk/pdf/past_present_future.pdf.

13   *Modern Railways*, February 1977, p. 74; *Railway Magazine*, July 1978; *Britain's Growing Railway*, p. 71.

14   *Modern Railways*, August 1993, p. 461.

15   Alan Millar, *British PTEs: 1*, Strathclyde (1985), p. 42.

16   http://www.jhowie.force9.co.uk/strathclyde.html.

17   Colin Speakman, *Public Transport in West Yorkshire: 10 Years of Achievement*, Metro-West Yorkshire Passenger Transport Executive (1985), p. 25.

18   Geoffrey Hurst, *Register of Closed Railways*, Milepost Publications (1992), p. 74, ref. 3256.

19   Colin Speakman, op. cit., p. 28.

20   'Traction and Rolling Stock Special' in *Modern Railways,* 1996, p. 52.

21   *Modern Railways*, June 1978, p. 250.

22   http://www.thetrams.co.uk/supertram/history.php.

23   'South Yorkshire Review' in *Modern Railways*, August 1991, pp. 418–23.

24   *Modern Railways*, January 1985, pp. 31–6 and August 1991, pp. 418–23.

25   *Modern Railways*, 1974, p. 371.

26   Terry Gourvish, *British Rail 1974–97*, p. 87.

27   *Modern Railways*, March 1976, p. 113.

28   John Gough, op. cit., p. 9.

29   Michael Harris, *BR Mark 2 Coaches*, pp. 92–3.

30   *Modern Railways*, July 1974, pp. 254–5.

31   http://news.bbc.co.uk/onthisday/hi/dates/stories/october/4/newsid_2486000/2486817.stm.

32   Mike Vincent and Chris Green (eds), op. cit., p. 23.

33 *Speed for the Seventies HST*, British Rail Board (1970s), p. 1.

34 Roger Ford and Brian Perren, op. cit., p. 47.

35 *Modern Railways*, December 1973, p. 490.

36 Ibid.

37 Neil Wooler, op. cit., p. 194.

38 *Modern Railways*, August 1978, p. 345.

39 *Modern Railways*, June 1978, p. 250.

40 *Modern Railways*, December 1981, p. 533.

41 *Modern Railways*, November 1977, p. 449.

42 The Southern Report, December 1972.

43 BRB Reports and Accounts, 1976, p. 18.

44 *Modern Railways*, June 1978, p. 247.

45 Brian Boddy, *It's on the Cards that Some Things have got Worse*, Transport Ticket Society (2001), pp. 2–3.

46 Roger Ford and Brian Perren, op. cit., p. 164.

47 'Optional Travel Boom in The West and Wales' in *Modern Railways*, September 1970, p. 413.

48 Keith Parkin, op. cit., pp. 166 & 168.

49 *Modern Railways*, October 1978, p. 439.

50 Charles Long, 'Twelve Years of Golden Rail', in *Modern Railways*, August 1982, p. 349.

51 BRB Reports and Accounts, 1973, p. 5.

52 *Modern Railways*, January 1975, p. 4.

53 *Modern Railways*, February 1981, p. 56.

54 Brian Boddy, op. cit., p. 4ff.

55 Ticket Inspectors' Handbook O.3 1975 gives the expiry date as 31 March 1976. *The Inter-City Story* (first edition: p. 159) gives the start date as 1 April 1976 but this must be a year out based on Ticket Inspectors' Handbook.

56 BRB Reports and Accounts, 1975, p. 14.

57 *Modern Railways*, May 1979, p. 207.

58 *Modern Railways*, February 1980, p. 55.

59 John Glover, op. cit., p. 24.

60 *Modern Railways*, December 1980, p. 531.

61 *Modern Railways*, December 1979, p. 523.

62 *Modern Railways*, February 1980, p. 55.

63 *Modern Railways*, December 1981, p. 531.

64 Ticket Examiners' Handbook B.19, issued June 1975.

Chapter 9

1   Brian Murphy, *ASLEF 1880–1980 100 Years Strong*, Associated Society of Locomotive Engineers and Firemen, p. 48.

2   Charles McLeod, *All Change: Railway Industrial Relations in the Sixties*, Gower Press Ltd (1970), chapter 5: 'Easing the Hardships of Redundancy', pp. 56–65.

3   British Transport Commission: Recruitment and Training Arrangements, report by Stanley Raymond, March 1956, p. 7.

4   Michael Bonavia, *Birth of British Rail*, George Allen & Unwin (1979), p. 89, col. 2.

5   British Transport Commission, op. cit.

6   British Transport Commission, ibid., p. 9, para. 31.

7   British Transport Commission, ibid., p. 9, para. 34.

8   Training for Transport, British Railways (Western Region) London Lecture and Debating Society, session 1964–65, No. 489 'Training For Transport' by Mr M.R. Bonavia (Director of Education and Training, BRB), p. 8.

9   'It relies on the doubtful judgement of an untrained interviewer', British Rail Southern Region: National Examinations Board in Supervisory Studies Project Report: Recruitment, Selection and Training of Railmen and Leading Railmen in the Surbiton Area, 9 July 1971, A.G. Robbins, p. 9.

10 British Transport Commission, op. cit., p. 8, para. 28(d).

11 British Rail Southern Region National Examinations Board, 9 July 1971, A.G. Robbins.

12 Diana Robbins, *Wanted: Railman. Report of an Investigation into Equal Opportunities for Women in British Rail*, Equal Opportunities Commission, HMSO (1986), p. 6.

13 Ibid.

14 Valerie Stewart and Vivian Chadwick, op. cit., p. 45.

15 Anthony Hidden, *Investigation into the Clapham Junction Railway Accident*, Department of Transport (1989), pp. 16 & 76–77.

16 Ibid., pp. 16 & 77.

17 Ibid., pp. 16 & 78.

18 Michael Bonavia, op. cit., p. 90.

19 Michael Bonavia, *British Rail: The First 25 Years*, p. 216.

20 Stephen Poole, *Behind the Crumbling Edge*, The Book Guild Ltd (2002), p. 201.

21 Ibid., p. 202.

22 Terry Gourvish, *British Railways 1948–73*, p. 226.

23 *Modern Railways*, July 1974, p. 254.

24 Terry Gourvish, op. cit., p. 490.

25 Terry Gourvish, *British Rail 1974–97*, p. 157.

26 Court (Plenary) Case of Young, James and Webster *v* The United Kingdom (Application No. 7601/76; 7806/77) Judgement, Strasbourg, 13 August 1981.

27 BBC, *Inside Story: Old, Dirty and Late*, 1993.

28 Charles Klapper, *London's Lost Railways*, Routledge & Kegan Paul (1976), p. 74.

29 David Holmes, *The Life and Times of the Station Master*, Silver Link Publishing (2007), p. 7.

30 *Modern Railways*, April 1965, p. 199.

31 Harold Pollins, *Britain's Railways: An Industrial History*, David & Charles (1971), p. 74ff.

32 *Modern Railways*, June 1965, pp. 335–9.

33 Stephen Poole, op. cit., p. 173.

34 Ibid.

35 Ibid.

36 See BR87109/21 Revised Rule Book 1972, which provides a list 'Showing disposition of former rules in the New Rule Book'.

37 Frank McKenna, *The Railway Workers 1840–1870*, Faber & Faber (1980), p. 37.

38 G.F. Fiennes, op. cit., p. 134.

39 G. Freeman Allen, *British Rail after Beeching*, p. 352.

40 Terry Gourvish, *British Railways 1948–73*, p. 162.

41 *British Railways Magazine*, Western Region, Insurance Edition, Vol. 8, No. 1, January 1957, pp. 5–6.

42 Valerie Stewart and Vivian Chadwick, op. cit., p. 25.

43 Interview with the author.

44 Sir Godfray Le Quesne QC, Monopolies and Mergers Commission: British Railways Board: Network SouthEast, p. 77, para. 8.44.

45 *Modern Railways*, June 1973, p. 238.

46 *It Takes All Sorts*, 1978, British Transport Films Collection Vol. 9: 'Just the Ticket', British Film Institute.

47 Report on Revision of Passenger Train Services to Combat Air Competition on the East Coast Route, British Railways, Eastern Region Liverpool Street, 5 December 1956, pp. 24–5.

48   Helena Wojtczak, *Railwaywomen: Exploitation, Betrayal and Triumph in the Workplace*, Hastings Press (2005), p. 254.
49   *Work Study and You*, British Transport Commission (1958).
50   Valerie Stewart and Vivian Chadwick, op. cit., pp. 50ff.
51   Terry Gourvish, *British Rail 1974–97*, p. 374.
52   Roger Ford, 'Traincrew In Action' in *Modern Railways*, May 1989, p. 241.
53   Mike Vincent and Chris Green, op. cit., p. 164.
54   John Rose, *Solidarity Forever: 100 Years of Kings Cross ASLEF*, Kings Cross ASLEF (1986), p. 49.
55   Philip S. Bagwell, *The Railwaymen, Volume 2*, George Allen & Unwin (1982), p. 276.
56   John Rose, op. cit., p. 49.
57   Philip S. Bagwell, op. cit., p. 276.
58   Helena Wojtczak, op. cit., p. 250.
59   Ibid., p. 277.
60   Ibid., p. 283.
61   Ibid., p. 316.

Chapter 10

1   http://hansard.millbanksystems.com/commons/1968/nov/29/commuters#column_950.
2   See Department of Transport Statistics, Great Britain 1979–89, p. 128.
3   The Commuters' Charter, June 1981, p. 3.
4   BRB Reports and Accounts, 1976, p. 7.
5   Charles E. Lee, *Passenger Class Distinctions*, The Railway Gazette (1946), p. 50.
6   Edwin Course, *London's Railways*, B.T. Batsford (1962), p. 201.
7   Ibid., p. 201.
8   Ibid., pp. 197–8.
9   Ibid., p. 198.
10   Alan A. Jackson, *Semi-Detached London*, George Allen & Unwin (1973), pp. 228–31.
11   'The Bournemouth Electrification – The First Five Years' in *Modern Railways*, December 1972, p. 455.
12   Alan Williams, *Southern Electric Album*, Ian Allan (1977), p. 85.
13   Alan A. Jackson and Desmond F. Croome, *Rails Through the Clay*, George Allen & Unwin (1962), p. 178.
14   Reshaping Report, p. 21.
15   T.C. Barker and Michael Robbins, *A History of London Transport*, Vol. 2, George Allen & Unwin (1976), pp. 343–4.
16   *A Cross-London Rail Link*, British Railways Board Discussion Paper, November 1980.
17   Michael Bonavia, *The History of the Southern Railway*, Unwin Hyman (1987), pp. 185–7.
18   S.W. Smart, Former Superintendent of Operation, Southern Region, 'The Southern Needs No Centralised Control' in *Modern Railways*, July 1964, p. 49.
19   *Modern Railways*, July 1964; ibid., p. 49.
20   'Station Control Rooms at Southern's London Termini' in *Modern Railways*, July 1969, p. 363.
21   *Modern Railways*, February 1963, pp. 73–5.
22   *Modern Railways*, July 1964, p. 49.
23   Train, Locomotive and Traffic Control System Embodying the Standard and Local Instructions as Applicable to the Southern Region, General Managers Office, Waterloo, January 1967.
24   *Modern Railways*, July 1969, p. 363.

25 John Glover, op. cit., p. 30.
26 David Brown and Alan A. Jackson, *Network SouthEast Handbook*, Capital Transport (1990), p. 43.
27 Ibid., p. 46.
28 David Brown, *Southern Electric: A New History*, Capital Transport Publishing (2010), p. 176.
29 *Modern Railways*, June 1965, p. 307.
30 G. Freeman Allen, *The Southern Since 1948*, Ian Allan (1987), p. 146.
31 Ibid.
32 Brian Haresnape, *Railway Design Since 1830*, p. 105.
33 As witnessed by members of the Southern email group.
34 Colin J. Marsden, *Southern Electric Multiple Units 1948–1983*, Ian Allan. See the picture on p. 103. Mark Brinton has explained that adhesion testing had been taking place on the line the night before and a residue of liquid had probably been left over.
35 David Brown and Alan A. Jackson, op. cit., p. 102.
36 Ibid., p. 102.
37 According to G. Freeman Allen, LSE director David Kirby had dismissed the scheme as 'supererogatory' soon after taking office. *The Southern Since 1948*, p. 156.
38 David Brown and Alan A. Jackson, op. cit., p. 102.
39 See pp. 176ff.
40 Terry Gourvish, *British Rail 1974–97*, p. 278.
41 David Gibbons, *BR Equipment 2: Drawings from Railnews 'Stockspot'*, Ian Allan Ltd (1990), pp. 25–32.
42 Information from former employees on the Yahoo Southern email group.
43 *Modern Railways*, July 1986, p. 364.
44 Interview with the author.
45 M&MC NSE, 1987, p. 187.

Chapter 11

1 BRB Reports and Accounts, 1988–89, p. 12 and Terry Gourvish, *British Rail 1974–97*, pp. 149–50.
2 BRB Reports and Accounts, 1982, p. 75.
3 'Insight: Inter-City Under Pressure' in *Modern Railways Insight*, No. 2, 1982, p. 10.
4 Roger Ford and Brian Perren, op. cit.
5 Michael Harris, Brian Perren and Roger Ford, InterCity 21 Years of Progress, Ian Allan (1987), p. 29.
6 'InterCity Today' in *Rail Magazine*, 1993, p. 38.
7 Cecil J. Allen, revised by B.K. Cooper, *Titled Trains of Great Britain*, Ian Allan, 6th edn (1983), p. 63.
8 Alan A. Jackson, op. cit., p. 227.
9 James Abbott, 'West Yorkshire: Lightening the Heavyweight Railway' in *Modern Railways*, October 1985, p. 519.
10 Jerry Alderson, Ian McDonald and Alan Bevan, *Britain's Growing Railway: An A–Z Guide*, Railway Development Society (2010), pp. 115–26.
11 *Modern Railways*, May 1982, p. 196.
12 David St John Thomas and Patrick Whitehouse, *BR in the Eighties*, Guild Publishing (1990), p. 134.
13 Valerie Stewart and Vivian Chadwick, *Changing Trains: Messages for Management from the ScotRail Challenge*, David & Charles (1987), p. 40.
14 Alan Millar, op. cit., p. 112.
15 *Strathclyde Rail Network: The Way Ahead*, British Rail (Scottish Region), (1983).

16 Alan Millar, op. cit., pp. 112–3.

17 According to the brochure 'ScotRail Review 1984/85', published by ScotRail, this was spent on upgrading all of ScotRail, p. 3.

18 'ScotRail Review 1984/85', p. 3. Included in *Modern Railways*, September 1985.

19 *Britain's Growing Railway*, pp. 119–20.

20 Valerie Stewart and Vivian Chadwick, op. cit., pp. 98–100.

21 Ibid., p. 49.

22 InterCity Strategy, Director InterCity, June 1984.

23 'InterCity: Passenger Railway Without Subsidy', lecture given at the RSA, 24 May 1989.

24 John Gough, *British Rail at Work: InterCity*, Ian Allan (1988), p. 40.

25 *Modern Railways*, July 1993, pp. 373–6.

26 John Gough, op. cit., p. 56, col. 2.

27 *Modern Railways*, May 1985, p. 417.

28 Michael Harris, Roger Ford and Brian Perren, op. cit., p. 24.

29 Ibid.

30 Ibid., p. 25.

31 Charles Fryer, *British Pullman Trains*, Silver Link Publishing Ltd (1992), p. 217.

32 *Modern Railways*, September 1984, p. 463.

33 *Modern Railways*, June 1983, p. 297.

34 Terry Gourvish, *British Rail 1974–97*, p. 251.

35 David St John Thomas and Patrick Whitehouse, op. cit., p. 108.

36 BRB Reports and Accounts, 1986–87, p. 19.

37 BRB Reports and Accounts, 1987–88, p. 22.

38 BRB Reports and Accounts, 1988–89, p. 4.

39 Neil Wooler, op. cit., David & Charles (1987), p. 203.

40 Ibid., pp. 205–6.

41 David St John Thomas and Patrick Whitehouse, op. cit., p. 105.

42 Ibid., p. 107.

43 Mike Vincent and Chris Green, op. cit., p. 96; ibid., p. 107.

44 Ashley Butlin, *BR Coaching Fleet Mk2, Mk3 & Mk4*, Irwell Press (1993), p. 16.

45 *Modern Railways*, August 1981, p. 349.

46 Brian Haresnape, *British Rail Fleet Survey 9: Diesel Multiple Units, The Second Generation, and DEMUs*, Ian Allan (1986), pp. 42–3.

47 Peter Dickinson, *Still Nodding*, HMRS (2010), p. 5.

48 Ibid., p. 5.

49 *Modern Railways*, July 1980, p. 291.

50 Peter Dickinson, op. cit., p. 7.

51 Ibid., p. 7, 12ff.

52 Brian Haresnape, *British Rail Fleet Survey 9*, pp. 56ff.

53 Roger Wood, *British Rail Passenger Trains*, Capital Transport Publishing (1993), pp. 110–1.

54 Brian Perren (ed.), *The Renaissance of Regional Railways, A Special Rail Supplement*, Meridian Media Services (c. 1991–92), p. 4.

55 Keith Parkin, op. cit., pp. 123–4.

56 Peter Semmens, *Electrifying the East Coast Route: The Making of Britian's First 140mph Railway*, Patrick Stephens Ltd (1991), pp. 93ff, chapter 6.

57 Ian Cowley, *Anglia East: The Transformation of a Railway*, David & Charles (1987).

58 *Modern Railways*, March 1985, p. 119.

59 Peter Semmens, op. cit., pp. 148ff.

60 *Modern Railways*, October 1989, p. 518.

61 *Modern Railways*, June 1987, p. 283.

62 David Gibbons, op. cit., pp. 94–6.

63 Michael Bonavia presents a good history of the railway involvement in *The Channel Tunnel Story*, David & Charles (1987).

64 Ibid., p. 86.

65 Ibid., pp. 133ff.

66 Ibid.

67 Terry Gourvish, *British Rail 1974–97*, p. 335.

68 Ibid., p. 444.

69 *Modern Railways*, October 1989, p. 508.

70 Terry Gourvish, *Britain's Railways: Labour's Strategic Experiment*, OUP (2008), p. 190.

71 *Modern Railways*, September 1991, p. 454.

72 Mike Vincent and Chris Green, op. cit., pp. 112–3.

Chapter 12

1 Anthony Hidden, op. cit., pp. 163 & 173.

2 Ibid., p. 114.

3 Repealed by Inquiries Act 2005, c. 12 Sch. 2 para. 1 Sch. 3.

4 Report on the Double Collision that occurred on 8th October 1952, at Harrow and Wealdstone Station in the London Midland Region British Railways, Ministry of Transport, HMSO, 1953.

5 Ibid., p. 1.

6 Stanley Hall, *Danger Signals: An Investigation into Modern Railway Accidents*, Ian Allan (1987), p. 11.

7 Report on the Double Collision, p. 25.

8 Stanley Hall, op. cit., p. 16.

9 Ibid., pp. 16–7.

10 Report on the Derailment that occurred on 5th November, 1967 near Hither Green in the Southern Region British Railways (1968).

11 Report on the Derailment that occurred on 15th July, 1967 near Amble Junction between Acklington and Chevington in the Eastern Region British Railways (1968).

12 Railway Accidents: Report to the Minister of Transport on the Safety Record of the Railways in Great Britain during the Year 1966, HMSO (1967), p. 78.

13 Report on the Derailment that occurred on 5th November, 1967, p. 21, para 161.

14 Ibid., p. 139.

15 Railway Accidents 1966, op. cit., p. 78.

16 Report on the Derailment that occurred on 2nd July 1971 at Tattenhall Junction near Chester in the London Midland Region British Railways, HMSO (1972).

17 Stanley Hall and Peter Van Der Mark, *Level Crossings*, Ian Allan (2008), particularly pp. 27–36.

18 Report of the Public Inquiry into the Accident at Hixon Level Crossing on January 6th, 1968. Presented to parliament by the Minister of Transport by Command of Her Majesty, July 1968, HMSO, para. 25.

19 Ibid., p. 39, para. 114.

20 Ibid., p. 28.

21 Stanley Hall and Peter Van Der Mark, op. cit., pp. 47ff.

22 Level Crossing Protection Report, HMSO (1978).

23 Stanley Hall and Peter Van Der Mark, op. cit., pp. 58ff.

24 Report on the Fire that occurred in a Sleeping-Car Train on 6th July 1978 at Taunton in the Western Region British Railways, HMSO (1980).

25 Ibid., p. 26, para. 98.

26 *Modern Railways*, August 1979, p. 359.

27 Terry Gourvish, *British Rail 1974–97*, p. 444.

28 Anthony Hidden, op. cit., pp. 92–3.

29 Ibid., p. 97.

30 Ibid., p. 95.

31 Stanley Hall, *Hidden Dangers: Railway Safety in the Era of Privatisation*, Ian Allan (1999), p. 31.

32 Ibid., p. 26.

33 Ibid., A just summary of Hidden, in my view, p. 26.

34 Anthony Hidden, op. cit., pp. 120–1, paras 13:20ff.

35 Passenger Falls from Train Doors: Report of an HSE Investigation, Health and Safety Exectuve, HMSO (1993), p. 6.

36 *A Fair Test: Selecting Train Drivers for British Rail*, Commission For Racial Equality (1996), p. 17.

37 Stanley Hall, op. cit., chapter 6: 'The Purley Collision: The Driver As Scapegoat', pp. 41–5.

38 Ibid., p. 45.

39 http://news.bbc.co.uk/1/hi/england/7140326.stm.

40 http://news.bbc.co.uk/1/hi/england/7966402.stm.

41 *ASLEF Journal*, February 2008, p. 10.

42 Stanley Hall, op. cit., pp. 38–9.

43 Terry Gourvish, *British Rail 1974–97*, p. 345.

44 Railway Safety: Report on the Safety Record of the Railways in Great Britain during 1990, HSE/Department of Transport, p. 1.

45 Stanley Hall, *Railway Detectives: 150 Years of the Railway Inspectorate*, Ian Allan (1990), p. 139.

46 The Ladbroke Grove Rail Inquiry Report, The Rt Hon. Lord Cullen QC, 2001, Part 2, chapter 10.

47 Railway Safety Report 1990, p. 1.

48 A Report of an Inquiry into the collision that occurred on 21 July 1991 at Newton Junction, Health and Safety Executive, HMSO (1992), pp. 38ff. Stanley Hall, *Hidden Dangers*, op. cit., pp. 46–58.

49 Railway Accident at Reading: A report on an accident that occurred on 1 August 1990, 7 December 1993, by Health and Safety Executive; A report of a train accident that occurred on 22 August 1990 at Hyde North Junction in the London Midland Region of British Railways, 15 November 1991, by Health and Safety Executive; Report of the Inquiry into the collision at Bellgrove Junction on 6 March 1989, Department of Transport, 28 February 1990.

50 Peter Rayner, *On and Off the Rails*, Novelangle Ltd (1997), p. 11.

51 Ibid., p. 11.

52 A Report of an Inquiry into the collision that occurred on 21 July 1991 at Newton Junction, Health and Safety Executive, HMSO (1992), p. 2.

53 Ibid., p. 40, para. 330.

54 Ibid., p. 2, para. 14.

55 Stanley Hall, op. cit., p. 53.

56 Peter Rayner, op. cit., p. 373.

57 Ibid., pp. 12–3.

Chapter 13

1 Piers Brendon, *Thomas Cook, 150 Years of Popular Tourism*, Martin Secker and Warburg (1991), pp. 278–97.

2 Roger Freeman and Jon Shaw (eds), *All Change, British Rail Privatisation*, McGraw-Hill (2000), pp. 2–3.

3 Terry Gourvish, *British Rail 1974–97*, p. 39.

4   BRB Reports and Accounts, 1980, p. 11.

5   Jon Shaw, op. cit., pp. 9–10.

6   Roger Freeman and Jon Shaw (eds), op. cit., p. 9.

7   Terry Gourvish, *British Rail 1974–97*, pp. 249–50 & 444.

8   Ibid., pp. 249–50 & 444.

9   Christian Wolmar, *Broken Rails*, Aurum Press, 2nd edn (2001), p. 60.

10 Roger Freeman and John Shaw (eds), op. cit., p. 11.

11 See Railway Finances, Report of a Committee chaired by Sir David Serpell KCB CMG OBE. Department of Transport, 1983, p. 30, para. 6.9 for an example of this.

12 Ibid.

13 Roger Freeman and Jon Shaw (eds), op. cit., p. 15.

14 Terry Gourvish, *British Rail 1974–97*, p. 384.

15 HC Deb, 26 November 1990, Vol. 181, cc. 606–7.

16 http://news.bbc.co.uk/1/hi/uk_politics/2286008.stm.

17 Jon Shaw, op. cit., pp. 206–10.

18 http://www.independent.co.uk/news/people/obituary-robert-adley-2322808.html.

19 Roger Freeman and Jon Shaw (eds), op. cit., p. 25.

20 Remark made by Christian Wolmar at Woking RCTS meeting.

21 Roger Freeman and Jon Shaw (eds), op. cit., p. 128.

22 Ibid., p. 127.

23 *Modern Railways*, August 1993, p. 455.

24 Jon Shaw, op. cit., p. 127.

25 Ibid.

26 *Future Rail – The Next Decade*, British Railways Board (1991), p. 4.

27 *Rail Magazine*, 13–26 September 1995, pp. 24–6.

28 *Modern Railways*, August 1993, pp. 460–1.

29 Terry Gourvish, *British Rail 1974–97*, p. 309.

30 Ibid., p. 444.

31 *Rail*, No. 175, 27 May–9 June 1992, p. 9.

32 *Modern Railways*, December 1992, p. 644.

33 *Rail*, 27 May–9 June 1992, p. 5.

34 BRB Reports and Accounts, 1995, p. 3.

35 BRB Reports and Accounts, 1995, p. 29.

36 BRB Reports and Accounts, 1995–96, p. 8.

37 BRB Reports and Accounts, 1995–96, p. 31.

38 Complete list of sales can be found in the board Reports and Accounts for 1995–96, pp. 74–5; 1996–97, p. 52.

39 BRB Reports and Accounts, 1995–96, p. 3.

40 *Rail*, No. 261, 13–26 September 1995.

41 Valerie Stewart and Vivian Chadwick, op. cit., p. 153.

42 *Modern Railways*, August 1993, p. 459.

43 Terry Gourvish, *British Rail 1974–97*, p. 440.

44 National Audit Office, Department of the Environment, Transport and the Regions, Privatisation of the Rolling Stock Leasing Companies, HC 576 Session 1997–98, 5 March 1998.

45 National Audit Office, *The Flotation of Railtrack*, November 1998.

46 http://www.independent.co.uk/news/business/the-player-chris-green-chief-executive-of-virgin-rail-right-man-to-tackle-mission-impossible-1071327.html.

47 BRB Reports and Accounts, 1996–97, p. 52.

Chapter 14

1 http://www.rtcbusinesspark.co.uk/.
2 *Modern Railways*, September 1991, p. 448.
3 Marcus Binney and David Pearce (eds) *Railway Architecture*, 1st edn, Orbis Publishing Ltd (1979); 2nd edn, Bloomsbury Books (1985), p. 12.
4 Bevis Hillier, *John Betjeman: The Bonus of Laughter*, John Murray (2005), pp. 573–4 and plates opposite pp. 363 & 555.
5 http://www.martinjennings.com/Betjeman.html.
6 Alan A. Jackson, *London's Termini*, Pan Books (1972), p.40.
7 See Gilbert Walker, *Road and Rail*, George Allen & Unwin Ltd (1947).

Index